Also By John Nichols

Fiction
The Sterile Cuckoo
The Wizard of Loneliness
The Milagro Beanfield War
The Magic Journey
A Ghost in the Music
The Nirvana Blues

Nonfiction
If Mountains Die *(with William Davis)*

The Last Beautiful Days of Autumn

John Nichols The Last Beautiful Days of Autumn

TEXT AND PHOTOGRAPHS BY JOHN NICHOLS

HOLT RINEHART AND WINSTON NEW YORK

Published by Holt, Rinehart and Winston,
383 Madison Avenue, New York, New York 10017.

Published simultaneously in Canada by Holt, Rinehart
and Winston of Canada, Limited.

Library of Congress Cataloging in Publication Data

Nichols, John Treadwell, 1940–
  The last beautiful days of autumn.

  1. Nichols, John Treadwell, 1940–   —Homes and
haunts—New Mexico. 2. Novelists, American—20th century
—Biography. 3. New Mexico—Biography. 4. New Mexico—
Description and travel—1951–   I. Title.
PS3564.I274Z469   813′.54 [B]   81-7228
                         AACR2

ISBN Hardcover: 0-03-059254-2
ISBN Paperback: 0-03-059253-4

First Edition

Designer: Robert Reed
Printed in the United States of America
10 9 8 7 6 5 4 3 2 1

Lyrics from "Divorce Me C.O.D." by Cliffie Stone
and Merle Travis. Copyright 1946 by American
Music, Inc. Copyright renewed. All rights
controlled by Elvis Presley Music & Unichappell
Music, Inc. (Rightsong Music, Publisher.)
International Copyright secured. All rights
reserved. Used by permission.

Grateful acknowledgment is made to the following:
Simon J. Ortiz and the INAD Literary Journal for
permission to reprint from "No More Sacrifices,"
excerpted from *Fight Back: For the Sake of the
People, For the Sake of the Land,* by
Simon J. Ortiz, copyright © 1980 by
Simon J. Ortiz.

To reprint from "Advice to our children," *Selected
Poems* by Nazim Hikmet, translated by Taner
Baybars. Copyright © 1967 by Nazim Hikmet.
Distributed in America by Grossman Publishers,
Inc. Used by permission.

To the estate of Pablo Neruda for permission to
reprint from "The Morning Is Full," *Twenty Love
Poems and a Song of Despair* by Pablo Neruda,
translated by W. S. Merwin. Copyright © 1976.
Jonathan Cape Ltd. Used by permission.

This book is for Sylvia Landfair, whose blythe spirit enriched many of these adventures.

Then it is for Charley and Lois Reynolds, and Evelyn Mares Valerio and Isabel Vigil. Their courage and humor through all the hard times have been inspiring.

Too, it is for Rini Templeton, who defends the land and the people with her whole heart every hour of her existence.

It is also for Craig and Jenny Vincent; their lifework ensures our American future.

Special abrazos to Bill Davis, whose photographs inspired this book; to Doug Terry, who somehow survives our friendship laughing; and to Marian Wood, who—with much love—endures.

And to all Taoseños, the guardians of this fragile and beautiful valley.

IN MEMORIAM

Louis Ribak
Justin Locke
Cowboy Joe Vigil

My grandfather, John T. Nichols, passed it on.

We lived in that country long enough to have seen it in a great
variety of circumstances and moods, and gradually every part of it
acquired significance; the whole area became charted with our
experiences, many of which I shall never forget.

—Niko Tinbergen
Curious Naturalists

There are songs
about the rain,
so beautiful.
White soft mist,
gentle on the land,
flowing in rivulets,
stone shining,
so beautiful.
There are songs.

—Simon Ortiz
Fight Back: *For the Sake of the People,*
For the Sake of the Land

CONTENTS

AUTHOR'S NOTE

Almost every time I went fishing in 1980 I carried a pack full of photo equipment; it weighed a ton. Yet for a number of reasons I had trouble taking pictures down in the Rio Grande Gorge. To begin with, the trout usually start hitting flies about the time shadows reach the water; this made for an impossible contrast situation, where either half the gorge and the sky were washed out, or the shadowy part of the canyon was almost totally dark.

The enterprising photographer might quickly point out that had I entered the gorge a few hours earlier I could have captured the entire chasm in daylight. That is correct. Unfortunately, I would have caught very few trout. And for a year and a half my fisherman's instincts overwhelmed my photographer's desires; I had a bona fide block against arriving at the river before the trout started hitting. Some pictures included in this book, of the entire river in sunshine, are posed shots—that is no time to be snagging fat rainbows in white water.

Probably I should confess outright that catching trout *always* preempted the pursuit of esthetics. And if I was down on the river with my friend Charley Reynolds, I found it especially difficult to pause for a few carefully-considered transparencies. For this reason, although he is a major hero of this book, Charley's feats are little recorded. On the Rio Grande together, we always moved in opposite directions, because neither of us was eager to share the other's river. Put bluntly, I figured that any section of water Charley had touched was pretty much emptied—so I stayed as far from him as possible when trout were on my mind. Hence, my only photograph of Charley Reynolds holding up a lunker trout was taken during a rare outing together on the Red River. And the nineteen-inch rainbow in Charley's fist happened to emerge from the river on the end of *my* fly line. In fact, it came out of a riffle that Charley magnanimously bequeathed to me as he surged forward to grab a deeper pool. I explain this because Charley is a stickler for accuracy, and would never deign to claim a fish he didn't nab himself. The photograph is accurate in most other details. That's the famous "rubber" .32 on his hip, and you can see the lead-filled killing bat stuck into his britches like some horrible gangster blackjack. The bearded face looks properly scrufty, and the hat—lawd God!—is the very headpiece Tom Mix bequeathed to Andy Devine, who later passed it on to Slim Pickens.

The waders we can forget about. I've seen Charley in waders on only one other occasion during the three years we've angled together. But it was a cold Wednesday, and he didn't want to get his feet wet. He regretted wearing the damn things all day long.

The spirit of my lunker in Charley's fist is totally accurate, however. That's the kind of trout he hauls out of the Rio Grande with regularity; and he can out-lunker me four out of five trips to the river with ease. I remember an evening last year when he called to say, "Guess what I just pulled out of the river?"

I swallowed, gulped, and grumbled, "What?"

"Well, my smallest was a fourteen-incher."

I waited, knowing I was about to take a real beating.

After a moment he said, "Aren't you gonna ask what was my biggest?"

In a clear, cold voice, I growled, "Screw you, Charley."

"It was a twenty-one-inch brown. But that ain't all. . . ."

Charley is a man who can rub it in. Bleakly, I muttered, "Oh yeah?"

"Yup. I also got a couple seventeen-inch rainbows, and a sixteen- and a fifteen-incher. I hadda quit and come out early my sack was so heavy."

Never one to go down without a fight, I said, "Put Lois on the phone."

When his wife came on, I asked, "Is that unprincipled galoot telling the truth?"

"I'm afraid so. That's the best mess of fish I've seen him come out with in a little while."

When you are up against a talent like that, it's hard to stop concentrating long enough to take a picture.

J.N.
July 11, 1981

PROLOGUE

Statistically, the probability of any one of us being here is so small
that you'd think the mere fact of existing would keep us all in a
contented dazzlement of surprise.

—Lewis Thomas
The Lives of a Cell

I live for autumn. All year long I have reveries of those cool beautiful days to come, and memories of Octobers past. It is the most alive, the most heartbreakingly real season in my bones. I love the chilly winds and dying leaves and the first snow flurries that sweep intermittently down this lean valley. I adore the harvest smells around me, of ripe and rotting fruit, of the last alfalfa cutting. Nervous horses with their heads raised, flared nostrils tautly sniffing arctic odors, make me feel like singing. And I long for the gorgeous death of that high-country season when the mountains pulse with a pellucid varnish of winter whiteness, and the spears of a million bare aspens—only moments ago bursting with resplendent foliage—create a soft gray smirrh across jagged hillsides.

All the respected clichés apply. Geese are flying south; ducks land in the stock tanks, irrigation ditches, and swampy lowlands of the Taos Valley. One day my crab apple tree, bursting with crimson fruits, is full of tiny warblers, pine siskins, and other migratory birds; next day the branches are forlorn and jagged, as stark as a ghost-story metaphor. Deer hunters are sighting in their rifles, football games are back on TV, baseball's World Series is coming up, or just over—the mountain lakes are freezing. Evening killdeer scoot over stubbly fields screeching shrill hibernic warnings. Magpies are noisy and nervous, gathering in raggedy cottonwood trees. At night, I lie in bed listening to leaves tick against my tin stovepipes. A cow is groaning two pastures over; dogs are barking.

I cherish the loneliness of autumn. And experience a great lust to disappear into the Rio Grande Gorge, there to spend afternoons among basalt boulders, plying the low clear river for trout. Everything physical seems to come together—in my body and on the surrounding land during this time of death and dying.

There's nothing morbid in it for me. I accept autumn as a ritual of celebration. All life is heightened and precious; all anguish is bittersweet, unfailingly real. It is like a sexual climax to me. Earth, water, sky, my own flesh become attuned and important. I know that all impermanence is immortal. I want to make love, be in love, sow silly

3

and wonderful seeds of carnal desire. Growing giddy in the windy shadows of brittle leaves, I have a powerful need to dally with what is plump, voluptuous, kinky.

And I have no fear of winter.

Life might be perfect if I could adjust my emotional thermostat so that it always functioned in a mythical sense of autumn. I respond to springtime in off-balance rhythms, nervous and apprehensive: it never falls into place before summer abruptly takes over. And summer chills me with disorganized dread. Everything is too full, heavy, green, hot, inevitable. Though we have a short growing season in this valley, June, July, and August weigh me down with a sense of never-ending opulence; I grow squeamish in the lush green folds of a forever season. Granted, I like to irrigate my small fields, grow a garden, deal with all the busywork of the midyear. But what a relief when Labor Day is here and gone, the hills are empty of tourists, and the rivers are dying and lucid!

I am forty, I have become mortal. I have no further psychic, emotional, or intellectual need to prolong summer seasons, and it is only when autumn begins its play that I can truly focus on the rich and vital life I am living. All of a sudden I grow alert.

October is a hallelujah! reverberating in my body year-round. A thousand rattletrap pickup trucks are in action, gathering winter wood supplies, chugging and careening along rough dirt arteries, raising dust that dissipates slowly into the limpid blue atmosphere. Wood gatherers are picking up slash in the shadow of Tres Orejas Mountain, they are cutting green piñon trees south of Route 96 near Ojo Caliente, they are finding huge logs west of Tres Piedras, they are scavenging along Pot Creek, the Rio Chiquito, and the Little Rio Grande in the Sangre de Cristo foothills.

I, too, am out in the hills, hunting down fuel, reveling in the sweaty work. My hands become callused and battered. The water I guzzle during breaks never tasted sweeter. The hot scent of dead piñon is an aphrodisiac. The air is dusty, it smells of dry pine needles; yet I sense imminent ice in the clear blue sky.

Sometimes, on warm October days, a solitary blue spruce tree, simmering coolly as if powdered with a pastel rime of midwinter frost, takes my breath away.

Every few years the clean blue autumn has a trick of enduring almost beyond belief. One incredibly clear day follows another, through October, into November, occasionally into December. We all wait for the mountains to release dark storm clouds over the Taos Valley, brutally terminating the idyll. Yet willfully, mischievously, those tempests tarry. And the high country lingers in exquisite languid suspension. The preposterous soul-stirring arrogance of aspen-yellow hillsides flames brightly and subsides; swooping high drifts of crinkly brown cottonwood leaves bunch against the wire fence of my chicken coop; the bolls of wild sunflowers along the edge of my garden have been picked clean by migratory seed predators . . . and yet the valley still dawdles in a sunny dream the likes of which I have never elsewhere so consciously enjoyed.

Every morning we all awaken, expecting to find snow on the ground, our distant horizons eradicated, our haystacks dulled by a surly gray drizzle.

Yet each day the valley accepts a reprieve, twenty-four more hours of precious borrowed time. I awaken with Easter exuberance, thrust aside the stone blocking my cave, and embrace another daily resurrection. How I appreciate everything . . . *fully!* After all, tomorrow this reprieve will be buried by blizzards, crushed under slabs of doomsday ice. I can't waste a minute indoors! I must take advantage of this gift, wedged so tentatively between summer's hectic somnolence and winter's harsh apogee.

I'll drive to the top of Picuris Peak and overlook the valley. Or stalk trout in a crystal stream only inches deep. Or gather wood, take a picnic, go hunting, rake hay. Or perhaps bend a lover over an old log on a high slope and gloat through the golden afternoon, happy that I still feel eighteen though I'll be forty-one next summer!

Each perfect day, I know, is going to be the last beautiful day of autumn. Tomorrow, everything will be kaput. But sometimes the valley tantalizingly coasts forever, like a game bird with set wings slowly gliding toward earth, describing an exquisite parabola, remaining buoyant far past any logical landing point, so egotistically thrilled by the beauty of its prolonged gracefulness that it wishes never to touch earth at all.

PART ONE

Nothing is hard in this world
If you dare to scale the heights.

—Mao Tse-tung

ONE

The Socialist poet Walter Lowenfels once wrote a small prose work entitled *The Revolution Is To Be Human*. In it, he says many things that I am always quoting to people, in speeches, in everyday conversations. One of them is: "not to know and love the tragedy of your own life is not to know the joy of being here at all."

The tragedy and joy of my own existence begin with landscape and weather, natural things. The sounds, odors, shapes, and colors of the wild world. Birdcalls, the shadow of a hawk, river boulders, watercress, least weasels. Simple and direct. The mood of clouds, aspen leaves, distant thunder, coyotes barking, pink rain, any and all snowfalls. These things are my first positive assumption. All else follows.

Soon clouds, mottled bark, sourbugs, and rainbow trout are interspliced with bodies. My own, with its athletic past and slowly deteriorating present. And the deeply tender and brutal moves of making love. Naked women, as well as imaginary icebergs, manipulate the foundation of my passions, they fabricate the intimate veins accelerating my erratic heartbeats. Lovemaking intrudes most beautifully—and most dangerously—upon my instinctive loneliness. I am irrevocably drawn to secret situations: a ribald and sorrowful lust, triggered in me by rain, magpies, and the intricate magic of huge pebbly anthills, has commandeered much of my sensibility. I'm grateful for all the joy I have known. Sometimes I am befuddled and fatigued by the pain that has accompanied the bawdy intimacy of sex.

After that, crowds of people circulate, creating a fantastic hurly-burly I wish both to embrace and to run from. At heart, I am afraid of prostitutes, presidents, cops, insurance agents, and the family next door. Though outwardly obnoxious, brash, even brazen, I am a timid soul, a Caspar Milquetoast, a Walter Mitty. My social energy is a bluff. I have hermitic instincts. When not fascinated by the human carnival, I am appalled by it. Deep down, I am afraid of interactions. I could get along nicely without human intrusions. In his book *Report to Greco,* Nikos Kazantzakis laid his finger on my predicament:

> I have always loved people (from a distance) and whenever someone came to see me, the Cretan in me awoke and I took a holiday in order to welcome a fellow human being to my house. For a good while I would enjoy myself, listening to him and entering into his thoughts, and if I could help him in any way, I did so joyfully. But as soon as the conversation and contact became too prolonged, I withdrew into myself and longed to be left alone. People sensed I had no need of them, that I was capable of living without their conversation, and this they found impossible to forgive me. There are very few people with whom I could have lived for any length of time without feeling annoyed.

I can relate to that. I wish nobody would ever come to see me. Yet everything I know, all the ways I relate to history, to the natural world, and to the universe, I learned, of course, from others. Still, I often feel more comfortable contacting people through their books and movies and paintings and photographs than through their actual selves. Constantly, I find myself in a panic because I am bombarded by visitors. I don't know how to deflect them or send them packing. I'm terrified of saying no, of being thought a son of a bitch. I give away money to try and placate them (and because I am appalled by the unequal distribution of wealth). People whom I passionately adore are horrified when they realize that if they left tomorrow, I might shed a tear, but I would also kick up my heels and go fishing. I don't think anybody can manipulate me anymore by threatening to remove themselves or their favors from my life. I love being without them just as much as I love being with them.

Recently, I had my phone number unlisted. It was heaven . . . yet I also felt guilty for cutting off so much world. I waste too much time talking with friends, neighbors. Yet I love to talk, and can easily charm most folks. It is assumed I am a gregarious and outgoing fellow, at ease among populations. Yet on many levels I hate to confront my fellow citizens. I suffer nervous diarrhea days before giving a speech. Still, I have talent for winning over an audience. I kill 'em with my humor, my charm, my shit-eating grin. My willingness to fashion a public sort of frankness and intimacy catches listeners off guard. I give political, Marxist speeches, which folks often find palatable despite themselves. Or they tell me, "I don't agree with what you say . . . but let's go fishing sometime and discuss it further."

If the public only knew how happy I might be letting my hermit's genes hold forth, locking my doors to all busybody ministrations. If the world's oxygen were magically cut off for ten minutes, and only I, who happened to be in a greenhouse full of photosynthesizing jungle plants, were to survive—I doubt I would despair. Imagine: I could travel from El Paso to the Galapagos Islands without fear of being bombed, chopped, garroted, or run over. I could search for quetzal birds knowing they now had a chance not to become extinct.

It seems as if I hardly ever make The First Move. I sit in my little house, puttering, farting a lot, overeating and cursing myself for overeating, yet never growing fat. I shove logs into my woodburning kitchen stove, doing everything possible under the sun to put off writing, and waiting in dread for my important activities to be interrupted by somebody who doesn't realize how precious my hours are. I scatter hen scratch on my birdfeeders and for hours watch grackles do their marvelous territorial dances over the grain. I read newspapers from front to back and devour entirely such heady magazines as *People* and *Time*, as well as *The Guardian*, *The Nation*, and *In These Times*. I make endless lists of things to do on old envelopes and promptly lose the envelopes. I stack mounds of letters to be answered on my kitchen table, then brood over them guiltily without slipping paper into the typewriter to reply. I put an Inti-Illimani record on the stereo, follow it up with a Victor Jara, a Georges Brassens, an Edith Piaf, a Dave Dudley, a Jerry Lee Lewis, a Roosevelt Sykes, or a Dolly Parton, or an Arthur Rubinstein, or a Yehudi Menuhin. My entire living room is walled with bookcases, and I spend a lot of time wandering about, plucking a volume here and there, reading ten pages of *Lolita*, twenty pages of *The Forty Days of Musa Dagh*, an entire chapter of Ray Bergman's *Trout*. Then a horse clops up the driveway, a man named Candido Garcia dismounts and bangs on the door, eager to share a beer and palaver about the state of the valley . . . but I tell him frantically that I am *at work*, and cannot be disturbed.

Well, people are here to stay (at least for a while longer), and I know they are bound and determined to hound me to my grave with cries of execration. No doubt I will die as always, befuddled by the capacity for cruelty and loving that is the dual disease of humankind.

Because of people, my own tragedy ceases to be personal. It has been replaced by the sum total of the world's past, its present, and its future. When I see Salvadoran soldiers posed in a truck full of bodies on the front cover of the *New York Times Magazine*, needles of ice perforate my own heart. That's my dead thigh pressed against my friend's lifeless buttocks. I am both outraged and absorbed by that moment. I have a fascination with the enemy, with intimations of universal hostility. I read about my personal triumphs, and my epitaphs, on the front pages of the daily papers, in the national and international newsmagazines. An important part of my credo is the old Donne saw that no person is an island, apart from the main: and for sure every person's death diminishes me. Likewise, in the great victories of humankind, I unabashedly share. And I willingly claim some of the credit for myself.

Who's winning? Who's losing? I can't tell. I know it is terribly important who wins and who loses. I know it is important to tote up the evidence and choose sides. There is no such thing as an objective observer or an apolitical human being. "Passivity" is an active stance: only the lingo is obfuscating. If you are not against the extermination of the Jews and the Cherokees, you are for it.

The battle has always been as simple as that. Ignorance is not an excuse, it is approval of atrocities.

My soul bears the scars of bayonet thrusts, sizzling bullets, jellied gasoline. Sometimes I despair over the anguish of the planet. I feel faint, demoralized, suicidal. I can't understand why the death squads are so successful. Then I pluck my courage from folks like Walter Lowenfels. Who also said: "When the tragedy of the world market no longer dominates our existence, unexpected gradations of being in love with being here will emerge."

I count on it. I know it is possible. If there were just one germ of that love, in just one human being, I would believe in the future, I would believe in those unexpected gradations of "being in love with being here." And I know this will come about because I, for one, am already in love with being here. The terrible smell of cordite will never overwhelm me for long, it will never overwhelm the wonderful smell of gambas and langostinos in garlic oil, rotting bark, a horsehide baseball, sagebrush, white thighs, or victory in Cuba and Nicaragua.

Plus I have friends, lovers, acquaintances the world over whom I will never meet, who have this thing in common with me: a great "love of being here." Some of these people are dead, but they are alive in me, and in millions of others. Scott Fitzgerald, George Sand, Bertrand Russell, Isadora Duncan, Isaac Newton, Lucy Parsons, Che Guevara, Margaret Mead, Babe Ruth, Patsy Cline.

Amen.

I live in a beautiful, high-country valley.

On the eastern side of Taos the Sangre de Cristo Mountains rise up to thirteen thousand feet. West of town the broad sagebrush mesa is bisected by a magnificent narrow crack in the earth, the Rio Grande Gorge. The heart of the Taos area is productive, wet, verdant. Dozens of irrigation ditches, and their many smaller veins, branch off of nine major streams, forming an arterial system that sustains a dwindling number of small fields and farms.

Twelve years ago, when I first arrived, this was a more agriculturally productive and coherent valley. Since that time, the remains of a functioning subsistence infrastructure have been all but eradicated. And the esthetics have come under relentless fire. The valley has been opened up whole hog to a middle-class expansion. It has fallen under the spell (or should I say bootheel?) of progress, American style. A local population of largely Spanish-speaking, and once land-based people, is being displaced by middle-class newcomers like myself, eager to exploit the area in various business or countercultural fashions. Money has brought about a pizzafication of landscape, so that physically the valley now has the cluttered, flabby, monochromatic look of much of commercial America. In the process, the area's once powerful sense of community is disintegrating. The drive to make this a middle-class, monocultural replica of the tasteless and sullen development that plagues much of the USA is dismal to behold. The alienation that proliferates among the valley's denizens is a shame. Old-timers are befuddled and embittered by it, newcomers take it for granted. Crime is on the rise: everybody has a gun. Burglaries are endemic. The *Taos News* is constantly advising us to call the Police Crimestoppers number, squeal on somebody, win a reward. Zoning laws are few, and the development philosophy that prevails is: Grab all you can get as fast as you can without worrying about the consequences. Traditions that held the valley together are dying. The society here is becoming transient.

A tension arises from the economic, physical, and emotional turmoil. I tend to steer clear of local bars, all too aware of underlying antagonisms between races, between classes. There is a disturbed and unsettling mood that pervades the boomtown atmosphere. Taos is very chic, very poor, very cranky. Most residents feel helpless to change anything, even though they realize we are creating a bitched future. The litany is: "Well, you can't stop progress." Or: "I know it's not good, but what can you do?"

There is still a balance in the Taos Valley. In 1981, a majority of the population remains Spanish-speaking, although census figures suggest that within a decade Anglos may outnumber Chicanos. Certainly, a vast majority of the valley's businesses are owned by relative newcomers, who effectively control the economy. But there are still some land-based old-timers, their children, and a few concerned newcomers struggling to keep the more important traditions intact. These folks have a respect for community, a respect for each other, a compassion for all living things, a sense of humor, and pride in themselves coupled with a humility that comes from instinctively understanding their places on earth.

One such person is my longtime friend, Andrés Martínez. A quiet, dignified, and outwardly mellow man, a lot of renegade dwells beneath his distinguished exterior. We have been in many battles together, and in my book, Andrés is one of the honest-to-God keepers of the flame. I respect him as a human being, as a fighter, as a man with curiosity, conviction, and humor. I love him as I would a brother or a father. I envy him his life, because I believe he has come through his adventure intact. At eighty-two he is wide awake, alert, interested in the world, concerned for the welfare of his fellow citizens, and eager to work his personal magic on the future of his community. He likes politics and enjoys engaging the foe. Yet he also steers clear of all the ugly gossip that chatters back and forth across this valley in noisy, bitchy waves. Somehow, while in the thick of it, Andrés is also above it all. His honesty and humility do not—contrary to popular opinion— make him vulnerable. He understands power, does not shy away from it, and tries to wield it on behalf of things he believes in.

Most deeply, Andrés believes in the land. He has worked hard to protect it, and to preserve sensibilities that venerate it. The basis upon which his life and vitality is founded is the understanding that when you kill the land, you destroy the human soul.

Not long ago, Andrés said he wanted to climb Tres Orejas, the odd mountain that rises from the sagebrush plain west of town, on the other side of the gorge. Although just turned eighty, he had never climbed that three-eared cerro, a physical and spiritual reference point throughout his life. As a young boy, during the first decade of the twentieth century, he had herded sheep on the plain surrounding the isolated hill. But he had always been too busy to climb it.

Then he left Taos for many years, going to school, teaching, traveling, starting a family, holding down different jobs. He ventured as far west as Pasadena, and as far north as Salt Lake City working on the railroad. Occasionally, he rode the rails and was hassled by yard bulls. He remembers wide cotton fields and vast pecan orchards outside Phoenix, where he once journeyed to shear sheep in January. Then he moved north with spring, pruning as he went, reaching Wyoming and Montana in June. Other adventures took him east to the Kansas wheatfields, where he labored in clouds of thresher dust that he claims gave him the emphysema he suffers from today.

For a while, with his first wife, Dorothy, Andrés ran a Navajo trading post in Atarque, New Mexico . . . and that is one of his favorite places, though it is all gone now. He enjoyed working among the Navajos and learned much from them. For example, they taught him to smoke his clothing before hunting. They never taught him how to avoid rattlesnakes, however. One day, in the store, Andrés heard a strange swishing sound, like a piece of paper rustling across the floor. He turned in circles, seeking the cause of the noise, but failed to find it. Then abruptly he glanced straight down, and discovered that a small rattler, which had struck without warning, had its fangs caught in his dungarees.

"I jumped right over that counter, I was so scared!"

Nothing in his life was easy, but Andrés always came through. In Atarque, he ran a bunch of sheep. One winter, a terrible snow fell, he couldn't feed them properly, and lost seventy lambs. But at the last minute he sold the ewes to the government for $2.50 a head; and, having paid a buck per animal for the lot, he just broke even.

A man named Dent, who owned a castle near the Garden of the Gods in Colorado, hired my friend. Later, he wanted to set Andrés up with some cattle over in the Texas panhandle. But Dorothy exclaimed, "Oh my God, not the panhandle! All those *winds!*"

So instead, one day after World War II, Andrés and Dorothy blew back into Taos, and launched a small dairy farm in that section of the valley known as Talpa. From the top of his outbuildings, and from his haystacks, Andrés could gaze across the plain to that distant three-pronged peak, in whose shadow he had spent many a boyhood day, tending Gregorio Mondragón's sheep.

Still, he never got over there to climb it. His son Peter grew up, went away to school, became successful, got married, and died of cancer much too young. Andrés and Dorothy struggled to keep afloat in the dairy business, but eventually lost out to corporate dairies commandeering the Taos market. Finally, they retired and moved to a trailer in Cañon, closer to town. Then Dorothy died, and Andrés lived alone for a while, farming land for his church, irrigating two of his own acres, gathering wood each autumn, drying fruits and vegetables, making chicos of white corn, and in general keeping busy and keeping fit.

In his late seventies, Andrés drove off to California to visit an old family friend, recently widowed. And he returned to Taos shortly thereafter with a new wife, Jeannette, and a desire to climb Tres Orejas while still in the pink of condition.

I said, "Sure, why not?" After all, I had been in the valley ten years already, yet I had never climbed that mountain myself.

Our ascent of Tres Orejas is a special day in my life. Nothing traumatic or earth-shattering happened on the climb. It was not as if an eighty-year-old and a thirty-nine-year-old somehow managed, without oxygen tanks, and under the severe conditions of a Himalayan winter, to conquer Mount Everest through a series of dizzying and dangerous traverses up awesome icy couloirs. Tres Orejas may look sort of formidable from a distance, but up close it is a friendly little bump, only eight thousand feet high—a moderately steep, but not foreboding climb of about an hour.

Yet something did happen during our trip. Watching my friend relate to stones, deer tracks, and the bleeding wounds chewed by porcupines into piñon trunks, I learned the mountain through the eyes, memory, and excitement of an aged pilgrim experiencing for the first time a piece of geography that had long lain importantly in the bosom of his personal faith. This fact immediately birthed in me a profound sympathy for the mountain.

Since then, I have returned often to Tres Orejas, snooping around on its slopes, in its saddles, among its rotted piñon trees and narrow arroyos. I have spent evenings on its rocky summits, lulled by the surrounding vistas, commemorating my lofty perch in romantic and heartfelt rhetoric. It is, for me, a special place, and I hope that its magic lasts forever. And I am very grateful to Andrés Martínez for sharing it with me.

The great moments of lasting adventures are often composed of benign trivialities. So that bright autumn day began as we rolled back a frost-resistant plastic sheet from the Martínez tomato garden. Jeannette had packed a prodigious picnic. On the verge of our departure, she hurried from the trailer, exclaiming, "Wait, you forgot to kiss me!" And Andrés and Jeannette gave each other a friendly buss, while I wondered if Jeannette was wondering if Andrés had chosen this cloud-less October morning in 1979 to commit suicide on a mountain.

I'll admit, I had misgivings. About what, exactly, I'm not completely certain. Did I fear that a forced march up the slopes of a symbolic hill would be curtains for my pal's ancient ticker? Or was I worried that the stress of lugging him back to the car after his heart attack might trigger in me a cardiac caper of my own? After all, I suffer from tachycardia, a collapsing mitral valve, and other coronary anomalies, not to mention an asthma problem severe enough to keep an Alupent inhaler on my person at all times.

Or what about this scenario: I check in with the initial heart attack, then my friend commits suicide lugging *my* 180 pounds back down to the fabled sagebrush plain!

Even worse: twenty yards below the middle summit I collapse with a variety of heart-asthma ills, and Andrés flops me over one shoulder, trots down the mountainside to our vehicle, and drives lick-ety-split across the dusty mesa to the local hospital, in which I awake a week later to be confronted by banner *Taos News* headlines announcing the award of a glittering medal to my stocky friend for having saved the life of a cultural pillar of the community!

Whatever the case, on a bluebird October day in 1979, Andrés and I bid Jeannette adiós, stopped at the Cañon Phillips 66 station for four dollars of gas, aimed south on the main highway through Ranchos and Llano Quemado, and turned right onto Route 96, a dirt road heading west through deserted sagebrush to the Rio Grande Gorge and Carson beyond.

Actually, "once deserted sagebrush" is the description that now applies. For of late various oddball dwellings have begun to crop up among the faintly rolling hills and intriguing arroyos.

And of that old dirt road they have now made a paved highway.

But in October 1979 progress had not yet stricken that dusty terrain, and we cruised easily while Andrés pointed out landmarks that were intuited more than seen. Like the ancient Acequia de los Americanos, which once irrigated the desolate sageland where a huge orchard existed . . . and now not a tree stump nor a fence post remains. The youngster Andrés and his dad cut cedar posts in the mountains, selling them to the Ranchos Land and Orchard Company for ten cents apiece. Of all those posts, of the company itself, nothing remains today except vague memories and yellowed survey maps and plats in the county courthouse.

But Andrés recalled when thousands of apple trees dotted the plain, watered by the Acequia de los Americanos. I let my eyes drift, envisioning that vast orchard far from town in an early autumn snowstorm. Slow, mutating whiteness swirled like cosmic filaments out of a misty low ceiling that nearly touched the earth. Countless wet red fruits sparkled dimly. And raucous black-and-white magpies cavorted among the branches, their noisy calls defused by a billion muffling snowflakes.

Then one day the money dried up; and with it, the water. For years, the fruit trees struggled not to die. But finally roots shriveled, branches withered, leaves ceased to appear. Only twisted black silhouettes remained of the groves. Roots lost their grip in the loose soil, and trees were blown over . . . or carted away for wood.

"Someday," said Andrés, "I'd like to search around and find one of those old posts my father and I cut down, and take it home for a souvenir."

Other childhood memories returned. Andrés and his pals often drove sheep from Ranchos and Llano Quemado west to Los Cordovas, slightly north of the old orchards. They spent the daylight hours in the rich pasturelands near the Pueblo River, letting the sheep graze. The young herders went skinny-dipping in the clean stream, "and, under the hot sun, our backs would get covered with blisters."

Then, in the cool summer evenings, as lightning flickered over the northern mountains and rain sprinkled upon the Talpa hills, the boys drove the sheep back to Llano Quemado.

At the lip of the Pueblo Gorge I braked so we could gaze down several hundred feet to the river. Birthed at the Indian's sacred Blue Lake, it travels down through the Pueblo, is joined by the Rio Lucero north of Taos, swings around through Upper Ranchitos, picks up the Rio Fernando de Taos and then the Little Rio Grande (which is also composed of the Rio Chiquito and Pot Creek waters), and finally descends through a narrow gorge to the big daddy, the Rio Grande.

I used to park on the cliff, descend the steep talus slopes, and fish north, back up through the deserted canyon where my sole companions were water ouzels, enormous dragonflies, and swallowtail butterflies. But then effluent from the old Taos sewage plant, dumped raw into the river, fouled the stream. Gravel beds were coated in a green scum and I felt uncomfortable eating the brown trout I caught. Eventually, I abandoned those waters.

We descended the narrow, precipitous road. Close to the confluence of the Pueblo River and the Rio Grande, Andrés pointed to a grassy area around a spring clogged with watercress, and explained that a mill once stood there. On a winter night years ago he had been trapped in a snowstorm after a trip west, and passed the dark hours at the old mill with a group of woodcutters (called leñeros), huddled around a fire as huge snowflakes quietly fell through the starless darkness.

From the gorge bridge, the paved road continues south beside the Rio Grande to the main highway at Pilar. Ugly concrete picnic gazebos have risen beside the river. At newly constructed parking areas there is a charge for camping. Sometimes you can't see the forest for all the Winnebagos among the trees.

We turned onto the gorge bridge. A decade ago, swallows still built their mud nests on the girdered underbelly of the bridge. I often sat beneath it, taking movies of the busy graceful birds. But then the picnic areas arrived, and there wasn't room enough for both birds and people. Somebody destroyed the nests, and the swallows took their breeding elsewhere.

We ascended the twisting dirt road toward the Carson mesa. At the last dangerous U-curve, I paused to gawk at my favorite rock formations. They are like huge tumbled crystals, those monstrous lichen-covered boulders, resembling ancient megaliths. Behind them, seemingly balanced atop the eastern rim of the gorge, stretches the Picuris chain of hills; farther north lie Taos Mountain and its associates.

Finally—alley oop!—we chugged over the lip onto the Carson mesa. Immediately, a paved road snatched us again. I remember when this section too was dusty, washboarded, and uncomfortable, and I would slalom among the anthills on my way to gather wood.

A mile west of the rim, Carson is a fine, bustling metropolis. That's Boxberger's house on the right, Shneider's trailer and chickens on the left. Our friend Bernabé Chavez actually attended classes many decades ago in the boarded-up old stone schoolhouse. The Verde Shupe residence completes the picture: Carson, New Mexico. We blinked . . . and missed it.

A few miles later we turned off the pavement and headed north toward the peak on a very rocky dirt road. An old stock tank by the road still held a little water. Some desultory cattle lolled about sleepily. Earlier in the year the pond had been full of water and rich with wildlife. I had spotted killdeer, snipes, mourning doves, and swallows, ruddy ducks, bufflehead, and coots, an occasional mallard and goldeneye. Myriad flowers blossomed nearby, tall slender crimson things, also fluffy yellow pollen-rich daisies. Hummingbirds buzzed through the desert air, weaving among big fat bumblebees. Flycatchers perched atop sage plants: a black-and-white shrike observed the scene from a fence post.

But not for long, that kind of idyll. A realtor had subdivided the eighty-acre stock-tank plot into small development lots, with guaranteed rights to a community water well.

We climbed laboriously past a trailer, up over the hill toward that wide expanse of sagebrush bisected by veins of crested wheat, where our friend Pacomio Mondragón brings his sheep in the springtime for lambing, shearing, and castrating before heading farther west to his summer quarters near Canjilon.

And shortly thereafter we parked at the base of the mountain.

It sits in the middle of an ocean, a unique and fascinating silhouette. Though owned by the U.S. Forest Service, it belongs to people like Andrés and me, and my friend Julian LeDoux, who all his life has gathered downed piñon wood from its slopes. Sage and juniper private-property foothills at the northeast base were long ago platted by subdividers. But so far no orgy of housebuilding has taken place on the waterless plain.

At ten o'clock we began. Not a cloud in the glaring hazy-blue sky. A decade ago, the sky used to leap at me like an aggressive Pepsodent smile, brimming with pretentious clarity. Clear days were the rule, not exceptions. Even during a drought, the crystalline blue atmosphere seemed always to have just been washed by recent rains. Then smog drifted up from Albuquerque. Plumes of dull smoke wafted over from the Four Corners Power Plant area. Burgeoning under the middle-class onslaught, Taos itself cast forth billows of gunk, soon becoming one of the more polluted areas of New Mexico, in competition with several open-pit copper mines, and the busiest boulevard in Albuquerque.

Five years ago I stood near the summit of Wheeler Peak, New Mexico's tallest mountain. The surrounding atmosphere was so milky I doubt that I could see for more than forty miles.

Which might sound like a lot to an Angeleno or a New Yorker. But to a Taoseño, such limitations of view are a tragedy of our times.

During the past year—as I began to take photographs of the valley—I have come to realize there is almost never a truly "clear" day. Always some disruption hovers, clouds are flattened by the thin haze, outlined in a metallic glare. I learned not to aim my camera south; to keep the sun behind me, always. Then the northern skies, particularly in the late afternoons, appeared fancifully etched in unblemished clarity.

An illusion, of course. But that is what we have come to settle for.

As we started up, Andrés deserted his English and began speaking Spanish. We moved easily through juniper and piñon forest. Fresh deer tracks crisscrossed the loose, dusty earth: flickers disappeared into the trees. I picked up a piece of dark gray stone that looked as if some native American, a century and a half ago, had begun to chip out a weapon before discarding it for better material. We paused and gathered piñon nuts, shelling them between our teeth, gladly tasting the meat already roasted by weeks under a hot sun.

Zigzagging, we selected the easiest route. Andrés stopped occasionally, gazing up at our destination, enthralled by the unique summit shapes. Little spiny lizards flicked out of sight behind reddish volcanic rocks. Or they froze, waiting for our shadows to trigger their flight.

Birds sang, unleashing a crescendo of incongruous warbled notes. Beneath a relentless sky the landscape seemed arid and desolate and lonely, yet a virtual orchestra of birds—I guessed sage thrashers or Townsend's solitaires—made it seem we had somehow stumbled into a fertile and dripping wet English country garden!

We proceeded through the lyrical racket. Large black-and-orange wasps floated on the warm currents. Deer tracks multiplied, as if a vast herd had migrated across this southwestern tundra and galloped up the mountain. Limestone rocks were scattered across the slopes. In former times, explained my friend, people extracted the lime for cooking uses—in posole, in their beans.

"You had to use everything in those days." So saying, Andrés plucked a herb that he calls chimajá: "It's good for stomachaches."

We climbed without stopping. It took forty-five minutes to reach the shadow of the southeast summit. A rock cone rose abruptly, uncomfortably steep on the south side. So we swung around to the north and Andrés started ahead of me. I stayed close behind, worried a little, my eyes on his old leather boots, the soles worn smooth: I was scampering about on herringbone sneakers.

He grabbed a thornbush, cursed, and latched on to something else. A wren on a nearby rock dipped nervously, then disappeared into a little cave. In a few moments, we reached the top and stood with our hands on our hips, panting and exhilarated. On boulders framed by yellow flowering rabbitbrush lay deposits of weathered deer droppings. I thought of deer and elk in regal lookout postures on the crest.

Below, the plain seemed placid, rather dull. The Sangre de Cristos some twenty miles east were dimmed by haze, almost boring. As usual, in violation of all environmental laws, the Llano Quemado dump was burning. Way down south, near Chimayo and Española, hills were almost totally obscured by smoke.

I was prepared to settle down and let my aged friend savor it however he desired. But Andrés was impatient to tackle the second summit. He was, in fact, determined to climb all three "ears."

In the first saddle between summits, Andrés stooped, plucking up a tiny green plant. The earth was parched and dusty. "Where do you suppose it gets water?" he asked, pinching the roots. They were ever so slightly damp.

A few seconds later he remarked, of a bush: "Deer love to eat that." The wind plucked words from his lips before I could hear them, but I think he called it a paloduro.

Atop the middle summit we settled down and began to catalogue all the valley's landmarks. Like hawks, above it all, we searched the monotonous plain for a negligent prairie dog, a little mouse, a venturesome sidewinder.

Vegetation on the mesa forms an uneven quiltlike pattern of gray (the sage) and yellow umber (the blocks and strips of crested wheat). The grassy patches curve and swirl, giving a sense of motion to the pastel carpet of chamisal.

Directly west of the mountain is the infamous reservoir, built in the thirties to bring irrigation farming to Carson. An earth-fill dam blocks the Aguaje de la Petaca, an arroyo that begins thirty miles north near Tres Piedras (thirty miles west of Taos), and enters the Rio Grande Gorge south of Carson, near Pilar.

Probably the reservoir seemed like a good idea at the time. In those days, Carson, or more properly its nearby sister town of Taos Junction, on Route 285 about ten miles west of the mountain, was booming. The Chili Line narrow-gauge train came up the gorge from Santa Fe, climbed to the top of the Carson mesa, and stopped in La Barranca, Taos Junction, and La Servilleta, on its way to Antonito, Colorado, and Alamosa.

According to Carson old-timer Verde Shupe, Taos Junction had a train station, a couple of diners, two grocery stores, a post office, and a dance hall. Verde carried the mail for a while. His dad had brought him to Carson as a ten-year-old in 1912, and he still lives there. And remembers when the dam was built. People bought bonds to finance the work, mortgaging their land to do so. And that first year, the reservoir filled up with water. It looked like boom times. Acequias were trenched, sending veins out to the Carson homesteaders south of the mountain, who cleared their lands and prepared for prosperity.

Then blowholes appeared, the water disappeared into subterranean caverns, and the reservoir scheme became a fiasco. Nobody seems real clear as to the logistics of the swindle. But most of the land south of Route 96 was forfeited to pay for the bonds; it passed into private hands and was sold out-of-state in a variety of fly-by-night land scams to people in Chicago, Cleveland, New York, and Oklahoma, who own it to this day, may have never seen it, and sell it as investment property.

Verde Shupe had no cash and lost half his land. The Chavez clan, a noted sheepherding family, lost much of their land, too, and with it their large herds that had roamed the area.

Not long after, in 1941, the Chili Line was discontinued and Taos Junction dried up, blew away. Today, it's only a roadside café.

Far beyond the empty reservoir are the hills around Canjilon and Tierra Amarilla. More to the north lies the big, round hump of San Antonio Mountain, on the way to Alamosa, Colorado.

To the east, and closer by, is a bumpy gentle hill called Cerro de Taos. At its foot developers have bulldozed the grid patterns for some future community of little houses.

The next hills, in a clockwise direction, are located near Questa and Cerro, villages a half-hour north of Taos. Cerro Montoso is round, breast-shaped, with a curious nipple-like indentation. A nearby low round hill is called Pot Mountain. A more jagged peak on the edge of the gorge is Chiflo. East of the gorge, Guadelupe Mountain rises sharply. Beyond these layered hills is a high round cerro, up by the Colorado border in Costilla, where occasionally I go dove hunting in October: it is called Ute Mountain.

Impossible, because of the haze, to see beyond to the jagged, snow-covered peaks of Blanca Mountain, at Fort Garland, Colorado.

Sweeping farther east, our eyes traveled down the snowcapped Sangre de Cristos. Just north of Taos stands melodramatic, bald Valecitos, lording it over Arroyo Seco. Next comes Taos Mountain . . . the Mountain of the Pueblo. On the mesa north of town we could distinguish some features: a landing strip for the airport, and the high steel bridge crossing the gorge, eight hundred feet above the river.

Immediately south of Taos the Sangre de Cristos diminish into foothills that barely cast shadows on Cañon, Talpa, and Llano Quemado. Then they rise again, southeast of us, now, to the heights of Picuris Peak. Beyond Picuris, we could make out the jagged Truchas Peaks in the Pecos Wilderness Area.

Andrés pointed out a gouge in the Picuris foothills where for years people have mined tierra blanca for whitewashing the interior walls of their adobe houses.

Closer to us, though still beyond the gorge, we could see tiny silver cars traveling the highway that loops around the Arroyo Hondo above Pilar, and then disappears into the gorge, heading for Rinconada, Embudo, Velarde, Española, and Santa Fe.

Still circling clockwise, we came to the smoky silhouette of the Jemez Mountains, above Los Alamos. Then, nearly completing a full circle, we arrived at the flat-topped mesa-mountain of Abiquiu, called Pedernal.

Landscape—as much as the air would allow, as far as the imagination could hope to wander—completely revealed. The entire universe—ladies and gentlemen—about which, in this book, I am going to speak!

Andrés pointed to a small wooden structure just beyond the eastern foothills of Tres Orejas: "Those corrals belong to Delfino Valerio." A half-mile to the south an abandoned house was surrounded by dead trees. "That's the Graves place," he said. "But nobody lives there anymore."

Miles farther south we could see the five or six buildings comprising the mighty township of Carson, on Route 96. Other than that, very little broke up the beautiful monotony. A tiny weathered ruin, a couple of isolated adobes—like small boats on the otherwise deserted and becalmed sea.

Dreamily, my friend speaks. He remembers the sheep camps from seventy years ago, and where they were stationed. On that hummock, the Martínezes; over by that arroyo, the Mondragóns. The Petaca

Arroyo, he speculates, might have been caused by earthquakes originally, not by eroding water currents. He points out a new route our friend Pacomio Mondragón might take with his sheep over to Canjilon, after the lambing. In the old days, all the land below was richer with native grasses; and the sagebrush was twice as tall. The sheep could survive easily in the snow, they had more protection.

Once Andrés became lost in the tall sage, after bringing the sheep up late from a trip to the river. At age nine he couldn't see over the sage. So he made camp by the rim of the gorge, and waited. Dusk—that enchanted crepuscular peace that made religious the area on a daily basis—lowered. No airplanes relentlessly laid their contrails against the sky. Stars had a clarity back then never since duplicated. Coyotes jabbered, out hunting, seeking the boy and his vulnerable flock. On horseback, adults arrived in the nick of time, and herded the sheep back to safety.

One day, Andrés remembers, two men divided their flock in order to camp on a ledge in the gorge. Confused by the narrow space, about twenty sheep tumbled over the cliff onto murderous rocks below. Their bones, no doubt, still lie among the impervious boulders. That was when—in 1910? 1911? Hard to remember anymore. One of the herders was so-and-so. But: "He's long dead now."

Ghosts take flight off the tip of his Spanish tongue. They float into the dusty mauve landscape, inessential shadows. Sheepherders, homesteaders, old pals, fellow children who grew up, left Taos, disappeared into history. Others remained in the valley, hanging on to their sheep, clerking in grocery stores, teaching school—outstanding citizens and goofy outlaws . . . all gone . . . *difuntos* . . . dust.

He points out where roads used to meander through the mesa, along the rims of certain arroyos—but they are no longer visible, they fell into disuse, were obliterated by wind, sagebrush, time.

Quietly, I listen to eighty years of memories. Wind ruffles his white hair, but he does not seem cold. With an amused smile he pictures how the area must have looked underwater, millenniums ago.

You can find fossil shells in the arroyos, and little trilobites immortalized in stone.

At the turn of the century, says Andrés, you could ride out and make a camp anywhere and nobody came to ask for a permit, heckle, read riot acts. Hardly any fences enclosed the territory in those days. Some men drove their herds overland as far west as Navajo country. Nothing impeded their progress between here and the horizon—no barbwire, no cities, no private property.

He points out the locations of La Servilleta and La Petaca, little towns northwest of us, hidden from view in canyons and forests. And over there is Huérfano Mountain, a smaller volcanic eruption than our own. And he recalls that brief moment when the reservoir held water, and thousands of ducks bobbed happily on the bluer-than-blue wind-churned waves.

Finally, Andrés sucks in a breath and says thoughtfully: "This is a glorious day for me. I always wanted to do this before I died. I thank God for letting me live long enough to have this experience."

We joke a little about that. I suggest that every autumn he should plan to climb another mountain. And God would always let him live another year in order to realize this new ambition. "Climb a mountain every year," I tell him, "and you'll live forever."

Laughing, we head for the final summit. On the way we lift a loose cornice of rock off a boulder, slip a dollar bill and a quarter in the slot, then replace the chunk over that hidden treasure for future generations to cast their adventuring sights upon.

The third summit is steep, and slightly dangerous. But Andrés scampers agilely ahead. Pausing occasionally, he wonders what kind of mouse or little rat has left its tiny pellet doodles in small protected crevices. Below us, the lyrical birds still faintly fill the air with their dazzling melodies.

Sheltered by rocks, we eat sandwiches and apples and sip hot coffee. Three ravens circle curiously, then plane off on the gusting wind. I am excited by the idea of spending a night on the mountain, waking up at dawn bathed in a sagebrush mist, my nostrils smelling the piñon trees. I would sit up in my sleeping bag and gnaw on a piece of jerky as the sun burst up from behind Taos Mountain. . . .

Andrés points out a protected cubbyhole I could sleep in. There I would be in the cockpit of my universe, a perfect place from which to sing these admiring hosannas.

It was steep and hot, heading downhill in the sunny midafternoon. The footing was rocky and uncertain. We circled around the jagged branches of dead trees littering the severe slopes. The bird symphony crescendoed as we reached lower elevations. Andrés stopped, pointing out little holes scuffled in by tiny animals, or very large insects. Then he spotted coyote tracks at a small cantilevered rock under which a rat or a gopher had been munching piñon cones.

Andrés remembered that as a kid, herding sheep, he used to find many arrowheads. Once he had a whole bag of the souvenirs, but he lost it somewhere.

By four o'clock we were back in the van, jouncing along raggedy dirt roads. A faint track disappeared into the dry reservoir. We crossed the dusty floor and aimed northeast toward the Tres Piedras Highway near the high bridge, which would lead us into Taos from the north.

The only structure between the mountain and the bridge is the Martínez sheep corral. In the springtime, a herd hangs out there for several months. But right then it was deserted. Tumbleweeds were stacked up against the rickety fences. Layered sheep manure coating the earth was so dry it had no smell. Wind hissed lazily through rusty tangles of discarded barbwire.

A lonely outpost, thought I: tough, fragile, doomed.

A jackrabbit loped across the road. A shrike on a fence post didn't even budge.

Behind us, it took the dust forever to settle.

PART TWO

The time has come for a respect,
a reverence, not just for all human
beings, but for all life forms—as we
would have respect for a masterpiece of
sculpture or an exquisitely tooled machine.

—Carl Sagan
The Cosmic Connection

THREE

Autumn begins in the high country.

Sometimes I have awakened beside alpine lakes on an August dawn to find the water filmed with ice. Years ago I was almost caught in a blizzard trying to hike out of Bear Lake on Labor Day weekend. Sometimes slabs of last winter's snow still glimmer in shaded mountain gullies when the new winter snows commence.

Starting in September, in the valley, our eyes rise toward the mountains, waiting for the aspen to launch their melodramatic spectacle. Say what you will about their picture-postcard souls, the aspens make it official. If it is a bland, dry autumn, they take forever to turn. In other years, dampness and early frosts can trigger their excesses prematurely, and the show dies aborning. Occasionally, the foliage never truly ripens: it starts to flare, then suddenly nose-dives into mottled beiges, browns, and even blacks. And that robust cliché yellow we love to gawk at never happens.

But oh, when all the elements fall together and great swathes of mountainside blossom with that scintillating radiance! Never mind if it has been versified and adulated to death, each year that the aspens truly turn gold renews our faith and our amazement. I nurture no belief in God, but when this beautiful death goes down I'm willing to grant to those who do trust in some hallowed deity at least a clever and arrogant magician out there, mischievously and with acute dexterity, amid a swirl of star-bedecked Arabian robes, working his or her overweening, and yet totally captivating, sleight of hand.

A brazen display. Yet how I love to wallow in it when everything falls together. At the very least, I make sure my wood runs coincide with the glory of the aspens.

I'll head up the Little Rio Grande, fish for a while, gather wood for an hour, then just loll about in the afternoon's waning warmth, marveling at the gaudy (shameless!) aspens. Though a thousand poets have gooily gushed rhapsodic about those shivering yellow scales and altogether too-perfect slim white trunks as symmetrical as Jesus, I could care less. Gratefully, I cavort in the perfection. I love to be seduced by the corny dramatics. I gorge, visit the vomitorium, then gorge some more until I stagger from the hills, dizzy from sensual overload.

Is it art? Who cares! Does it have a good move to the left? I should worry! I don't haggle with Dolly Parton, I just accept her.

Nothing can go wrong among the aspens. They remind me of virginity: slim, pure, obnoxiously unblemished. Pristine and serene, they do not dominate, are too pretty to be useful. As fuel, they can't compete with piñon—they die too fast and leave a lot of ash. I consider them above it all, a ruling class—trees without calluses. Could they but speak, their words would descend from those giddy heights on English accents. Don't tell anybody, but I also suspect they are rather stupid.

Nevertheless, when first they turn, I willingly gasp, tingle with excitement, feel good all over. And leap into my VW bus, eager to indulge myself by roaming through their resplendent cliché like an actor through a remake of *Elvira Madigan*, enthralled by their overt blond preening against the hokey sky.

Ain't nothing like a true-blue autumn aspen to put clear-eyed zest in your life. We zoom away from the valley on one of those days when you wake up, take a glom out the window, and exclaim, "Land sakes alive, child—I must of died overnight and gone to heaven!" The sky is so blue you could eat it on a silver spoon and shit perfect periwinkles for a week. The air smells like a lover's lips two seconds after sucking on an orange Popsicle. A few woolly little clouds are as white as the South Pole, too clean to be true. Once in a lifetime—today!—the air is so clear that the silhouettes of trees and mountaintops seem etched with utmost skill upon priceless Florentine crystal. Even everyday birds sluicing through the pellucid ether resemble animated figments of venerated Chinese art.

You couldn't ask for more chutzpah. By the time we reach the mouth of Taos Canyon, my decrepit VW bus has metamorphosed into a sleek overconfident conveyance heading toward Camelot. Narrow meadows flanking the route have just dribbled off a Disney paintbrush. Yellow flowering rabbitbrush and legions of iridescent mauve cornflowers are singing cornball melodies. Obviously, this road leads to some placid wonderland, at the heart of which rises a big rock candy mountain, surrounded by lemonade springs and warbling bluebirds.

I almost want to pull onto the shoulder and holler an obscenity at this goody-two-shoes apparition of a Friday afternoon: the old blasphemy-in-a-church syndrome. Instead, we just toddle merrily along, in no mood for denigration.

Up, up, and away we go, turning right at the Valle Escondido, and right again on Floresta road number who-can-remember? Jouncing and weaving, we cruise under a magic canopy of leaves above Garcia Park, leap from the car, tear all our clothes off, and pose nude for each other's cameras in the middle of the dirt road, hands arrogantly on our hips, legs spread defiantly, our heads thrown back in Moses-reading-the-tablet poses, our white skins bathed in buttery, leafy-veined sunlight, our curly locks made glorious by fantabulous aureoles of golden branches.

Like the surrounding forest, because we got it we have decided to flaunt it.

Oh golly, oh gosh—I sure do feel pugnacious, ma'am. Let's play Satyrs and Nymphets, okay? Ready? Bueno. Lie over there in the grass, on your belly . . . spread your legs . . . and just lemme feast lecherously on the translucent shadows bobbing against your round buttocks.

Ouch, dammit—bit by an ant!

So it's "alley oop!" and up again, and off to wander. These snow-white tall trees Monet would have envied. The impressionistic foliage overhead is like a gilded parachute that keeps me floating.

A grouse? I barely saw it. Just heard the abrupt chugging flutter of panicked wings, and caught a flash of movement before it disappeared.

Lazy and aglow, we inspect the luminous world. Sunlight and bright yellow leaves sap our energy. I feel too lazy to bend over and tie my sneakers. You ooh and ahh like a kid at the circus.

The windy clarity and cleanliness reminds me of fresh laundry— fluffy terrycloth towels, crisp white sheets, athletic socks paired neatly in plump, perfect bunches. How might good old Thoreau respond to the situation? What about the following?

"All nature is doing her best each moment to make us well. She exists for no other end. Do not resist her."

Not me. Not today, for sure. Not ever, if I can help it, will I resist her.

High on a straw-colored hill in the windy open, we can gaze into the forest below, where all those alabaster spears are hidden by untold shades of gold, cadmium yellows, soft oranges, luminous lemony tinctures, and pastel canary greens.

Down below we tiptoe across mossy logs into mellifluous gloom. I take a picture of you, the wanton wood nymph. We laugh, fart, and await a bird of paradise. Aspen leaves twirl on the surface of a little spring. I keep expecting very indolent bears to turn the iridescent corner and halt.

Back uphill, where the tallest aspens grow, it's time for a photograph I've planned all afternoon. A cornball earth-mother shot, to remember—a hundred years from now—the sexy and healthy hyperboles we feel. I snap on the twenty-millimeter lens, you shed your clothes again and stand over me, and I take a photograph that is solid fecund kitsch, and delights me immensely.

One thing leads to another. And in the drowsy late afternoon we celebrate our love in the tangles of sticks and layers of fallen leaves, thinking, as we happily ball away: *D. H. Lawrence, eat your bloody heart out!*

Afterward, Father, I cannot tell a lie—we committed a crime. I outed with the old pocketknife and applied the dull blade to the bark of a large tree. Carved the date, of course, and then your initials joined to mine. And finally the cryptic message: *screwed here.*

East from Garcia Park the road twists and curves around steep hillsides until it enters the canyon of the Rio Chiquito. There we stop, kill the motor, get out, and gaze across the narrow canyon at entire hillsides drenched in lavish autumn yellow. I take a photograph, then give up. The sun is setting. I smell earth in your hair, and brush particles of rotting leaves off your shoulder. The last sunshine rays fire up the highest trees, then shadows loop over the ridges, and twilight arrives.

We reverse direction at the Borrego Crossing, heading back for the park. On the way, of course, a large doe poses among sapling aspens and crisscrossed fallen logs beside the road. We return her calm stare. Then she saunters to oblivion among young spruce trees, and we push on.

At the park, first a fire, then a cool beer, some soup. Across the meadow an owl hoots. I reply, mimicking—three notes every time. It answers. And circles toward us in the trees, stopping every few yards to hoot back. Soon it arrives in the enormous dark spruce towering above our heads. We never saw it approach, never heard the wings. Just all of a sudden there it is, real close. Time passes, I hoot some more, but receive no further answers. Asleep? Or simply flapped away on those enormous soundless wings to murder mice?

The sky positively reeks of shooting stars. Coyotes bark, commenting on the short-lived blazing meteors. The fire dies down, and we lie in snug sleeping bags in the open van, not far from the glowing coals.

At dawn, all the grass in the becalmed meadow is frosted. As the sky begins to glow, the aspen color returns. Leaves that can be set atremble by puffs of air as faint as mouse exhalations, do not stir. To get from here to there I tiptoe.

Another favorite and easily accessible high-country place is Bernardin Lake. Small and man-made, it used to be a lumber-company wash pond. Then, for a while, Fish and Game stocked it with cutthroats; we used to catch them on little dry flies. But they quit planting trout, I suppose because of winterkill. One autumn I hiked up with my fishing rod, and, instead of trout, I found an empty pond hosting what looked like a demolition derby between a handful of bulldozers.

After that, the lake filled up again. But trout never reappeared. In their stead was a vast population of juajalotes, big mean water salamanders (about which more later). So the kids and I caught juajalotes instead of cutthroats, and carted them back alive as part of our summer nature-studies program.

Evidence that beavers are active in the area is copious—they have made mincemeat of entire sapling forests around the shore . . . yet we have never actually seen a beaver. A reason may be that my kids, Luke and Tania, and their friends always amuse themselves by rolling huge logs down the west-side cliffs into the water, or by peppering the glassy surface for hours with skipping stones. Yet, even when I have been at the lake alone, seated quietly on the bank opposite the mound, I've never seen a beaver.

All the same, and especially in the fall, Bernardin Lake is a favorite haunt. Though tame and accessible, it is not that often visited— usually I have it to myself. A person can be reflective there—it's a good place to just sit around, waiting for deer or some oddball birds to make an appearance.

On the south ridge above the lake, the aspen forest is made up of many young trees, growing very close together. I enjoy resting in that reedy grove, or prowling through it feeling a bit like plankton sifting through a huge whale baleen. Captured among all those slim spears, I experience an excitement of place difficult to explain. Maybe that secretive grove reminds me of childhood hiding places. Perhaps I am touched again by the thrill of a five-year-old's breathless anticipation . . . when I used to crouch among lilac bushes in Montpelier, Vermont, or in evergreen trees behind the house in Wilton, Connecticut, cap pistols cocked, waiting to ambush a playmate, or one of my little brothers.

Usually, by early November, winter snows have effectively shut down the dirt road leading to within a mile of Bernardin Lake. But in the autumn of 1980, few storms invaded the local hills. And when Luke and Tania and my friend Sylvia Landfair entered the forest for a Christmas tree, we were amazed at how little snow had fallen. All the roads were passable. A few days later, we decided to try and reach Bernardin Lake. The drive up was easy, the hike in a bagatelle. Yet even though a scorching sun blazed in the cloudless sky, and temperatures exceeded sixty, the lake was frozen solid.

Next day, the kids and I returned with skates and sleds, accompanied by my avuncular pal Leo Garen, his girlfriend, Billie Beach, and Leo's sweet skinny dog, Peaches. Once again the ridiculous sky was swimming-pool blue and unblemished, absurdly mild for December. Still, some ice remained slick and hard, and with nary a false start all of us tumbled into an enchanted afternoon.

Leo Garen is a man of many talents who currently writes movie and TV scripts. We go back about a decade, to that day he first showed up in my kitchen with Dennis Hopper, and we killed a gallon of wine together. Leo himself is The Man Who Would Be Famous, who, through a series of heartbreaking and frustrating events, failed to grasp the brass ring just when it looked like a sure thing.

But let us return, momentarily, to the days of yesteryear, when, as a tough Philadelphia kid, Leo commenced his meteoric rise. His first great triumph was a contest won by selling subscriptions to the *Philadelphia Inquirer*. His prize?—Batboy for a Day with the old moldy Athletics. In fact, Leo perched right next to Connie Mack at the game. And remembers the dugout was traversed by a gutter full of running water in which the ballplayers expertly plunked their throat angels.

Fraught with ambition as the result of early triumphs, he left home at the tender age of fifteen, headed for New York, fell by accident into the world of theatrical make-believe. Next, he tackled Provincetown on Cape Cod to consolidate his early gains. And wound up processing fish in the local icehouse.

"Picture this thing that's like an enormous ice-cream cone, made out of wire mesh," says Leo. "The wide end stuck out over the ocean. All the boats that came in full of fish dumped their catch into the cone, which was constantly revolving. On their way down the cone, all their scales were stripped off. Then they came out at the narrow end, where I held a pan full of water for them to fall into. I sloshed them around so they'd settle perfectly, and then passed the pan down along a traditional conveyor belt—you know, on little rollers. I wore a rubber suit, but I got scales under my collar, up my sleeves, everywhere. I was in Provincetown for three days, at the start, just trying to find a room. Nobody would rent to me when I said I worked at the icehouse. But finally an old lady took pity and gave me a room; her husband was a fisherman."

From the icehouse he graduated to a more perilous trade, working as crew on a party boat, baiting hooks for fifty fishermen, dealing out the beer. It should have been a cushy job. But that summer the Cape was surrounded by sharks, and most of the fish caught were sixteen-foot blues, eighteen-foot makos.

"One of the strongest memories of my youth," says Leo, "is of being sixteen and hanging by one hand over the stern of that fucking boat, clubbing sharks over the head with a two-by-four! Then people wanted the jaws of those damn beasts for souvenirs, so I had to cut them out, and that nearly destroyed my hands. The jaws are all bone and cartilage and gristle. My hands were torn, chopped up, all raw, and the cuts were soaked in squid juice and shark juice. They swelled to double their size. . . ."

So he dropped that shtik, and began writing art reviews for the Provincetown paper. He knew absolutely nothing about painting, but soon found himself interviewing such luminaries as Hans Hofmann.

Though not for long. He returned to the Big Apple, applied himself, and began directing plays. He was good, and staged major productions of works by LeRoi Jones, J. P. Donleavy, Jean Genet. He directed Norman Mailer's *The Deer Park*, ran in a fast crowd, and knew everybody in America who was anybody in America. It was a heady time, and for a while he believed that the sun rose or set according to the fortunes of Leo Garen. That he enjoyed himself immensely goes without saying; that he was a gifted and highly respected professional is a matter of record. And when he had squeezed enough juice out of the Apple, he made the jump to Hollywood. Where (after a stint working for Ray Stark) the folks at Fox gave him a bundle to make his own movie. Titled *Grasslands* (and later retitled *Hex* by the studio), it starred such soon-to-be-illustrious actors as Keith Carradine and Gary Busey, and was released briefly in Europe—where it garnered fine reviews—though never in America, where it was shelved by the studio.

Leo fought for his picture, and the ensuing squabble broke his heart, also his will to hustle the Hollywood game. Penniless and tired, chased by credit-card companies and his shattered dreams, Leo staggered wearily into Taos seeking succor in a more spiritual life, paid some dues at a local commune, joined the Native American Church, lived here and there and everywhere mostly by the skin of his teeth, and tried to retrench. He went through a period of intolerable despair—yet somehow survived. Finally, he rented a little house full of mice, threw in a couple of cats, emerged from his wrestling match with the devil still coherent and profoundly in love with Taos, figured out that after all life could be beautiful, and made a number of wood runs in a rattletrap blue pickup truck by way of starting over.

Then, cautiously, he resurrected his career.

So there we were: Leo and Billie and Luke and Tania and me, high in the heart of a Christmas season, looking to perpetrate a little old-fashioned fun.

Leo is no exercise fanatic, and at first he monitored us from a pasha position onshore, deriding our antics with typically witty and ironic comments. Billie twirled about the ice on imaginary skates, singing show tunes. I donned my blades and dashed down the length of the lake and back before collapsing from an asthma attack. Then the kids piled onto the sled, and I threw a rope over my shoulder, tugging them at high speeds along the ice for a hundred yards, before abruptly stopping to crack the whip and send them catapulting across the frozen surface.

Next, we lured Leo toward the field of play. He protested, we insisted. Slowly, he lowered himself onto the sled. I grunted, huffed, took a hit of Alupent, got the sled moving, picked up speed . . . and then we sailed across the lake like two characters in an Edith Wharton novel (or was that a Ken Russell movie?), until I cracked the whip, and Leo held on for dear life!

Next, Tania loaned her skates to Billie, and away went that genteel and whimsical Angeleno, purty as a picture.

"Ah, yes, Ivan," Leo croaked in his finest Russian accent. "It vas vonderfool, in de old days, how de serfs vood pull us arount on de sleds in de middle ov vinter. You did so good today, Ivan, ve are gonna trow you an extra bone. . . ."

The last act, final scene, played like this: as the sun westered and cool air emerged from the pine forests and nudged out onto the ice, the children and I held an Olympic pairs skating championship, twirling hand in hand along the ice, while Billie and Leo sang the theme song from *Dr. Zhivago*.

They judged us harshly, but who cared? We skated backward without falling, Luke and Tania and I. Then we actually leaned forward, lifting a leg off the ice—in a "camel" is it called? And in our own minds won every competition in a walk.

Finally . . . there's no punchline. Our little band of Merry Revelers simply departed, heading down the mountainside glowing from the simplicity of that fey time on the isolated lake in December, while "Lara's Theme" died away, and the beavers, secure in their mud-encrusted compartments, removed cotton wadding from their ears.

FOUR

So it begins in the high country, and then moves to a lower elevation, in the shadow of icy mountains.

At first, the autumn is a lonely time for me. The kids have returned to their mother and school in Albuquerque. Suddenly, my little house reverberates in silence. Shell-shocked at my kitchen table, I wonder: What next? Time to work, repair damages of the summer holocaust, gather wood and chop it, refocus, push on. The growing season was so short and hectic. In May, I planned a thousand adventures with my kids; in September, it seems I failed miserably to give them quality fun. I wish we had played catch or Frisbee in the back field more often, or chased butterflies, or made another expedition after lizards in the gorge. I could have strummed my guitar more often at night, or told them bedtime stories. I feel queasy, almost despairing because I never got organized. During the summer—a raucous carnival played at a hundred decibels—I never had time to think. Quiet times alone together eluded us. *Now* I think I could do it . . . but the kids are no longer with me.

It's okay. For a few days I wallow in self-pity and self-recriminations, then I adjust. For better or for worse, the summer is over, September is upon me. I need go nowhere in search of holy grails— they come to me. Apples have ripened in the mini-orchard; hard little pears dangle from brittle limbs outside the kitchen window. A neighbor, Tom Trujillo, has cut and baled the front field. Killdeer have become frenetic, preparing to migrate; and the nesting boxes in my elm trees are finally emptied of starlings. In the mornings, when I go to care for my son's pigeons, I walk through a tunnel of stiff brown sunflower stalks taller than my head. Ice coats the pigeons' water pans; I lift out thin frozen ovals and dump in fresh water.

Warblers appear in the trees, flitting inexhaustibly for a few days, then disappear. One day the siskins arrive, falling out of the north busily atwitter to pluck the sunflowers clean. And although in the hills the aspens are turning, around my house the cottonwoods remain stubbornly green, and the Chinese elms seem determined never to exercise their deciduous options.

Still, by mid-September every night produces, or sincerely intimates, a frost. Long ago all the squash plants turned black. Too soon the weather may grow permanently arctic. Nightly, I cut off the water into my leaky faucets so an exit pipe into the front field won't freeze. With the rainy season ended, dryness accumulates, so I turn on a humidifier when I sleep, hoping to breathe better. I make my annual pilgrimage to the back field in which I harvest by hand all the prickly brown seeds of the careless weed, a plant to which I am most allergic. Ritual burnings of the seeds occur in my driveway; applied also to the pyre are sheaves of hand-pulled blond foxtail grass, which each summer threatens devastating inroads on my two diminutive fields.

When I shake the apple trees, hard, glistening fruits bounce painfully off my head. They land in thick swirls of long grass. I hunt them down like Easter eggs, place them on layers of straw in cardboard boxes, and know I'll still be gnawing them in April, wrinkled skins and all.

The rotten apples go to my friend Candido Garcia, who gathers them for his goats and hogs. We crab humpbacked through the orchard amid swarms of honeybees and yellow jackets, plucking rotten fruit from the clutches of busy honey makers. And later on we might share a different adventure together.

For example:

Three A.M. . . . November . . . a deer-hunting weekend.

From the overcast sky a few snowflakes are dawdling. Candido removes the saddles from an old car sinking onto rusty axles beside the corrals. Patiently, tamping their hooves a little, the horses whinny softly, commenting on the cold. In the glare of his pickup headlights, Candido tightens cinches, packs gear in the saddlebags. Andrés Martínez has loaned me his father's .30-30; I slip it into a saddle scabbard, then lift a liquor bottle from Candido's hand and take a bitter sip of cheap bourbon. Wind is gusting out of the south. Too bad more snow hasn't fallen, for then tracking the deer would be easier.

Mounted up, we ride. Along a damp dirt road through the sage-brush, into an arroyo, up the other side. A gate opens onto the highway. Two miles north, the Raton bypass takes us east toward the mountains. No cars pass. Cold and hunched over, we allow the horses to proceed without much conversation. A millennium has passed since last I rode a horse, and it takes a supreme effort of will to remain upright in the saddle.

A mile south of Carlos Trujillo's bar, we veer off the road onto a trail, and enter the forest, climbing. Stray flakes float coolly past our faces, but the ground is bare. Quickly, in darkness, we rise up the steep trail. Within minutes we can look down on the twinkling town from alpine country. It is colder, and of course you can smell the difference. My old horse is no fan of this exercise: she balks, I dismount and lead her a ways, then grapple back on board.

Beyond civilization, Candido grows more chipper. He talks, sings, nibbles on the bottle. Strange man, loner, small farmer, he takes care of his widowed mother. Recent changes in the valley are not for him. His sisters have left the valley. Candido's last trip abroad was to Korea, compliments of the U.S. Army. Now he confronts a world that considers him an anachronism. His farm is in Ranchos, near Highway 3, in a prime development area, increasingly hemmed in by the convoluted dwellings of a middle-class culture. But he does not want to let go. Goats and pigs, a few horses, and some cattle live on his minifarm. He has chickens, a few geese. Grows corn. And puts the hay up by hand, in a huge mound, instead of baling it.

Especially, Candido loves horses, and rides every day when he has the time, canvassing the valley, visiting friends. Once, when I was playing tennis at the town courts on the Middle Road, I heard a galloping horse, looked up, and there was Candido, one hand clamped to his hat, racing joyously along the dirt road. He drinks, occasionally seems disoriented, and is tired of all the bullshit changing the valley. Who cares if we bag a deer? He just wants to be on horseback, in the hills, away from it all.

When darkness is replaced by a thin chilly dawn, we are miles above the valley in a different world. Sprinklings of snow powder the brown grasses of small clearings. Pausing to rest the horses, we dismount, let the reins dangle, and devour candy bars. Full and tall, the forest is silent. At the edge of the clearing, we find fresh hoofprints— probably of a buck and a doe. Candido studies them for a moment through his dark glasses. He is wearing a floppy hat, a faded dungaree jacket over his shirt, old chaps, and ancient heelless cowboy boots. No dyed-in-the-wool nineteenth-century western geezer, dollar poor and hardscrabble ornery, ever looked more authentic.

"Have another drink, John. Then we'll say, 'Sayonara. . . .'"

The tracks head east, along a ridge, easy to follow now that snow consistently powders the trail—until abruptly they swing down a steep hillside. Dismounting, I lead my horse a ways, begin to flounder, realize it's hopeless, turn around, and retreat to the trail. Candido laughs, nonplussed, offers the bottle again, and breaks into song: "I'm an old cowhand, from the Rio Grande. . . ."

Doubling back, we pick up another deer, and resume the chase in a different direction. Gray daylight, tentative penumbra of winter gloom, has risen. Lustily, Candido crows out a long corrido about love and death and the Mexican Revolution . . . and finally I accept the fact that we are not really hunting deer, we are just up in the mountains, wandering around without tension, feeling loose and goosey. Our guns will never leave their scabbards. And more snow than this will never fall.

"Allá en el Rancho Grande," "Cielito Lindo," "Muñequita Linda," and a host of other songs fall to our hoarse and cheerful voices. Around noon, we guide the horses over a divide and down to the Rio Chiquito for water. Up high again an hour later, we loll against rotten logs, munching on sandwiches, apples, oranges, and the bourbon dregs. Weather has turned blustery, but not too cold. A few sunny rays punch through cracks in the clouds. Gratefully, the horses slouch along an old logging road, from which, occasionally—through breaks in the foliage—we can overlook the entire valley bathed in summery sunshine.

By late afternoon, when we leave the hills, not a cloud mars the boring sky. Deliciously tired, we amble into an arroyo and follow its sandy, shadowy bottom. A dog barks, then flees. Smelling home, the horses prick up their ears. Reaching the dirt road where the day began at 3:30 A.M., my horse breaks into a gallop, and I let her fly, clinging to the saddle horn for dear life!

At the corrals, irrigation water has overflowed the banks of a nearby ditch. Swallows are darting. Candido strips off his saddle and chucks it into the backseat of that derelict Chevy. I am exhausted, saddlesore, and happy. And the deer won't have to quake in trepidation before our merciless onslaught for another season.

I awaken at 10:00 A.M. The sun is stupendously shining. The frigid air of my yard is spotless. But the eastern hills are vague silhouettes behind a thick haze over town—caused by a thousand wood fires burning. In my kitchen stove I light newspapers and kindling, then dole out grain to the birdfeeders. Instantly, flocks of iridescent black grackles arrive and start posturing belligerently at each other, snapping up tidbits between pufferies. I carry a cup of coffee to the outhouse, and sit with the door open, still groggy. The black cat, Duke, out all night on a hunt, angles up to say howdy. As I pull burrs from his tail, he flops on his back, playfully batting my fingers. Then he hops lightly onto an old sawhorse and settles there, sleepily observing some juncos in the woodpile. Harbingers of cold weather, those gray little birds have only recently materialized.

Or perhaps Duke saunters across the dusty driveway, pursued by a half-dozen angry magpies, one of whom is bold enough to land right behind the cat and nip at his tail. Duke, of course, pays no attention.

I sip my coffee and grin idiotically at the juncos. The orchard and garden area today is host to a flight of black-and-white warblers. Plus a half-dozen western grosbeaks. But the last meadowlark has migrated; the redwing blackbirds will soon be gone. A faint odor of skunk lingers near the outhouse; that, and burning cedar, and a murky redolence from the bogs behind my back field, a mixture of horse dung and mildewed grass.

All summer I let spiderwebs accumulate in my home, to trap insects that invade the porous structure. But it's almost time to jab the webs with a broom. I watch the kitchen windows at night to determine the best time for this operation: the moths are my barometer. As long as they batter against the dirty glass, the spiderwebs are safe. Each evening, though, as September approaches October, fewer moths attack the windows. Underwings, sphinx moths, Isabellas, tiger moths, caterpillars, tiny fragile moths with raggedy transparent green wings, and other little humpy numbers, with short fat antennae, that resemble teeny owls.

Absorbed in work one night I absentmindedly listen to rain pattering against the portal roof. But when I look up, I discover the sound is caused by an army of moths fluttering against the windows, trying to escape the frosty darkness. A week later, half of them are gone.

Soon, only a few moths are spawned each night. Nearly inert, they cling to the cement wall by the portal light bulb, so lethargic my fingertip fails to arouse them. With that, I know the mosquitoes too are gone, and raise my broom to the spiderwebs.

September and October are months for doing chores, repairing the ravages of summer, putting things in order. I recondition fences, sink new posts, mend gaps in the barbwire with baling strands. Knock down weeds, perhaps, rake 'em up, have a burning. Leaves I let stay where they fall, to rot and crumble, enriching the earth. Dry stalks along the ditch beside the driveway go up in smoke. I lean on my rake, captivated by soporific flames, growing drowsy from "fire laziness." Fence posts smolder at their bases, I scrape away glowing cinders. A dragonfly flip-flops through the smoke, disoriented and dying.

The lower part of my field is drenched. Cattle trampled the ditch bank two fields north, and that water is flooding me out. So I don irrigation boots and head for the break. A Wilson's snipe jumps from the bog. Ocher locust leaves are caught in an eddy at the curve in the ditch. Underwater, long vibrant algae plants undulate over tawny pebbles as I chip away at half-frozen earth, plugging the gap.

After the front field is cut and baled, I rake up the stray grass and pile it on top of the small protruding roof of the garage. On my back on that roof, I relax, staring at the sky and at big cottonwood leaves beginning to mottle; at intervals they click off their branches and—*de-ci de-là*—drift earthward, landing with scratchy ticks among raspy sunflower stalks or atop the chicken-wire roof of the pigeons' flight pen. In the sky, fantastic clouds shaped like atomic mushrooms undergo leisurely transformations. I am blissfully tasting salt above my upper lip when somebody fires a high-powered rifle down by the road—*boom!*—and a lead slug chatters through the locust trees along the front ditch by the house, chipping off branches, and spooking Tom Trujillo's horse, who stumbles—leaping the ditch—and almost breaks her leg, then gallops crazily into the field, wondering how to escape the danger.

Rolled over on my belly, I cringe, pressed flat, my heart thumping apprehensively. But that's it, all over . . . quickly gone. Seconds accumulate into minutes, and serenity floods the area.

Several years ago I had a pet goose, a quiet and gentle soul. She loved to snuggle her head in the heat of my armpit. When I hosed her down she insisted on sticking her face—open-eyed—into the jet stream. Come September, she fashioned a nest in leaves beside the front irrigation ditch, laid three eggs, and settled in for a long spell. Though the eggs could not have been fertilized, I didn't have the heart to remove them. I'm not sure why; but she seemed so maternally intent on brooding.

Day and night she warmed her eggs; I brought grain to her place. Leaves piled up around her, but she never lost faith. Temperatures dropped, and in the morning she would be nestled imperviously among the frosted grasses, her breath emerging in tiny plumes. One night I looked out the window and it was snowing. At 2:00 A.M. I walked over to the nest and sat down beside her. Snow approached the earth as if each flake—attached to an invisible thread—were being lowered meticulously to protect it from damage. My goose stared into the night, rigid and protective. I waited awhile. Despite the quiet storm, no breezes stirred: the air actually felt cozy and warm. A white layer built up on her back, and I brushed it off. I talked to her, but she didn't acknowledge my presence. Finally, I apologized for letting it go on this long, reached beneath her breast, and appropriated the eggs. She raised no protest, uttered not a sound. I flung the eggs far into the darkness, stuck around a moment longer, then went inside.

Next morning she left her nest, returning to a more sensible routine among the chickens.

I noticed that the four young aspens along the south side of the garden had oystershell-scale disease. So I stopped at the Lilac Shop in town and asked how to combat this scourge. They sold me a can full of something with "ortho-" on the label. It contained malathion. I read the directions carefully, shit a brick, and figured: I can't spray this poison onto my trees, I'll kill everything within a hundred miles!

The alternative was a chair, water, and steel wool. Carefully I scrubbed the aspen trunks, scraping off the oystershell scales, trying not to damage the bark. A decade earlier, my friend Justin Locke had brought the trees up from Santa Fe, and helped me put them into the ground. For years, they remained stunted, on the verge of dying. I refused to water them. "Sink or swim on your own initiative, trees," I snapped heartlessly. And for a long spell it appeared they might succumb. Yet while they went nowhere above the earth, their roots must have been probing down through the caliche an inch at a time, reaching for an aquifer. Because suddenly, two years ago, while seated in the outhouse admiring their golden foliage, I realized they had gotten *tall!*

October. I decided to use the kitchen hose to wash my car. But it was frozen. So I brought it inside to thaw out. It sat on the kitchen floor by my feet, warming up as I typed. Several hours passed. Then, out the corner of an eye, I noticed a movement on the floor. And from one end of the hose emerged a little water snake, thoroughly puzzled by its interrupted hibernation.

Okay, so it's autumn, time for work, and I'm steaming along strong on a novel. Sometimes, in the wee hours, I take a break, make coffee, sink my teeth into an apple, flick on the radio, and read the paper. The station I tune in to most often is WBAP, Fort Worth–Dallas, my favorite country-and-western clear-channel broadcaster. Bill Mack's "Open Road Show," to be specific. With all the latest eighteen-wheeler information, and featuring Harold Taft, The World's Greatest Weatherman. Wee Marie handles the telephones, taking requests originating from everywhere in America. Rangefire Rita's husky voice warns truckers not to throw them smokes out the window into dry prairie grass, starting something they can't handle. The music is comprehensive, both modern and historical: Tex Ritter, Hank Williams, Bob Wills and the Texas Playboys . . . also Merle Haggard, Loretta Lynn, and Dolly Parton. The wind is howling outside, but I'm snug in my disorganized, comfortable kitchen, listening to Merle Travis sing:

> *"If you want your freedom P.D.Q,*
> *divorce me C.O.D."*

Pitch-soaked logs are burning ferociously in the stove, giving off waves of heat. When I shove in another, there's a moment of relative silence, then suddenly the log goes *whoosh!*, catching fire, damn near exploding. And the words roll off my typewriter in droves.

The old conscience is never really clear, though, until I have laid in a monster supply of timber for the winter. Even if I had no need of fire, wood gathering is a ritual I would ignore at my own peril. But I tend to put it off, often almost beyond the point of no return—don't ask me why. My laziness seems to be an inherent part of the ritual. Yet finally an early snowstorm triggers my panic button, and I awaken one morning ready to head for the hills.

A stunning day is hanging out at my windows like an irresistible nymphet, crisp and unblemished except by a line of clean upturned clouds over the eastern mountains that look like spindrift off ocean breakers. Tiger, the wild Siamese cat who lives in the roof, limps down the portal ladder (which I use for turning the TV aerial—north for channels seven and thirteen, south for channels four and five), and meows for breakfast. A pair of Lewis's woodpeckers under the pear tree are stabbing rotten fruit. Some cat has ripped apart the hornet's nest in an apple tree, and the intricate imprisoning branches are decorated with its pale gray tatters. Yawning, I fling an ax and a shovel into the bus, add an apple and a jar of water, and then can't resist an urge to answer the jangling telephone.

It's Andrés Martínez, in search of a partner with whom to gather wood.

Made for each other? Don't you believe it! I shudder as he nonchalantly lays out the plan. For Andrés is no casual Sunday plucker of genteel dry branches, but a man who believes in The Real Thing. Chain saws, gasoline, double-bladed and razor-sharp axes, and overloaded pickup trucks! Heavy green wood is his game, and he fells it amid cries of "Timber!" Though in his eighties, he can chop me right under the table—and demolish a twelve-course meal after the outing into the bargain!

Although he has no fireplace or wood stove in his trailer, Andrés usually buys a permit in the autumn and collects as much wood as he can, laying it on friends. In every inhabitant of the valley, I suppose, beats the stubborn corazón of a pigheaded leñero. I suspect that for some folks around Taos, heaven is a piñon forest, a sharp ax, a lightweight chain saw that never breaks down, and a permit from the U.S. government to amass as many cords of green piñon as a person could assemble throughout eternity.

I have gathered wood a few times with Andrés. Let me declare right now that I abhor the cutting of green piñon trees. But there's something about a local yokel that loves the ear-splitting howl of a cantankerous, erratically functioning chain saw gnawing through the pitch-filled yellow wood of a gnarled piñon, the corner-boy, inner-city hoodlum evergreen of our coniferous forests.

Andrés and I first jounced off together to level a portion of the Carson National Forest in September 1978. He had a decrepit Pioneer chain saw, constructed during the Neanderthal age of chain-saw evolution. It weighed a ton, but he wielded it with impunity. When I took over the first time, it nearly dislocated a shoulder, clunked out of my hands, and almost butchered my foot. Five minutes later, my back ached; I thought blood must be dribbling from my ears. Youthful and proud, however, I staggered on and managed to level a few trees. Collapsing for a break, I guzzled a half-gallon of water, wondering how much a good neck brace would cost and if the cramps in my forearms and fingers would ever go away.

Nearby, scornful of "breaks," my friend effortlessly pruned off branches and partitioned the trunks, using a double-bladed ax sharp enough to split hairs. And while I spent hours sucking on old apple-juice jars filled with cool water, Andrés disdained even to moisten his lips, claiming he wished to avoid dehydration.

The ground was littered with annoying prickly-pear cactuses whose vicious spines probed through the fabric of my sneakers, making me yelp, curse, and limp about. Although Andrés wore his tattered boots, which appeared eminently vulnerable to cactus attack, he seemed to receive not even a solitary quill.

Well, we chopped up all the wood and loaded the '66 Ford. We piled wood up to the gunwales, then up to the top of the stock sideboards. There I suggested we stop. For the sake of the truck, of course. Not to mention the sake of ourselves should the pickup collapse out there in the middle of nowhere.

For Andrés, though, as for most of the hardy, long-time Taos wood gatherers, a truck filled with heavy green piñon only up to the top of its side racks is a half-filled vehicle. If the tailpipe isn't scraping the ground, you've still got a ways to go.

Keep in mind, too, that the underside of the bed of a properly filled pickup is meant to rest not upon its metal springs or shock absorbers, but directly upon the rear axle.

So Andrés had me drive around, knocking over—with his truck's front bumper—huge dead stumps, which we heaved up to the Olympian heights of our massive cargo.

Prepared at last to depart, I figured no truck that overloaded could possibly survive the primitive dirt roads and the steep descent into, and ascent out of, the Rio Grande Gorge, which lay between us and home.

I am what is known in the trade as a "worrywart." Andrés is what is known as "a laid-back human being." So off we rattled in a half-ton truck with its twelve-ton cargo, grading the road behind us with the tailgate. I kept tensing for blowouts, but Andrés chattered unperturbedly about other things: over there our mutual friend Pacomio Mondragón used to winter his animals; and they say that several year-round springs exist down in the Petaca Arroyo. . . .

Cutting wood seems to make Andrés grow younger. Myself, I aged a half-dozen years trying to maneuver our absurd load safely home from the western forests. Then, swinging cautiously around the final dead-man's curve on the descent stage of the gorge road just above the Route 96 bridge, we had a blowout. We neither wrenched outward and plunged to our gory dooms, nor careened out of control to smash (and explode) against the left-hand cliff. At two miles an hour, and tipping the scales as we did, the truck simply clunked to a standstill like a poleaxed elephant, and simmered.

No problem, however. We had two jacks and a spare tire. In deference to my friend's age and wisdom, I did the jacking, removed the flat, bolted on the bald spare, and lowered the truck onto the fresh tire—which had no air.

"Don't panic, John." Behind the cab seat Andrés located a brilliant gadget, an airhose with a bunch of spark plug–shaped attachments. Simply remove a spark plug from the engine block, select the corresponding-sized attachment and fit it onto the hose, screw the hose into the block, brace rocks in front of the truck's tires, slip the gearshift into neutral and start the pickup, then press the nozzle of the airhose to the intake valve on the deflated tire, and—presto!—in no time flat that piston has obligingly pumped the tire full of air!

Unfortunately, in this case, one spark-plug attachment for the airhose was missing—the one that would have screwed snugly into *this* Ford's engine block.

I fluster easily, but not Andrés. Better than me he understands that life is long, and rarely a smooth ride. And anyway, an incontrovertible axiom of Taos wood gatherers is this: given that you are always behind the wheel of dilapidated vehicles held together with prayers and baling wire, toting ten times their allowable capacity, you must *never* be prepared for emergencies.

This provides the marvelous opportunity, on almost every wood run, to prove you are an inventive genius as, somehow, you manage to triumph over the disasters that inevitably darken your adventure.

Having discovered—tch, tch!—that our ingenious airhose lacked a single propitious gizmo necessary to its proper functioning, we began flagging down the occasional passerby in search of a solution. In due course, sure enough, an old fellow behind the wheel of a rattletrap wheezed to a rickety stop, and ceremoniously handed over a bicycle pump.

One hour later, as I writhed on the edge of the cliff in the clutches of near-fatal fibrillations, I gasped triumphantly for the heavens to note: "I inflated that damn spare tire, by God!"

As always, whenever Andrés was guiding us through these perilous adventures, we arrived home in plenty of time for one of Jeannette's mouth-watering meals, which are always complemented by several unbelievably tasty glasses of homemade chokecherry wine.

When I'm alone buscando leña, it's a different story. Amateur-ville, to be sure . . . but not without charm. I pilot the old VW bus up the Little Rio Grande, catch a few trout, bathe, perhaps, in the icy water, then leisurely scavenge the detritus of past years, or pick at other leñeros' leavings. Wandering across permit-area hillsides where Texas chain-saw massacrers have butchered countless pines, I salvage the small waste branches that will perfectly fit my kitchen stove. I heave these branches up and down steep hillsides into a dozen piles among the ruins; later I stack them so deliberately in the bus that I leave with almost a full pickup load.

Collecting on weekdays, I have the forest to myself. That is the great good fortune of my métier: it allows me, if I want, almost always to be alone.

Returning from Pot Creek, or from the Little Rio Grande, I often pull off the highway overlooking a roadside meadow in which the stream has been widened by beaver dams into tranquil pools. Inevitably, the brown trout are feeding. The dimples of bigger fish are hardly detectable as they slurp in bugs—minuscule rings quiver where their snouts barely break water. The little fish are enthusiastic acrobats, however, leaping high and twisting like rodeo stock before slapping back into their home territory, rocking the water with waves enormously disproportionate to their size.

If I have remembered my rod, I scurry downhill, circle a bushy cedar at the water's edge, duck through the barbwire, and enter the meadow, quietly laying down dry flies at the end of a long thin leader to catch some of those trout for dinner. I may even wander along the grassy stream banks until well after dark. . . .

At home, another beloved ritual: unloading the wood in the dark. First, though, I sit on the portal, nursing a beer, listening to Tiger pacing the roof overhead and meowing insistently. Then I stagger tiredly over to the bus and begin to fling wood onto the woodpile. My old tattered work gloves provide scant protection for my gouged and battered fingers, but I kind of like the wounds—they are a connection to the feel of my wood. Perhaps the moon is bragging; maybe its reflected glory highlights sinuous veins of silvery foliage curving along the rough contours of my potholed driveway. And cats are scampering, excited to have me home, splashing playfully in the leaves.

When the work is done, I retire to the bathroom, plug in an electric heater, draw a tub, settle luxuriously into the steaming water, and open a book. Tina the bulldog arrives and assumes a pose in front of the heater, her nose practically soldered to the bars. Duke hops onto the edge of the tub, dips a paw into the water, and reaches out to paddle my knee. Then he arranges himself into a sphinx and regards me sleepily. With my index finger I paint a drop of water on his nose, and sadly remember his mother.

Loretta was born during the summer of seventy-eight, out in the woodpile, daughter of a wild breed. Her infancy passed in secret. I knew she existed, but just barely. Slouching toward the outhouse in the morning, I might catch a blur of gray and white disappearing into the woodpile. A squirrel, I'd think, and pay little attention. The animal was so small and shy that I simply never got a good look.

Winter that year savaged autumn prematurely. By mid-November, temperatures had dropped to well below zero. During Thanksgiving week every night saw temperatures of twenty below. Even the clearest sunniest days seemed unable to rise above zero.

One evening, I heard a kitten mewling. When I opened the kitchen door, a shadow flickered under the car. I put out a plate of milk and some stale catfood. At the time, I had no animals, and no desire for any, either. Life, I thought, should be kept as overtly simple as possible.

The milk disappeared, also the catfood. Next day I replenished the meager rations, waited patiently, and then burst outside to catch a glimpse of the animal. Trapped in a corner of the portal by the woodbin was a filthy and exhausted little kitten, its back arched, hair frizzed, fierce mouth hissing and spitting.

Obviously iced through to the bone, it also shivered uncontrollably.

I backed off. The kitten glared with frightened wild eyes, unwilling to move until I had retreated inside.

A week of standoffs ensued. No Taos weather had ever been more bitter. The frozen kitten ate on my porch, then slunk into a cardboard box in the woodbin. I had determined to be hardhearted. If it survived wild, fine. But I wanted no pets intruding on my solitude.

The antagonisms were mutual. The wild kitten ate in secret, retreated to the box, and grew more sickly. Snot dribbled from its nose and further caked knots of dirt in its pathetic fur. Despite the food, it was soon so weak it began to defecate and urinate in its box. Finally, I decided to end the suffering with my son's pellet gun.

Instead, I put on a padded ski glove and went to grab the kitten. Though almost dead, it went rigid with powerful fury and tried to kill me, clawing, almost biting through the glove, spitting angrily. A more ferocious and enraged animal I have never handled. Opening the kitchen door, I tossed the stinky bundle inside. It landed on the floor, already flying, and zoomed beneath the stove.

That was November. I never saw the kitten again until mid-January. In the meantime, I figured the animal lived because its water went down, food disappeared, and little turds appeared in the Kitty Litter.

Night after cold winter night I sat at the kitchen table, typing on my novel. Gradually, the offensive smell of rotting kittycat subsided. I shrugged, poured more food and water, forked shit from the Kitty Litter, and stirred the granules to dry them out. Naturally, I also wondered about life under my stove. No doubt the kitten was better, and growing stronger, perhaps also bigger, judging from the food it

demolished. Uneasily, a few times, I dreamed that I might awaken one night with a ferocious bobcat at my throat.

But I never caught a glimpse of it. Sometimes, lying in my living-room bed in the dark, I heard it crunching dry food in the kitchen. Yet for two months the kitten never left the shelter of that stove when I was present.

Came a midnight, though, when I happened to look down from my typewriter, and there sat a beautiful, fluffy kitten beside the stove, staring at me. I shifted slightly, and—lickety-split!—it fled.

I can't remember exactly the taming process. It happened slowly. I resisted giving a name, for I had no inkling of the beast's sex. Yet slowly but surely it began to venture from hiding to watch me at work. From the corner of one eye I saw it emerge, but continued typing. For at first, if I simply quit typing, the jittery kitten split. If it stayed, either I sat extra still or tried moving very deliberately. After a time, the kitten accepted these moves. Soon, it adventured a foot from the stove, then two feet. I dangled a string off the table edge, and one evening the kitten bumped into it accidentally, sprung a foot in the air, retreated, spent an hour analyzing the object, concluded it wasn't dangerous, and returned and gave the string a vicious swat with one paw. I chuckled, and the sound of my voice launched the kitten into its hidey-hole.

It grew more brazen by the week. I conversed with the animal in a low murmur, and it became accustomed to my voice. Every night, after I settled down, it emerged, batted the string, and explored further. So long as I made no sudden moves, it stayed in the open.

As soon as I went to bed, it began to get downright nosy. I heard it rustling around in the dark kitchen. Thumps and flopping noises accompanied its antics with the string. Finally, I heard it enter the living room, walking on tiptoes, sniffing at my blankets.

January, February, then March. Hidden during the day, the kitten came out regularly at night. I dangled more strings, put a golf ball on the floor, added other toys. I wriggled the string myself across the floor, and, waiving all caution, the kitten chased after it, absorbed in the game. Every day less fearful, it came closer to me. Finally, I reached out, patting it gently. Enthralled by the string, it paid no attention. So I stroked my hand down its back—and received a swift bap that tore open my flesh as the kitten screeched and jetted to safety under the stove.

But its resistance was wearing thin. That gloomy cave was no fun anymore. We had longer playful sessions. Outdoors, spring was making overtures. I went to pick the kitten up . . . and was painfully smacked again.

Nevertheless, we both persisted. Next time I grabbed the wild beast, shoving it quickly onto my lap, I held it tightly and stroked a little. Though it had decided not to bite, the kitten remained so tense I quickly set it free.

I decided then not to force the situation by trying to handle the animal. And inevitably, a night arrived when I heard my kitten enter the living room. It padded around, emitting unquiet lonely mewls from deep in its throat. For about an hour it paced, talking, then I felt weight land on the bed. The kitten held very still for ten minutes, waiting to see if I had any alarming gestures up my sleeve. Then it stalked onto my chest and settled there, its face just inches from my chin, and started purring. I counted to a hundred, then raised one hand and cupped its haunches—the animal kept on purring. I stroked it all over without incident. I even poked fingers between its hind legs and probed a bit to determine the sex, thus discovering what I had not known, while my peaceful new pal kept purring.

That night I named her Loretta.

In the wall of a utility room off the kitchen is a small hole through which the cats come and go. Most of their nights are spent outdoors, hunting. Loretta, that wild and skittish black-and-white beauty is one of the all-time one-cat mouse-demolition derbies. Her son Duke—beautiful, black, stupid, and lazy—is a different story. His idea of hunting is to jump his mom as she squeezes through the hole with a *Microtus pennsylvanicus* in her jaws, and heist the field mouse from her.

Duke's dad, the handsome remote roof-dwelling Siamese, never comes through the hole: he likes his wild kingdom. Sometimes at night I put down Tiger's catfood, then sit in the dilapidated portal armchair, watching him eat. Maybe it's snowing. Toward town, the misty sky shines. Tiger meows, always talking, always pained. When I pick him up he doesn't resist, but only suffers being cuddled, and never purrs. At the first opportunity, he jumps off my lap and walks away—stiff-legged, macho, undemonstrative, a loner. Yet I always hear him out in the dark, or overhead, mewing his remote Siamese anguish.

From time to time the autumn rodent slaughter gets out of hand. Exposed in the harvested fields, the mice are sitting ducks. Every half hour either Duke or Loretta appears in the kitchen, emitting a proud growly purr, and once again I am treated to a ten-minute corrida, the predeath dance of a valiant mouse. Mostly, they stand and fight, up on their tiny hind legs, snarling, dying with their boots on. Loretta rarely drags it out: her hunting instincts are too deep. She drives a tooth through their skulls and chomps them up in just minutes, leaving no traces. But her adolescent son is a buffoon, spoiled by his easy-street existence. Inevitably, his mice escape: they hide beneath the refrigerator, or in an irrigation boot, or in newspapers stacked by the stove. Wandering in a daze, Duke meows disconsolately, a chubby, inept, black velvet drone.

A spacey cat is Duke, also a trifle remote, like his dad. But once in a while he joins his mother on the bed at 2:00 A.M. and flips on his motor. Flames leap from his fur as I stroke it. Electricity crackles from that black pelt, scaring Loretta, who jumps up and backs away. But Duke could care less that he's on fire.

More than once I have awakened covered with junco feathers: much feasting has occurred over my sleeping body. In the springtime, I may leap from the hay to answer the kitchen phone and land squarely upon a half-chewed water snake!

But I love the cats. They touch my life without intruding. Friendly, independent, and largely silent, they move contentedly through their small universe without complaint, sleek and powerful and clean. We are attached to each other. When I reconnoiter the back field at dusk to clear my head on the mountain vista, they join me, bouncing playfully in the brown grass. Or, rolling onto their backs, they beg me to play with them. I scrabble fingers into their chests and tummies; they grab my wrist with their front paws as their hind feet thump me painfully in fierce delight. Often I don a ski glove, so they can bite and kick to their hearts' content.

Returning from town, I spy them in my neighbor's field, awaiting a telltale mouse movement in the grass. But as I enter the driveway, they gallop for home, arriving at the front door full of greetings just as I pull in.

The idyll, as usual with Taos animals, is short-lived. One day, Loretta simply never returns. I look for her beside the roads, perhaps hit by a car, and find nothing. My guess is she wandered too far afield and was gratuitously offed by some kid with a .22.

Shortly thereafter, Tiger disappears for a month. I miss his lonely nocturnal noises. Finally, I hear his plaintive song in the orchard, and discover him dying in the tawny growths beneath the crab apple tree. Light as a feather and all chewed up, he has one hind leg badly mangled and infected. I feed him and drive to the vet, who sees no way to treat the wound and puts him to sleep.

Don't ask me how moronic Duke, originally the least wild of the three, has survived so far almost a year beyond his parents. After their deaths, he grew up and became a relentless and successful hunter. I constantly feed him poison pills to knock out the worms he contracts from mice and birds. Not long ago, I awoke at 3:00 A.M. when he landed on my bed, freshly nailed by a skunk. I dragged him into a hot bath, scrubbed him down with tomato sauce and Breck shampoo, and locked him in the bathroom in front of the heater. But Duke is not—as my friend Mike Kimmel might say—wrapped too tight. After a two-day sulk, he went out on the hustings again, and promptly became the first animal I have ever known stupid enough to tangle a second time with a skunk!

Duke is not much of a fighter, either. Long ago his balls fell to a surgeon's knife. Pampered scion of a genteel upbringing, he suffers indignities with indifference. To get a worm pill into Loretta, I had to mummify her in a towel, wear gloves, and then pin her down with one knee while prying her jaws apart and jamming down the pill. Often she shredded the towel and half ingested my hand! By contrast, Duke simply purrs in my lap as I unwrap the pill. Then I prod open his mouth, pop in the pill, and clamp shut his jaws until he swallows. No gloves, no towels. The cat stops purring for a moment, swallows, and then restarts his contented feline mutter as I tell him he is a good boy.

Duke is not above defending his territory, however. He does it mostly by show, having a distaste for actual physical contact. In battle, he arches and frizzes silently, and tiptoes sideways in a threatening manner. He never backs down, but rarely seems to make his point emphatically. Over the past year various neighborhood interlopers have given him little if any respect.

One brazen tom started squeezing through the utility-room hole and poaching Chef's Blend from Duke's kitchen bowl. Hearing this illegal crunching, several times I roared in from the living room to arrest the impostor, but it always skedaddled before I arrived.

Soon I loathed that brazen cat. Duke grew ruffled, also, and began to show up missing great tufts of hair, licking his wounds. Obviously, the price of freedom being eternal vigilance, I had to shoot the impudent brawler. I loaded my .22 pistol and laid it on the bedroom desk. Immediately, the crucial moment arrived. A faint crunch issued from the kitchen as feline incisors chopped through Cheerios-sized kernels of Chef's Blend. Duke uncurled from his nest in my goosedown sleeping bag, ears pricked and eager. Together—stealthily—we tiptoed through the living room . . . and burst into the kitchen, finally catching the rascal by surprise.

I had psyched myself to start blasting in the kitchen—but how do you shoot a streak of lightning? We barreled into the utility room, and Duke leaped on the hindquarters still protruding from the narrow hole. A gluttonous eater, our trespasser was having trouble squeezing out. I jammed my foot up against a haunch, effectively halting his progress. He howled and twitched, but I couldn't fire, fearful of hitting Duke. Obviously, I could have crippled the cat by mashing hard with my foot, but that seemed too grisly. In the end, I lifted my foot, and the cat sprang free, yanking Duke through the hole behind him.

I stormed out the kitchen door. A gray streak zipped through swirls of driveway leaves and sailed gracefully off the ground, up the basketball backboard viga, and vaulted into obscurity beneath the eaves of the garage roof, chased by Duke, the mighty miniature panther.

I struggled up the viga, terrified of my own gun, never having chased anything with a loaded pistol before, and under such emotional circumstances to boot. Carefully, I reached up and deposited the pistol on the roof, then hauled myself up by means of wooden supports bracing the viga against the garage. It would be just my luck, I figured, to be accidentally drilled between the eyes as I poked my head over the edge of the roof.

By the time I cautiously clawed onto the roof, and gingerly availed myself of the .22, our prey was gone. Duke paced the old dirt roof beneath the new wooden one, growling nervously, obviously relieved that no fight had occurred.

Our terror campaign worked, though, and that bad cat never returned.

It's early, early morning. Duke is sleepily deployed on the edge of the porcelain tub, eyes closed, sensuously breathing in steam. I am browsing through Horace Judson's book *The Search for Solutions*, snuffling about in Einstein's theory of relativity, Newtonian physics, hydrogen bomb makers, the discovery of capillaries. A half-dozen crickets and spiders are floating in the water. The house is silent. Outside, falling leaves tick against the roof and windows like rain. No wind blows, but leaves are loose on their boughs, and a mysterious, swollen atmospheric pressure pops them loose, as if by magic.

I never rake fallen leaves. Wind sculpts them for me in drifts along garden sheep-fencing, in crevices of the woodpile, against the adobe foundation of the garage, around the roots of lilac bushes south of the kitchen. I can smell them through the open window, pungent, decaying, wistful. A light rain commences, instantly catalyzing autumn redolence. Especially the elm leaves carpeting the ground in front of the portal. Mocha, white, and beige, they gleam with an impeccable iridescence, like scales shocked from radiant fishes.

Tomorrow, Duke—an aloof Egyptian apparition—will prowl across the precious elm leaves. Just before dark, the leaves will emit a silvery glow reminiscent of peacock finery. Jaggedy teardrop shapes, rimed in fluorescence, delicate veins vivid in sterling relief. The argentine ripples caused by wind make them glitter like moonlit sea swells. Bit by bit I crush this perfection, tracking through the leaves with my wheelbarrow full of wood.

My friend Julian LeDoux has brought me a cord of piñon. Never have I seen such exquisite fuel. Dry and sharp and professional—it smells like turpentine. The color of this treasure, as I hack away at dusk, is vibrant gray, lucid and clean. Bigotes of furry-green Spanish moss cling to the bark. Each stick I split radiates a gemlike clarity, perfectly textured, a work of art. How can I stoop so low as to *burn* this stuff? Better to sculpt it, place it on pedestals, or just leave it be. So alive is this wood it makes me ache. A soul breathes, not at all inert. Dreamily, I split the tough chunks, feeling happy and sexy.

I can see my neighbors scratching their heads, bald-facedly puzzled or nauseated by such silly euphoria. Wood, after all, is wood. After sixty years of chopping it to keep warm, only the basics remain. It's a pain in the ass to split, cuate, but what the hell, it's cheaper than electricity or butane!

No matter, I'll take my fling and risk ridicule. If meddling with beautiful wood gives me esthetic joy, so be it. I'm not ashamed.

Green elm leaves dying, and the texture and smell of pitch-filled firewood, make me horny. Holding this blond and silvery log in my hand, I see and feel the swollen temptation of peachy breasts.

I halt the wheelbarrow on the mosaic of elm leaves. Mauve-green, gray-green, beige-green, bright and soft, apple and turquoise, dull and mute . . . moss green, olive and marine and sky green, intense and subdued, not quite dead, smelling funky. Duke slinks by, meows once in a singular fashion. Rich and dark, his fur glitters as if charged with electricity after being washed in mysterious gells and egg whites. In fact, that ebony fur is as wealthy-looking as midnight mink.

What's that smell from the garden? Garlic, of course. Rows once domestically planted have gone wild. Pigeons, in the far background, are burbling placidly, carrying on ineffectual little wars.

Standing in the tub, I peer out the small window—shit, it's *snowing!* Too, leaves are falling. A foggy luminescence lights up the sky. A skunk rattles around by the garbage cans. In the morning, before it all melts, I'll go outside and interpret stories in the white mantle. A dog trotted up the driveway, circled the VW bus, crossed the little lawn, and hopped through the fence into my neighbor's yard. Or cat pawprints—Duke on his nightly rambles? Crossing the driveway, they

enter the garage, then exit again, checking the outhouse, and pass through a hole in the chicken wire approaching the pigeon coop. Eventually, desultorily, they stalk off through dry sunflowers into the back field.

Blissfully, I sail my bathtub outside. Slouched under the steaming water, I let leaves gather on my belly, they form reefs around my knees. I captain my tub across the little yard, indulging in chauvinist reveries. You put on a garter belt, silk stockings, creamy high heels, and bend over happily leering, playacting a lurid Klondike moll. One sneeze, though, and we break up into carnal rag-doll guffaws. Gusts of autumn burnish your silver and ashen curves with rusty, ocher, and birch-gray highlights. I'd like to write your name in the air with come. Or carefully paint your plump lips with jism, then kiss, touching tongue tips through the sticky plasm.

Such strong aches. Tonight, alone, I lie in my sleeping bag, cupping my testicles like a little boy. Nearby, in the darkness, a magpie scrawks—a rare occurrence . . . scavenger nightmares? I think I can hear the stars twinkling, sounding like Alka-Seltzer. The Milky Way, semen of the universe, palpitates across the icy night. I love you. And I can feel the presence of gawky long-legged mosquito hawks floating on transparent wings across the dark diaphanous silence of my room.

I jump as the cat lands on the piano keys, playing an atonal arpeggio in the other room. Next—such quiet! Even dust holds its breath. Duke floats onto the bed. Brief rivulets of sparks chatter off his shoulders as he shifts into a more comfortable position, too tired from mouse hunting even to purr. Wind minces at the window, peeping inside, hoping for a glimpse of tiny murders. Bits of adobe roof dirt dislodge, sprinkling through cracks in the ceiling onto the desk.

I cast my imagination across the mesa and into the Rio Grande Gorge. Tomorrow, the snow will melt, the sun will shine, the river will be low, clear, ready for fishing. Now that my wood is in, I'm ready to go. All year I have awaited this moment.

In June, again in August, I stared down at the river from the high bridge, measuring the water's depth and clarity. Slowly, a sandbar a half-mile north became revealed. Over the weeks it widened: the river became less murky, ready for fly-fishing.

So begins The Season.

They are waiting down there—mysterious, stupid trout. In my bed, thinking about them, I reconstruct the underwater river. Enormous boulders, convolutedly shaped and contoured, overshadow gravel beds. How dark and raging is the fast water, topped by white waves and turbulent foam!

Down deep, growing hungry, they watch the water clear up, eager to commence the autumn feeding. Rapacious, sinister sleek torpedoes behind rocks and in back eddies, fanning quietly to maintain their positions in darkness broken by vague pinpricks of starlight, or by the half-dissolved flutters of distant heat lightning.

Noisy currents rattle and crash around them. Yet, suspended in entropy, they expend little energy, in no mood to challenge the green gloom, unaware that tomorrow I'll be down on the river, hunting.

If only tonight I could experience those thundering depths, creep into the nocturnal shadows of boulders, insinuate myself into their stationary vigils, cold-blooded minimonsters at rest, eyes wide open . . . do they ever sleep? Do fish dream?

What a queer and voluptuous vision.

PART THREE

Then he steadied himself and began to cast
and the whole world turned to water.

—Norman McLean
A River Runs Through It

FIVE

Above all else, the gorge is a wild place.

Paradoxically, it is least wild in the well-advertised Wild River section an hour north of Taos, a stretch that has been promoted into a tourist delight because it was declared a national landmark. Up there the gorge is wide, the trails steep but amiable. Cabanas for overnight campers dot the landscape. I love that portion of the river, but usually steer clear of it until well after Labor Day.

Elsewhere, the river is difficult to reach and honestly primitive. For miles it trickles between dangerous sheer walls impossible to scale. The few difficult trails are traveled regularly by only a handful of hardy fishermen.

In olden days, these bajadas were used almost exclusively by shepherds, and they are still frequented by remaining herds. Laboriously, sheep clamber down rocky paths winding uncomfortably through steep talus configurations to drink in the Rio Grande. Half a day the animals may spend climbing out. Sometimes they rest overnight on ledge formations. Coyote and deer also frequent the bajadas at night. Often I spot their tracks in the sand of small riverside beaches, but I have never seen the animals themselves down there.

A bajada may have several names, depending on the individual who uses it. Bajada de la Víbora—Rattlesnake Trail. Bajada del Caballo—Horse Trail. Gutierrez Trail. Francisco Antonio. Miner's Trail. San Diego. La Junta. El Aguaje. Chiflo. Bear Crossing. Big and Little Arsenic. The names by which I know others may not be in common usage across the county. Rope Trail. Sheep Corral. Rockslide. Suicide Slide. Powerline. And Ox Trail.

No signs identify most trails. If you don't know exactly where they drop over the cliff, they are impossible to find. You might descend into a small crevice, or circle around a huge rock, or literally drop off the cliff into space—and suddenly there is a path to the river. Often, it is only by a few bent grasses that you can get your bearings. Last year, trailside rocks on two of the bajadas were spray-painted by enterprising fishermen, a garish and disrupting graffiti. But other seldom-used bajadas are invisible—instinct must carry you down through boulders and sagebrush to the river.

Powerline is among my favorites. Its difficulty makes it attractive to me. Often, I lose the trail entirely and launch a freefall journey down the steep incline. At the bottom is a wide pool with frothy ripples at the head, a deep channel swinging east, and shallow water and a sandbar below. On the western bank, vermilion-green reedy grasses grow thickly on a sandy beach. Because of a bend in the river, the autumn sun departs late, so fishing doesn't perk up until well into the evening. On several bluebird days I have shed all my clothes and skinny-dipped in the icy Powerline pool, then lounged nude on the warm rocks, luxuriously pummeled by sunshine before getting dressed and rigging up for trout.

Another bajada that sees little action is Rope Trail. It has a reputation for snakes, though I have never bumped into one there. More irritating is an infestation of small prickly-pear cactus whose harassing spines stab painfully through my cloth sneakers. Steep and short, the bajada offers a few adventures—two ten-foot cliffs, a narrow couloir that must be negotiated backward, a small minefield of prickly-sharp agaves, and an unstable rocky arroyo that arrives at a picturesque little beach by the water's edge.

A quarter-mile north is some fine riffle-fishing located directly beneath the high bridge. The banks are strewn with airmailed garbage, and you must stay alert for lethal rocks tossed by mischievous tourists. Nevertheless, I fish that section often, ignoring the dangers, because it teems with trout.

Suicide Slide is a tunnel of loose rocks that commences at the rim and funnels you without a twist or a turn straight down to the river. I consider it perhaps the most hazardous trail because the loose rocks avalanche easily and can suck under an ankle, chewing it quickly to a pulp. The trail hits the river at a classic fly-fishing hole a half-mile south of Rattlesnake. White water tumbles over rocks at the head of the pool and continues for twenty yards, shallow, fast, and foamy. I have rarely failed to raise a lunker in this pool: beaching that lunker has been another matter entirely.

Caballo Trail is easy to reach if you know the complicated network of mesa roads. The descent is routine. The riverside is open and grassy. On a nearby rock a fisherman spray-painted the following legend:

BEWARE BEN. 8/3/80 MARIO
M. AND FRANK G. KILLED
A RATTLER

Usually, I choose to head south and ford the river where it is wide and shallow at a beautiful island made up of small white stones. Fast riffles and small holes on either side of the island provide many trout. Farther downstream is a hundred yards of rocky riffles, shallow runs, and dynamite back eddies, another of the choicer fish habitats on the Rio Grande.

Way north on the west side of the river, little-used Ox Trail descends to a prime stretch of fishing. The dirt road peters out long before you arrive, and access is by pickup or a four-wheel-drive vehicle only. Piñon forest spills over into the gorge, and the area is chosen by many hunters during deer season.

Ox itself is fairly straightforward, and hairy. I once gazed at it from a lookout point across the gorge, incredulous that I had actually negotiated the trail. Beginning at a majestic, curved palisade, the trail teeters along the edge of a cliff for one-half mile before diving suddenly down toward water. On the upper portion, a slight misstep to your left (going down) or to your right (coming out in darkness), can lead to a fatal hundred-foot fall, straight down. It is on Ox Trail that Rex Dolmuth, a legendary Rio Grande fisherman, died some years back of a heart attack while happily carting out one of the better messes of trout that he had ever inveigled to his flies.

Though risky, the rewards Ox offers are worth it. I always head south to where the water widens and flows over, around, and between a thousand boulders. I can crisscross the swift water, leaping from stone to stone, fishing the entire river. It becomes the most varied, also most accessible terrain on the Rio Grande. And least fished, because few enjoy the challenge of Ox Trail.

Feeling free, then, absurdly youthful and athletic, I prance through the evenings, euphoric, scampering above the foamy spindrift of that wild place out of a childhood fantasy. Something almost illicit describes the ease in which I flicker across that dangerous water. As a kid, of course, I was dismayed at my inability to spread my arms and soar. Now it is as if, late in life, I have been granted such a wish by the Rio Grande.

The river, and my possession of it here, is natural, intricate, sensual. The mystery of boulders is for once exposed, as if an outrageous and maddening puzzle had been taken apart and all its secrets placed on display.

Passion for this adventurous place makes me jubilant!

Charley Reynolds has been fishing the Taos County section of the Rio Grande for thirty-three years.

First and foremost, he's a fly-fisherman, but he isn't that proud.

Spinning gear doesn't interest him: yet if need be, he'll throw anything into the river, from a worm or a salmon egg to a crawdad or a hand grenade, if that's what they're hitting. Last year, in fact, during the second week of January, he actually went ice fishing with a friend and pulled out a mess of trout using cheeseballs, corn, and salmon eggs—a "combo plate," he called it.

"That's Velveeta cheese," he phoned to inform me, after recounting the story in Dori's Bakery in Taos one morning. On certain points, the man is a stickler for accuracy.

But Charley's true artistry on the Rio Grande is with flies, and it begins in his home, in a cluttered workroom where he pours over books about nymphs and damselflies and caddis larvae and little crayfish, and how to imitate them artificially. A master flytier, he can create any sort of illusion, on any type of hook. He prowls the general stores for suitable yarns to spin around his fishhooks, often surreptitiously licking a strand of fluff to determine its underwater disposition. Owl pelts, coyote skins, rabbit fur, and jungle-cock feathers become exotic creations such as Wyoming Bucktails or big stupid Zonkers. He can tie up Montana Stone Flies, or Spruce Matukas, or Taos Badgers. And when all is said and done, he can also tie up a nondescript black, and a nondescript brown fly, unnamed, on a size-ten hook, and use *them* ninety percent of the time.

Arbiter and overlord of my discovery of the Rio Grande, Charley is not exactly your average sort of trout fisherman. But then, the thirty miles or so of Rio Grande that we Taoseños fish isn't exactly your average fabled chalk stream of British lore where Izaak Walton pursued in negligent outings his wily trouts, and found time, between casts, to reflect upon mating turtle-doves and flowers kissed by morning dewdrops.

Nope. No tweed hats, four-in-hand ties, Abercrombie and Fitch vests, or lightweight Orvis fly rods with precious size-twenty pieces of deer-hair fluff on the end of exquisitely hand-tied tapered leaders for us folks here in Taos. In fact, Charley often looks like a Bowery bum when he goes fishing. His pants drag halfway down to his ankles. His hat usually resembles something Tom Mix bequeathed to Andy Devine, who then willed it to Slim Pickens. And although Charley is over six feet tall, he simpers along in old army boots, limping and groaning from ancient injuries at each agonized step, so that you wonder how the man can successfully trek in and out of the gorge, let alone pursue trout with the finesse and expertise such stalking requires.

Under my friend's tutelage, the genteel image of the aristocratic angler is further savaged each time he kills one of his keepers with a lead-weighted wooden bat more suitable for use in a Mafia rumble! And as he stumbles about the boulders of our nigh-impenetrable gorge performing near-mortal pratfalls at every opportunity, does Charley place those keepers in a wicker creel? a canvas pouch? or perhaps in the waterproof pocket of an elaborate vest?

No way.

Charley Reynolds emerges from the gorge like a legendary fox escaping from a nursery-story hen coop, carting his fish out—Taos style—in a raggedy-ass gunnysack!

Should he snag a fly on a rare tree branch above the river, does this bear of a man laboriously squinch about on tiptoes, grappling for branches and bending the tree over double in order to pry off the fly, and—coincidentally—drive a barb through his thumb as the branch twangs backward? Hardly. Caught in this dilemma, my friend takes a backward step, outs with the old pizzolover—a .32-caliber Smith and Wesson, which he keeps in a hand-tooled holster on his hip—and shoots the offending branch, severing it in such a way that it lands politely at his feet.

Charley is no slouch with this gun, or with any gun, for that matter. Like immortal Pancho Lopez of yore, at thirty paces he can shoot out the eye of a bedbug, without bothering to aim. Not long ago, in fact, he was an avid hunter. Steeped in the lore of mountain men and women, he sometimes prowled the mesas during deer season with a replica of a Hawken muzzle-loader. Bewildered Taos citizens occasionally caught glimpses of Charley scurrying between his bank safe-deposit boxes and various southwestern gun shows toting a Santa Claus sack full of revolvers over one shoulder. Too, I have been privileged to watch Charley discharge a firearm, and I have concluded that if they still made silver dollars and I tossed one up, he could drill it six times and make change for me before it hit the ground.

Recently, though, Charley tired of guns, sold off most of his collection, and even lost interest in hunting, though he continues to craft lovely old-fashioned leather holsters and carved powderhorns, which he markets in a few shops around the Southwest.

And, of course, he always carries that little .32 into the gorge, not as a weapon, but as a valuable tool for removing snagged flies from high branches. More to the point—speaking seriously, now—should he bust a tibia, or find himself trapped on a narrow ledge just inches above one of the mountain lions that occasionally drift into the gorge, Charley can fire off three distress shots, alerting folks like me to come arunning.

My guess is that should Charley ever be in serious trouble on the river, his little gun would not fire, having been drenched and bashed silly from a half-dozen accidents en route. "Fact is," says Charley, "that little pistol has been in the water so many times, I might as well go out and buy a rubber gun."

A few years back, after inadvertently doing a somersault into the Rio Grande, Charley had to return later with a portable electronic magnet to ferret his revolver off the bottom of the river.

The man's accidents are legendary, and bear some cataloguing here, if only because a commitment to the Rio Grande seems to inflict all anglers with a most puzzling maladroitness on and off the river: Charley is merely one textbook example of the affliction.

I am writing this section in April 1981. Last week I fished with Charley down on the Red River. Thanks to a paralyzing drought, the water is low enough already to give us fair fly action. During our brief outing, Charley fell in the river twice and smashed the face and crystal off his watch. Next day, he traded a painting for a neighbor's motorcycle. Piloting the bike out her driveway, he lost control and plowed through a barbwire fence. Indomitable (and unshakable), he pushed the Honda onto the road and traveled almost to his own front door before dumping the machine again, this time in his own driveway. When I saw him in a supermarket next morning, he regaled me with tales of his moto misfortunes, said, "Yessir, hell ain't far away when you're on the brink of eternity," and generously offered to take me out for a spin on his new deathmobile.

I have no idea how Charley survives such misfortune. And yet he appears to be relatively healthy. No noticeable scars punctuate his face like grisly zippers. To be sure, as I've mentioned, he limps, the result of an ankle broken on April Fools' Day in the gorge five years ago. But his hands are the only dead giveaway. Big, strong, and blunt, they are also usually quite mangled, callused, bruised, and stained with leatherworking dyes. Several black-and-blue fingernails sport small round holes where Charley has relieved the pressure of blood blisters by drilling red-hot paper clips through the nail—one of life's more painful remedies.

Charley has always told me that he ain't much on doctors.

Or mechanics. Witness his 1973 red Dodge truck called Big Red (RIP). A sign on the driverside door said IT TAKES LEAD BALLS TO SHOOT MUZZLE-LOADERS. Big Red feared no terrain. The first few times I passengered to the gorge rim in Big Red, I felt like the inhabitant of a Sherman tank racing through pitfalls at El Alamein. Charley definitely liked Big Red to get him places *toot sweet*. Whenever we parked, he opened the hood and yanked sage branches out of the fanbelt. Then he shoved a large saucepan under Big Red to catch combustible fluids leaking from the truck's rock-dented gas tank, so that on our return we could pour gas back into the truck, and make it home.

Big Red is with us no more, even though at this writing he remains in Charley's driveway, awaiting a sucker with three hundred dollars to tow him away.

Charley, however, remains hearty and hale as he heads into the gorge looking like a cross between Wyatt Earp and Pappy Yokum. A self-admitted "bear cub in boxing gloves" who can swing a fly rod as well as Minnesota Fats handles a pool cue, Charley is, quite simply, one of New Mexico's premier precision sporting machines, a gallivanting conglomeration of guts, arrogance, instinct, and talent that can outfish, outhunt, outexplore, and outtalk anybody.

Charley arrived in Taos in 1946 with his famous artist father, and promptly set out to explore every nook and cranny in the valley. Today, there aren't many people who know more lore about Taos than Charley. As a child, he loved to run through the gray sagebrush on Pueblo land. He snooped up and down the edges of the Rio Grande Gorge, discovering old caves, burial grounds, ancient markers, Indian hunting blinds. He found arrowheads, old pots, and various tools. He learned to work with his hands—making wood carvings, leather goods, fishing flies—and developed into a fine craftsman. He read history books and dreamed of the old days. He had a fascination for wild things, ghosts, and colorful galoots.

Then he got married, and he and Lois had three kids: Steve, Alan, and Brian. To earn a living, Charley was in the art gallery business for twenty-five years, while Lois taught school. Charley did all right in the gallery, but never particularly cottoned to the job. Always felt kind of cooped up, in an alien world. And took off, whenever possible, into the hills, out onto the mesa, hunting, fishing, or just roving, looking for a rock on which somebody had chiseled their name a hundred years before, or for the weathered timbers of an old homestead, or for old bottles and old bones—the lonely signs in a wild country of folks and things that had gone before.

In 1976, age seventeen, the oldest son, Steve, had an accident that left him an articulate but severely brain-damaged quadriplegic, and all their lives changed radically. Alan has since finished trade school, and is living and working in California. Brian is in his last year at Taos High School, and preparing to head east for college. Charley has sold his art business in order to spend more time with Steve. And Lois has taken a sabbatical from teaching to work with Charley on a full-time rehabilitation program for their son.

At the time of the accident, nobody thought Steve would survive. Later, it seemed a miracle when his speech returned. Still, most doctors felt Steve would make little further progress. Yet today he has regained much use of his left arm, and volunteer groups from Taos arrive at the Reynolds' home three to five times daily, seven days a week, to exercise Steve in an attempt to repattern his brain. He is learning to bend his legs on his own, and is starting to crawl down a smooth, slightly inclined ramp.

"If I could ever see my boy walk again," Charley says, "well, I guess I would just break down and start blubbering on the spot."

So far the Reynolds have survived. In a sense, Steve's accident has made them grow up a lot. The strain caused from struggling to deal with the changed nature of their familial destiny has been fierce and unrelenting. At times it has pushed everyone right to the brink.

"I guess fishing," Charley once told me during our first year together on the Rio Grande, "is kinda what saves me my sanity these days."

Since Charley and I have not known each other that long, let me recount how I began to play a piscatorial Sancho Panza to my friend's angling Don Quixote.

I was sitting disconsolately in my kitchen along about 1:00 P.M. on a late summer day, contemplating suicide after four months of concentrated asthma attacks and heart fibrillations, when the telephone rang. Answering it, I got hit in the face by a voice so full of Oklahoma I frankly blanched.

Though Charley and I had never met formally, I had once, when purchasing art supplies at his gallery, timidly asked how he caught trout on the Rio Grande. His reply: "I just sort of skitter my flies across the water." Good advice: but I had never discovered just what, exactly, "skitter" meant. And so I dropped it, convinced that fishing pressure and pollution had pretty much rendered the Rio waters sterile.

But now that he had me on the telephone, Charley came right to the point. He had noticed in one of my books (*If Mountains Die*) that I claimed to be an angler. And he wondered if I would like to accompany him to the Rio Grande.

I hemmed, naturally intimidated, having heard through the Taos grapevine that this man was one of the best . . . and perhaps I had puffed up my own case a little too much in the book. But then I thought, Hell, he can teach me something, so I decided to be humble, and asked, "When did you have in mind?"

Never one to beat around the bush, Charley said, "How about right now?"

Two hours later I found myself on the western side of the gorge a few miles north of Arroyo Hondo, scrambling down treacherous rockslides to reach the bank of the Rio Grande just as the sun left the surface of the water. Across the river, two men were fishing. Charley called, "Any luck?" They shook their heads disgustedly: "It's real slow." The water was still high and a bit murky three months after a savage spring runoff had caused serious flooding in Taos and its satellite communities.

Charley just nodded noncommittally over the fishing report. Kind of offhandedly to me he said, "Hrmph. If I don't catch at least thirty fish this evening, I'll be disappointed." I nodded: yeah, yeah, sure. And thought: Nobody is that arrogant and gets away with it. For starters, only two hours of daylight remained. I made swift calculations and determined that Charley planned on landing fifteen fish an hour! Some more calculations brought me to the conclusion that he would probably need at least thirty strikes an hour, or one every two minutes, in order to capture thirty. Since not even in my wildest dreams could I imagine such productivity, I figured he had to be joking.

I was also growing impatient, for Charley dawdled, serene and overconfident in a way that seemed dementedly obnoxious. After all, I was used to laboring all day on this river in order to walk out with four fish! And here was a man lavishly squandering what little time we had.

If he noticed it, this strange man paid no mind to my squirming. Plunking onto a rock, he opened a soda pop and slowly drained it. Then, removing two spools of leader material from a shirt pocket, he ran off five- and four-foot-long strands of eight- and six-pound gut and spliced them together with a blood knot, leaving a five-inch dropper length dangling. A size-ten homemade black creation with sparse brown hackle became his tail fly; for the dropper, he used a brownish ratty-looking thing.

Finally, he stood up and ambled over boulders to the water and teetered a second, peering into the murky currents.

I said, "I might not fish for a while, because I really want to follow you and pick up some pointers, if that's okay."

He grunted approval and warned me not to stick my nose or an ear into the path of his back cast. Then he pulled out a little line from his reel, and with that the man was transformed.

Think of that moment in a Spanish *plaza de toros* when the trumpets blare, the toril gates open, and out surges the bull, muscles rippling and snorting fire, looking for something to kill. Take away the sand, replace it with water full of wild trout, blow a fanfare and propel Charley Reynolds out through the toril gates, and you have a faint idea of the electricity generated when my friend arrives at the edge of the Rio Grande.

I'll always remember seeing it for the first time. He became all smooth, fast, withering, master of the light touch and a dozen techniques, a veritable prestidigitator who could make trout leap out of the river like rabbits from a top hat.

"Is that what you call skittering?" I asked.

He was retrieving the flies across and up the current, the tail fly just underwater, the dropper fly wiggling slowly along the surface like a hatching and escaping bug.

"A-yup." Charley struck his first hit, landing a trout, and released it quickly. The two fellows opposite us looked up.

On his second cast, Charley caught another medium-sized rainbow. The third cast also netted a fish. By this time, our cross-stream spectators were gnashing their teeth. All of two minutes had passed. He was ahead of schedule. I gulped: "You mean that's *it?*"

"That's one way of skinning a cat."

I thought, My God, this lousy river is full of fish! "Let me borrow a couple of flies!" And I took off upstream while Charley headed south.

In the next two hours of "skittering" I landed, and mostly released, eighteen fish; I had missed twice as many strikes. I felt like Scrooge McDuck cavorting in a swimming pool full of silver dollars. I returned at dark to our rendezvous point positively breathless. I had discovered the Seven Cities of Cíbola, trout-fishing branch!

Giggling hysterically as my new friend laconically allowed as how he'd caught maybe forty trout, I peered into his gunnysack wherein a bunch of lunkers lay, and blubbered:

"Gimme some more of them killer flies!"

SIX

Funny how our lives change. New obsessions are born, passions we thought had died are rekindled. Up till the afternoon when I first hit the Rio Grande with Charley Reynolds, I had fished exactly twice in 1979. As September began, I had a severe case of the spiritual blahs. Then, abruptly, I realized the fish were up, and a haunting new piece of geography entered my life. All of a sudden I had a fever to be out in the free air, to be rugged, to seek trout, to study the river, to learn about the gorge. And in Taos, that picturesque and convoluted town where it often seems half the nation vacations, I decided to take a real holiday of my own for the first time in years.

I called Mike Kimmel, a writer friend in Philadelphia, and begged him to fly out for three weeks of gorge exploring, trout fishing, and Wild Turkey 101. Like Charley and me, Mike was in great shape. He had thirty-two bucks in the bank. He was spinning wheels on short stories and investigative articles and had grown momentarily tired of the free-lance hustle. So he snapped at the invitation.

Mike and I go way back. Guatemala in 1964, shortly after a state of siege, is where we met. Mike was at work in a small town for the American Friends. He is about five feet, four inches tall, and a very macho fellow in his black T-shirts, pegged dungarees, and black Wellingtons with Cuban heels. The outfit is belied by a pipe full of British blends constantly stuck in the center of his face, an incongruous sort of intellectual affectation. Mike comes on in a manner that might be described as "strong." Five minutes after we met he claimed he was the only guy ever number one in his major at Temple who could also run fifty balls shooting straight pool. Assessing him with a jaundiced eye, I figured he was too loud to be authentic, and accepted the challenge. Me, whose sporting career consisted of maybe ten games in a Utica pool hall and three viewings of *The Hustler*. Mike snapped, "I'll even spot you twenty-five balls." I replied, "Fuck you, I'll take 'em!" He won the toss and broke the rack. Ten minutes later he flubbed a ball at the end of his second rack, and I had a chance to play. I sank one ball, then scratched. I lost the match, 50 to 26, and took a closer look at Mike Kimmel.

Andrés Martínez gave me the Taos Valley, much of its history and water lore, the western mesa, and the old sheep camps in the shadow of Tres Orejas. Charley Reynolds offered the Rio Grande and the difficult prehistoric gorge through which it travels. Years earlier, Mike Kimmel opened up something different. He gave me city streets and stickball mythologies, Palestra chaos and corner boys in a cappella reveries, all that rough-tough, honky-yiddish-black-commie vital and aggressive and comic chutzpah. He made Damon Runyon blossom for me and opened up the Big Apple in a creative and boisterous way I never could have myself. He offered the rhythm of ghetto and city cultures on an energetic platter, taught me a delight in styles, counseled that the streets are nothing to be afraid of, proved I could learn to dig jive, and irrevocably altered the cadences—in my life and my work—by transmitting unashamedly a volatile, positive, proud, and argumentative energy and arrogance that has vastly enriched my life. A fine writer himself, he took seriously my art from the start, always offered cogent critiques, and, more importantly, believed unabashedly in literature with his whole heart, without cynicism, and in a fierce way that has invariably bolstered me during hard times.

Among other accomplishments, Mike is a *serious* fisherman. In the old days, when not carting trays in the Catskills, he was working party boats. Even today he'll take off on a weekend, drive to the South Jersey shore, rent a rowboat, and drift around catching flounders, just to be able to say he's "gone fishin'." Or on a Saturday morning he might hike over to the Schuylkill—the Schuylkill, for crissakes!—and catch a catfish or a bass.

Years ago, in the early seventies, when Mike first visited New Mexico, I stuck a fly rod in his hands, which had never held a fly rod, and packed him off to the minuscule Rio Chiquito, wherein mighty spooky little brown trout flourished. By then—already—I had tried to cultivate a handful of local fishing pals, but with small success. After a few times thrashing through impenetrable willows and thornbushes during hours of excruciatingly physical guerrilla maneuvering necessary to reach the stream without disturbing the jittery trout, my trainees denounced my sado-masochistic tendencies, turned in their rods, and fled to easier pursuits such as golf, or noontime Fooseball at Floyd's Café on South Santa Fe Road in Taos.

I figured: Now I punish Mike for that skunking in Guatemala. And, as he tripped over a vine, caught his fly on a juniper, and spooked half a mile of river, I chortled. At which point he raised his eyebrows, removed his pipe, and gestured emphatically with it as his upper lip curled into a fat sneer. Jaw jutted, he said, "Oh no, Nichols, wait a minute, not me—I ain't another one of your turkeys, I'll figure it out, you son of a bitch, then I'll mop the river with your ass!"

Later (rather than sooner), but still later (rather than never), he made good on this vow. It took him half a season, though, and it is probably the first time in New Mexico history that any significant

numbers of trout have fallen to an angler wearing a cobra-shaped pinkie ring.

We had some lovely adventures together on the small rivers, and up at the high-country lakes. But whenever we tried the Rio Grande—forget it. Zero. Zilch. We were shut out. Sunburned, blistered, and defeated after each sortie, we crawled out of the gorge and retreated to the realms of smaller game that we had learned so well to handle.

Soon physical catastrophes incapacitated us. Age thirty-five, I developed my asthma and tachycardia. Then I got divorced. Mike also joined the divorce sweepstakes, and celebrated by having a heart attack, age thirty-six. It began with an ache in his chest—he figured indigestion. When an electric pain shot down his left arm and *popped!* in his fingers, he figured "Uh-oh, maybe I'm in trouble." At dawn, a friend drove with him to the hospital. And I'll never forget Mike telling me over the phone:

"I get out right in front of the hospital, and I'm starting toward the emergency ward when this big yellow Oldsmobile zooms around the corner and almost takes my head off. Then it stops, and I start yelling at the driver. Where was he brought up, in a fucking barn? This tall black guy, maybe six-two, six-three gets out of the yellow Olds and he can't believe it! I told him to get the hell out of there, and stormed into the hospital to finish up my heart attack . . ."

He survived, and returned to New Mexico, eager to assault the high country again. First, however, a local heart doctor administered a treadmill test. Mike passed, so we stuffed our packs full of heart-patient goodies like beer and potatoes, parked at Cabresto Lake near Questa, and started climbing. After two quinaglutes and an aminodur I felt fine. At intervals, we paused beside a pristine little brook and gawked at each other, red-faced, veins bulging from our foreheads, wheezing stertorously, raggedy hearts like manic tom-toms . . . and we just giggled hilariously!

Later that night, as we lay packed tight in our robes beneath the snow, we actually read by flashlight from the trout-fishing section of *The Sun Also Rises*, and it sure felt good to be alive.

That was a season, then—the autumn of 1979. Subsequent years have been wonderful, but nothing will ever surpass that time when, thanks to Charley Reynolds, Mike and I learned the Rio Grande is indeed a spectacular and movable feast whose waters positively teem with silvery fish . . . and, what's more, you can catch 'em.

We caught them. And we lost them. I suppose mostly, in fact, we lost them. I still have dreams of all the lunkers I hooked that year: big rainbows tear upward toward the sky like miniature tarpon, dancing across ripples on their tails in great sprays of sun-drenched agua. Sometimes they dive to the bottom under heavy surging water, shake their heads twice, and are gone. On other occasions they hit my fly so hard and voraciously there's nothing but an abrupt *doink!* as leader and fly part company, and some monster heads downriver with the little barb stuck in its cruel-looking underslung jaw.

I soon started using a leader rigged with a tail fly and two droppers, and once hooked a twelve-inch trout and an eighteen-incher on the same cast. Gunshot-sudden, the bigger fish bellied over two feet above the river and snapped the line—but I landed the twelve-incher.

North on the river, between Bear Crossing and Ox Trail, Mike struck something that felt like a log. He tried to unsnag his fly with a tug, and up came the biggest trout he'd ever seen, perhaps in the five-pound class. Moving deliberately, the fish gave one smooth dolphinesque leap, spit out the hook, and reentered the water without a splash.

Mike was sitting on a rock, blue in the face, smoking his pipe and trying to regain his composure, when Charley approached and said, "Well, would you rather a not of hooked it?" Mike almost brained him with a rock.

The same thing happened to me in that pool at the bottom of Suicide Slide. I hooked an extra-large fish on a muddler minnow and played it for two minutes—quietly—deep under the water. Then it turned, started swimming away, and made a leisurely arc in the air, its sides that deep, rich crimson color of a King Kong rainbow. It reentered the water cleanly . . . and free.

Such experiences, we told each other mockingly, helped immeasurably to build character. Yet in that same riffle pool, on luckier days, I successfully landed three sixteen-inch trout.

I can't claim to have landed them in style, however. For starters, at first we never used nets on the Rio Grande. I'm not exactly sure why, given that there is little chance to begin with of coaxing a good fish out of the river: fast water, a rocky shoreline, and submerged boulders everywhere stack the odds in favor of the trout. If they run, it's usually through enough underwater garbage to slice a leather belt in two, let alone a six-pound leader. Often it's impossible to clamber after them on the treacherous rocks. And if you try to pull rein, they simply tear free, sailing frantically over glistening basalt barriers to freedom.

Still, we never took a net. Too clumsy, I suppose. Or possibly a macho affectation. In later years, I decided to carry a net, with mixed results. Yes, I wrested a higher percentage of trout from the river. Yet I also spent more time *in* the river, since my net inevitably caught on a bush or some driftwood as I leapt from rock to rock, tipped me off-balance, and dumped me into the drink. Landing the fish wasn't much fun, either. Each time I scooped out an energetically flopping rainbow, I had to spend half an hour untangling my trotline leader from the green mesh.

Nevertheless, I'm still experimenting. My friend Shel Hershorn, whose fatal flaw is that he's a dry-fly fisherman on this wet-fly river, has warned me repeatedly that it is undignified and insulting to land a trout without a net. I have attempted to treat his thesis with respect, although dignity, per se, is not one of my strong suits on the Rio Grande. And to date, the decorous netting of noble trout remains a far cry from some of the fish inelegantly beached by Mike and Charley and me.

Near Little Arsenic Springs, I hooked a two-pounder, tried to follow it along the rocks, slipped and toppled into the river, and finally, all trussed up in my own line, floundered ashore, dragging the fish behind me. Proudly, I posed for a picture, headband around my nose, fly unzipped, my dripping pants practically sagged to my heels, and my five-dollar TG&Y jogger's specials split at the seams and oozing little clamshells.

North of Big Arsenic Mike hooked an eighteen-incher, reeled in all his line until the leader knot jammed at his tippet, stood his ground with terrified calm for a few minutes praying the fish wouldn't bust loose, then waded into the water, worked the fish between himself and a tiny beach, kicked the fat trout ashore, tackled it in a style we had perfected some years earlier, and rolled over on his back, soaking-wet. Then, hog-tied in his own line, he placed the fish to his lips and gratefully kissed it!

Charley was not quite as clumsy landing them, though I once heard him holler and turned in time to see him thundering toward shore through a fast riffle like a bull moose in rutting season, his rod held high overhead, line flying every whichway, and a big rainbow skidding atop the foam behind him like a water-skiing hang-glider enthusiast trying to become airborne.

By and large, though, watching Charley work the river was a true esthetic treat. In 1979, after a week of perfecting my double-dropper technique, I grew unbearably cocky: one evening I actually brought to shore thirty-seven trout in about three hours! But Charley could catch that many trout in sixty minutes. Always moving, he seemed impatient as hell sometimes: his flies constantly flicked in and out of the water. He plucked at the current like an expert pickpocket, always laying his two flies down lightly, holding the rod high and mending his line immediately so almost nothing except the lures touched the water, then striking with an uncanny flick of his wrist that I cannot for the life of me imitate, no matter how much I strain to be alert and to use restraint.

But Charley could lose them, too. I was across river from him at Big Arsenic when a three-pound fish hit one of his size-ten brown creations. The rainbow sailed high a couple of times, flipping back with loud splats, but it couldn't throw the hook. Charley decided he had it conquered, especially because he had caught the lunker in a long, wide pool that offered plenty of room to run. Casually, Charley watched line sizzle out. Perhaps he even winked at me. But then the fish outran that tether, popped the hook, and evaporated.

Charley sat down, looking squeezed.

"Would you rather a not of hooked it?" I hollered heartlessly.

That combination of excitement and frustration comes with the Rio Grande. Never have I approached the river on any fishing afternoon except with a bounding excitement in my heart, an incredibly powerful lust to reach the water and begin, and an absolute faith that this day could be my best ever.

Almost always, a few hours later, I grope out of the gorge like a stunned troglodyte fresh from an eight-car collision. Though my sack be full of lucre, perhaps including a rare three-pound lunker, I have usually paid for this glory in much traumatic coin.

Though I used to think Charley Reynolds was downright clumsy in the gorge, I have now learned that nobody escapes the wrath of the river spirits and the gorge *duendes*. Charley has admitted that often he takes a dull or raggedy fly and ceremoniously sinks it into the sand, a tiny sacrifice to the river wraiths. But as far as I can figure, the river spirits could care less about his ineffectual offerings.

Entering the gorge is like walking into both a physical and a spiritual meat grinder. You have to run through Ben Davidson, Sam Huff, and Nick Buoniconti (repeatedly) to score a touchdown. Put another way, it is impossible to enter this particular ring without being punched silly.

Yet each day I tackle the river afresh, I forget all the lessons of past misadventures, and flounder stupidly into self-induced, metaphorical gang rapes.

There's no end to the fabled calamities served up by the mighty river: let me count the ways. Listen to this litany carefully, then, and abandon all hope ye anglers who dare to enter here. . . .

Every day always dawns perfect. But inevitably the weather changes. If a high overcast (suggesting my prey will be noshing all day) goads me into arriving early, at that second when I reach the water the sun will emerge to kill the feeding.

Should I depart the house on a picture-perfect placid afternoon, the odds heavily favor a weather change just as shadows strike the water: a mysterious storm materializes, the barometer nose-dives, and, their jaws wired shut, a million hungry trout, with aggravating indifference, watch my cleverly wiggled offerings swoop by.

Let's say all the instruments agree: Today is a one-in-a-million opportunity for overloading the old gunnysack with prime examples of the river's finest. Becalmed air, a warm atmosphere, the river low and clear—a perfect casting afternoon. Until—just as I strip out line and make ready my initial presentation—the river gods lower their howitzers and fire a windy tempest into the gorge. The direction of said gale depends on one of two scientific predilections. If my plan is to wander north, the hurricane will be roaring down the canyon, against me, sabotaging every cast I essay. If, on the other hand, I had hoped to fish south, the typhoon will be heading north. Little it behooves me to try and outfox these belligerent squalls. Should I reach a pool uncastable from below (thanks to the wind against me), and circle to the head of the pool in hopes of flinging my line downstream, the wind will immediately shift direction, annihilating the downstream option.

Now: suppose on a certain day the trout will only rise to lures fished in the skittering method. Without a doubt, a relentless breeze will appear, to quash all efforts at controlling this method.

Again: the day is tranquil. I enter the gorge at a productive spot just south of the Red River's confluence with the Rio Grande, rig up, and attract three mammoth strikes on my first series of casts. As I then salivate uncontrollably over the upcoming slaughter, it is almost certain that the water will grow cloudy and unfishable from an accidental tailings spill at the Questa Molybdenum mine. No need to panic, however: the river will clear up in due course . . . say about five minutes before quitting time.

All else being equal, the weather again perfect and overcast, the day warm, the barometer rising, and the fish feeding like starving barracudas just as I commence the afternoon's activities, the odds are nine to five that suddenly a little rain will fall. Accustomed to similar disturbances, the fish will continue their genocide campaign against various and sundry insect hatches. Unfortunately, though, all the boulders I have to dance upon in order to address the river will become so lethally slippery that to save my neck I'll have to quit fishing, or else crawl painfully over the rocks in slow motion, like a snail. Of course, I might decide to hell with the rain and proceed accordingly. I might slip and break my neck, also.

To give a more vivid perspective on the problem, let's create a Composite Day on the river, featuring Yours Truly, plus Mike Kimmel and Charley Reynolds. What I am about to recount is true—that is, everything happened. Not all at once, to be sure, but often enough to make the following history believable, strange as it may seem.

No trip to the gorge is complete without a flat tire. Charley is the king in this category. Once, while changing a flat by the rim of the gorge, he bounced a spare from the bed of Big Red onto the ground, and the spare promptly rolled off the edge of the cliff. I have suffered but one flat tire that I recall, yet my car has been vandalized and robbed several times, and once all my gas was siphoned.

In general, the puncture on a flat occurs on the way in to a trail; but the flat is not discovered until 9:00 P.M. when everybody is exhausted and desperate to go home.

But let's say that on this Composite Day we have made it to the trail, and are assembling our gear before the hike down. Naturally, everyone has forgotten a crucial piece of equipment. Charley has neglected his lunch, I've forgotten my canteen, all three of us have left behind the flashlights necessary to guide us out of this primitive place in pitch-darkness.

Or perhaps I've remembered my flashlight, but the batteries are dead. Had the batteries not been dead, and had I remembered the flashlight, then the night would be so clear, the moon so full, as to render a flashlight useless.

A further note about this disease known as Gorge Forgetfulness. To the best of my knowledge, never have I remembered to bring everything. If I packed the flashlight, I forgot the gunnysack. If I remembered the gunnysack, and it looked like rain, chances are very good I left behind my lightweight waterproof poncho. If snow or bitter cold was in the offing, I always managed to ignore my sweater and my special fishing gloves. On windy days I neglected to bring a fast-sinking line, which casts straight and true against all currents. On becalmed evenings, the only reel in my vest pocket contained that same fast-sinking line, which on a still day has a tendency to slap the surface like a beavertail.

On this, our Composite Day, Charley, Mike, and I have appeared on the river early. Our intent is to bait-fish while the sun is on the water, and later switch to flies as the trout start rising. On my belt hangs an ingenious contraption, a tennis can punched full of holes, stocked with grasshoppers laboriously amassed from my back field the evening before. Within ten minutes of reaching the river, the plastic cap pops off, and by the time I notice, all the grasshoppers have fled.

Dumbfounded at losing my wherewithal to catch trout so early, I flop down on a rock, remove my glasses, wipe my brow, curse myself unmercifully, then rise and traipse a half-mile upstream to borrow some grasshoppers from Charley. Because he is oddly fuzzy as I approach, I blink my eyes to clear them, then realize he's blurry because I'm not wearing my glasses. Pat my pockets?—no deal. I must have left them on that rock downstream. And for the next half-hour I search for that rock, finally locate it, and—thank God!—spot my glasses lying on a damp patch of sand between boulders.

All this negative activity has created a positive miracle—I have a great urge to defecate. In an appropriate spot I drop my drawers, and save some part of an afternoon I had begun to rue by consummating the act. But when I reach into my shirt pocket for some bumwad, which I *always* bring to the river, I discover that today I forgot.

Well, no problem. Behind me is a skinny little bush with pretty brown leaves. I grab it low on the stems and in a swift motion yank upward, stripping off the leaves. And also, incidentally, lacerating most of the skin of my palm, since this happens to be a nasty little thorn plant.

Howling, I jump up, stomping in my own stool.

Meanwhile, at other choice river spots, my friends are not escaping unscathed. Charley has already tumbled once into the river. He has no recollection of how it happened. One moment he was upright on a rock, next moment he was up to his neck in forty-six-degree water. Mike will later report, "I heard a yell and turned around. All I could see was this mustache and a pair of glasses!"

Mike has little time for ogling Charley's graceless shenanigans. Long ago he started his own disaster chain by unbuckling his belt in order to care for some daily needs. And now, upon reaching for his hunting knife, he discovers it no longer hangs on that belt. He has had that knife since childhood, cherishes it, and will be miserable the rest of the day wondering what happened to it.

Fortunately, his total preoccupation with the knife will soon be dulled by other goofs. The first involves a five-inch trout he strikes so hard that he loses his balance and takes a dunking, smashing his reel against a rock. Had he been using one of my ten-dollar Japanese reels—no problem. But today, eager to experience a little class, he borrowed an eighty-dollar Hardy from Charley.

Farther south, I have reel problems of my own. Only yesterday I bought an innovative new plastic gizmo for thirty bucks. Today I learn quickly that I'm in trouble. First, my line keeps twisting out of the spool, jamming the reel. Shortly thereafter, I hook a hefty fish, and the spool pops free of the reel and plops into the river, unraveling thirty yards of line. Laboriously, I retrieve everything, and try again. After crossing damp sand, I forget to scrape the wet granules off my sneakers, and immediately slip off a boulder, taking a wicked header, and fracturing my revolutionary reel.

Incidentally, I also splinter the crystal on my wristwatch.

Indefatigable to the end, however, I reach into my zippered vest pocket for my fly box. Unfortunately, the last time I probed this compartment I forgot to zip it shut, and somewhere in my pratfalls a fly box and a high-class pocketknife have tumbled into the water.

Refusing to cry over forty dollars of spilt milk, I locate another fly box, and rig up a fresh leader with two droppers and a streamer tail fly. Misjudging slightly on my first cast, I catch the streamer on some cross-river jetsam. An expert at dislodging similarly snagged hooks, I go through all my liberating contortions—but nothing works. Eventually, I must reel in line, point my rod directly at the snag, give a yank, and snap off the tail fly.

Instead, the blood knot at the second dropper breaks, and I lose all three flies at once.

Upstream, Charley is hard-pressed to keep up with my pace. He is an old pro, however, and not one to suffer a challenge lightly.

Promptly he latches on to a fine rainbow, wades onto a sandbar, bends over to gill his flopping adversary, and snags the dropper fly in his nose.

Ah, how vividly do Charley's howls echo through history to my ears, the pained exclamations of a master at his craft.

Out of my league though that stunt may be, I'm still competitive. Already, today, I've caught several hooks in the headband containing my hair. One might surmise that I wear a headband specifically to protect my brain from these onslaughts that occur frequently when the wind plays havoc with my flies.

Casting streamers in a wind is my pièce de résistance. If I try hard enough, I can always score a bull's-eye with the barb of a size-six Spruce Matuka in my right earlobe. But for a quirk in my casting style, I might pierce my lobes at regular five-minute intervals. However, I manage to break untold streamer barbs on rocks during my sloppy back casts. 'Course, when I'm plying streamers I regularly check the fly to make sure the hook is intact. Sooner or later, however, I grow forgetful and fail to check my Wyoming Bucktail after the third cast. Immediately, the four-pound rainbow tailing over in that shallow riffle chomps the fly, I strike, and it rockets clear of the water, giving me a good three-second ogle before it spits out the useless lure, and plummets into safety.

Enough of this nostalgia. The day is young, and we have still got a lot of hard knocks to accumulate. At the head of our line, Charley lumbers off to relieve his bowels, drops his drawers, and fails to notice that his slippery wallet plunked into a crevice. Under normal conditions no great tragedy. But today that wallet is guarding five hundred dollars, cash, with which Charley hoped to finance a trip to Denver, where Steve is slated to visit some important doctors. Naturally, Charley will not realize the wallet is gone until we reach the gorge rim in total darkness many hours later.

(For the record, I should note that Charley returned early next morning, his heart in his mouth, and—incredibly!—found that wayward billfold!)

Whose turn is it in the barrel—Mike's? Hooking a nice twelve-inch brown, he swings it onto the rocks, grabs his line, loses control of the rod (which clatters into the foamy whirlpool) and the fish—twisting free—slithers into a crack between boulders, and thence to the river.

Mike must now spend twenty minutes flushing sand from the broken Hardy reel.

A moment later he hurtles along the rocks up past me. Cheerfully, I ask, "How's it going, bro'?"

His greeting is an ugly snarl: "Just get out of my way, Nichols." For emphasis, he slips and clatters into the stones, almost breaking his neck. Scrambling back into view instantly, he whimpers, "I'm gettin' sick and tired of these fucking mastodons."

Angrily, he casts into the roiling waters, hooks a fierce fish, plays it a few minutes, and finally ekes it onto dry land and holds it up—a six-inch rainbow—cackling with sardonic glee: "Look what I got, everybody! My whole day is perfect!"

Ever the pragmatist, Charley mutters laconically: "Don't knock it. That's a fish."

And Mike, ignoring every gentleman's code of the sport and the river, hurls his minuscule sardine at our mentor!

So far, I'm having a stellar day on the river. Out of thirty hits I have managed to creel but three ten-inch browns. And now, as hints of darkness numb the surroundings, I experience an urgency to accelerate the pace. Who knows, Mike or Charley could be gaining on me. Promptly, I widen the gap by slamming my shin into prehistoric stone, aggravating my painful cellulitis. When I glance up, my features appropriately contorted in excruciation, a bald eagle is flapping silently by thirty yards away. I'm alone, maybe dying, and the symbol of America never flinches, just keeps on plugging. My agony flashes on that Auden poem "Musée des Beaux Arts," which refers to Breughel's painting of *The Fall of Icarus*.

Onward, through cretin boulders! Failing to notice a porcupine, I almost tromp on it—the beast clumsily rattles off. A large trout is feasting on a caddis hatch across the river; little bats flutter above the water. I cast for the caddis freak, but something snarls my effort. A midair explosion; my line crunkles and dies in crazy loops and snarled heaps of lime-green Air-Cel Supreme. A foreign body hits the water—*splat!*— and the dimpling lunker skedaddles. When finally I untangle the mess and reel in, I discover I've nailed a wee bat, hooked through the spine; its jaws grimace in half-drowned agony. Unable to release it without being bitten, I dash the weightless tyke against the rocks, feel miserable, contemplate using it for bait, then decide not to stoop that low.

Rerigging quickly, I maneuver into a better position, adroitly miscalculate a leap, and plunge headfirst into scary white water. Frantically, I scramble half onto a rock, notice my rod disappearing into a tumultuous froth, and dive to capture it. I emerge soaking wet, but gung-ho as always. Immediately, a wind rises, and soon I am half frozen to death.

Slightly befuddled, I march into the splintery broken shards of a dead cedar branch that gouges a small hole in my cranium. Instantly, geysers of blood plaster the fuzzy fabric of my headband.

Several days earlier, when my rod was stuck, I couldn't break it down. Nothing I tried could loosen the two pieces. In desperation, I wound a towel around the shaft, gripped it with pliers, and tugged—but no deal. Next day, Bill Vickers at Sierra Sports showed me how to wedge the rod behind my knees, squat, and yank it apart. Apparently, my machinations had forged a slight crimp in the delicate graphite. Now, as I cast successfully to a feeding fish, and strike hard, the rod snaps cleanly in two just above that juncture where the sections meet.

Refusing to panic, I compose myself and assess the situation. I find twigs and whittle them into splints. Band-Aids from the top pocket of my vest serve to bind the splice. And, after a fashion, I can still cast.

In fact, I catch two rainbows before we are forced to leave the gorge prematurely. Never mind how (or who), but one of us, sometime earlier, had sustained an ant bite on the tip of his pecker. Now this person feels sick and feverish. And when he unzips his fly to inspect the damage, we all nearly keel over in dead faints. Lobster-red and hideously swollen, that cock resembles a family-sized sausage with elephantiasis.

Immediately, the trout commence biting like crazy. But we must hike out. Halfway to the top, a black sky envelops the planet. Neither moon nor star illuminates our course. We have all forgotten flashlights, and soon find ourselves hopelessly lost. Back and forth we flounder, searching for an escape, stumbling in the rockslides, grabbing cactuses and cursing, gasping for water (nobody remembered to fill their canteen at the little spring we discovered).

Finally, I locate a path to the rim. Pig-headed, Mike and Charley take a wrong turn. At the foot of a cliff they call to me overhead for instructions on how to negotiate the labyrinth.

For half an hour they clamber, bitch, claw, and fumfer while I shout orders from above down into the pitch-black hellhole. It takes a while, but eventually they make it to the mesa, and feverishly suck on the extra canteens Charley always stashes in Big Red.

Mike sums it up for all of us:

"They beat me today, those fish, that river. I haven't been mugged like that since I was eight years old. It was like getting hit repeatedly by this jab I couldn't avoid."

He pauses for a moment, loads his pipe, lights it, then tilts back his head to confront stars, moon, galaxies, and offers the definitive comment on our day:

"They stepped all over my blue suede shoes."

SEVEN

I love it. Every last fatal, traumatic, and bewitching moment of my time on the Rio Grande. On each new trip, when I arrive at the rim and gaze down, it is like reaching the other side of a magic mountain and viewing a scene toward which my imagination has strained for ages. No two days are alike. Always, I expect some rare treasure to be revealed: of weather, mood, the animal kingdom. For centuries I suppose little has changed within that deep gash, yet it is always unpredictable to me, a wild and mystical environment whose rocky shapes, textures, and noises always knock me for a loop.

Up above, overlooking the river, I invariably anticipate adventures. That gruff rubble is so intimidating, electrifying, seductive. And I am a silly pink nudnik puttering clumsily across thundering accolades of muteness. Never one to seek danger gratuitously, I fearlessly embrace this peril with all my heart. Granted, the gorge is no inherently precarious environment. Few people are ever hurt down there, although turbulent springtime runoff waters regularly mutilate the occasional rafter. Otherwise, approached with moderate precautions, the gorge is a pleasant and amiable retreat.

My passion for it, I think, makes the river dangerous. My lust to cover ground, my intense fishing concentration, my fanatical need to push on around the next corner, even at the cost of retreating back two miles across boulders in impenetrable darkness, changes the nature of the experience—also its consequences. I adore the risk of staying keyed-up and perfectly balanced while rushing through the night, weighed down by my camera pack and a gunnysack full of lunkers, the whole universe captured tensely in the flickering beam of a flashlight across the cruel labyrinth of giant stones. Hard work, sure, but I feel terribly loose and rhythmic and cocky among the rocks. Not since college days have I reveled in a similar euphoria and confidence. Every muscle strains to react correctly, yet I am permeated by a languorous wild joy. Blind to my surroundings, I know exactly where I stand. Instincts attuned to the nth are almost erotic. The ambiance has become second nature to my heart, and to my muscles.

When I'm hot, I can measure the distance of my line as I cast for trout, not by looking, but simply from the feel of the instrument in my hand. The weight of line in the air tells me when to drop a fly within an inch of the edge of a boulder, judging exactly where a fish will strike. Sometimes everything comes together and I proceed without thinking, building an infallible poetry. Good pool shooters achieve the same intensely fluid rhythm as they circle a table on a long run, and every spectator is alert, enraptured by their effortless expertise.

A provocative sorcerer is the gorge. Within its narrow confines the most insignificant plant or animal is deified. A crayfish scuttling backward under a rock as my shadow strikes it is part of the hocus-pocus. Tiny sandy rivulets of clean spring water (flanked by sprigs of watercress) at which I drink are littered with minuscule white shells of freshwater clams. Across the sand scamper spiders, fragile wispy arachnids that, if caught by the breeze, would float away like weightless milkweed fluffs. Just once, I surprised a hairy tarantula; they frighten some travelers, but not me. Instantly, a childhood longing intensified: if only I could adopt it for a pet!

A willet whistles—Kay-ee!—and takes off from a rock; and a solitary Canada goose, preposterously hemungous, flaps upstream only twenty feet above the water.

On a break, seated, I eat an apple. A band of yolk-yellow sunlight gilds the top of the gorge. Shadows down here are cool. A dipper bird bobs cheerfully on a nearby slab, then loses all patience and flies upstream only inches above the splashing waves. Bats flutter jerkily through tenebrous fields of air. Moments ago, a beaver shocked me, slapping its tail like a gunshot: a geyser rose; I thought at first some prankster killer had pitched a rock at me. But then a head surfaced, and the fat brown animal slowly traversed the pool, waddled onto a beach on the opposite shore, and dissolved into chiaroscuro eddies at the base of the cliff.

A water snake wriggles past my toes; last lizards depart from the once warm, now cooling, black rocks. A Townsend's solitaire uncorks a silver threnody. Calcimine bird-splashes decorate the rocks.

Centered in that narrow band of cerulean blue above my head, the moon appears effervescent and transparent, a remote, blind, and tissue-thin trinket imbued with significant weightless romanticism.

A buzzard skirls down the western edge of the gorge, hunting. Rare butterflies are battered and ragged: autumn portends the end of their odysseys. I wonder if that pale monarch arrived accidentally, inadvertently blown off the earth into this spellbinding chasm.

Extending from the river to about thirty feet up either bank, the boulders are gray or black. Higher, they become mottled with sage-green lichens, splashes of yellow, veins of blue-beige growths. Among the boulders, scattered sagebrush bushes are putting forth yellowy-green blossoms. Rabbitbrush flaunts its eye-catching gold. Poison ivy has a slick crimson shine. To the branches of gnarled juniper cling small clumps of powder-blue berries. A large evergreen skeleton is burnished by water and winds, driftwood-white, lonely, alone, and imperial.

Every mile of the river has a unique personality. Here springs tumble noisily down cliffsides into the Rio Grande. There, ten-foot-high brown rushes rattle furiously against each other in the wind. On narrow plateaus above the river, head-high rabbitbrush and sage tower like jungle trees, and ponderosas rocket toward the late evening or-ange-sherbert sky.

Another area seems barren, nothing but talus slopes, a ponderous rumbling of frozen rocks slanting a thousand feet into the water.

In several gullies, near the rim, bright yellow foliage announces small stands of aspen trees, the most incongruous growth in the gorge.

In a few grassy, sandy areas grasshoppers are busy. Black dung beetles, asses aimed toward heaven, obliviously putter through the sand. Later in the evening, big dragonflies buzz among the bats. A cañón wren's diving song echoes loudly from the cliffsides; coyotes meander in and out. I have seen bobcat pawprints, raccoon tracks, also cougar sign. A friend tells me that a year ago, near the top of the Cedar Springs Trail, he came across a mountain lion dragging a small deer it had just killed.

And once, of all the times I have ventured into the gorge, I discovered fireflies. At Big Arsenic, with my friend Gabe Garcia and his son Sean. I have seen no other fireflies in New Mexico. But on that evening a bunch of the bugs were blinking over the grasses and boulders—as they once used to blink over my childhood lawns—si-lently, out of place, and thrilling.

Weather is especially unpredictable in the gorge because you cannot see it coming. The sky is never more than a narrow blue band high above. Storms sweep over suddenly, without warning. An abrupt shadow claims the landscape as if a giant had straddled the gorge. Hail erupts, then a stinging rain. I crouch in the lee of an enormous curved boulder, hollowed out underneath, cupped in a huge stone hand. Thunder booms, the glare of lightning rockets between the sheer walls. A dervish wind dries the basalt after a downpour, but the air remains cold and clammy, the fishing stays lousy.

Then *boom!* Another precipitous change. Enormous clouds stag-ger from the sky, squeezing their puffy bulks into the gorge, muffling, then suffocating the wind. The gorge is becalmed and misty, the air dead-still and warming. Soon, the fish start hitting again.

Later, the mist dissipates, revealing a clean dusky sky, except to the south, where a double rainbow haloes the chasm.

I am captivated by the capricious shifts of mood and temperament. On a clear sunny flat December day I descend Suicide Slide, and have little fishing luck. The air is still and icy. I enjoy myself, but soon quit concentrating on the hunt.

In a flash, the light changes, catching me totally off guard. As if the great oaken doors of a large cathedral (in a Hollywood extravaganza) had been opened, a luminescence floods the gorge. It stops me as cold in my tracks: has a rock just been levitated away from a cave in preparation for an ascension? An aureole glow, a shimmering, fantastic radiance infuses everything. Boulders pulse incandescently, seemingly as soft and fragile as inessential dream formations. Limbs of white driftwood and dry tumbleweeds shiver with silvery ivory phosphorescence. Everything acquires a vibrant damp luster that breaks my heart. Green grasses become so vivid they seem in the process of melting. I place pieces of wood against throbbing lichens and take their pictures.

All things bask in this splendid afterglow. I stare at rocks, shocked to discover them so beautiful. I gather some stones that shimmer like angels, store them in my sack, and lug them out of the gorge.

But up top the light has changed, and my stones are no longer almost transparently delicate and beautiful. I have removed them from Shangri-La.

Still, the sky is incredible. Pastel crimson-pink clouds, at once both demure and rococo, recall Victorian excesses, echoes of Maxfield Parrish. A large hoary bat lumbers by. Crickets raise their cheerful ruckus. Rambunctious swallows cleave with quicksilver moves through the scintillating airwaves.

Far away coyotes laugh obnoxiously.

At the end of a day we reassemble at the base of the trail, rest by the riverbank, compare our fish and clean them, and tell stories about whoppers, pratfalls, and other colorful sundries.

Charley's razor-sharp knives can split molecules. He squats on a sandbar, cleanly slitting his trout and yanking out the guts, regaling me with an account of The Big One That Got Away. He figures it ran to four pounds, and was over twenty inches.

"I saw it coming maybe fifteen feet away. You rarely have all that warning. It hit the fly and came right up out of the water, so I got a real good look. God, it had such a big mouth! I'd say easily over twenty inches. Then it took off across the stream to the other side, and got fouled up in the rocks and some debris. My line went kind of hard like, you know? Dead weight. I reeled in and tapped the butt of my rod against a rock, thinking if it was still on that'd jar it loose. Then I sat down and ate a sandwich and had a soda. Finally, I got up and pointed my rod straight across at the place so I wouldn't hurt it, and pulled on the line. I felt the leader snap. Both my flies were gone when I reeled in. What can you say about something like that? It's kind of like you're walking along with your best friend, and somebody comes up and shoots him through the heart and he's dead. There's nothing you can do about it. He's *gone*."

Later, we walk out slowly, exhausted, talking about other things: life, family, dreams. Charley dreams a lot. "Sometimes they're real nice dreams. I'll be out in the high country, just walking along, up above the tree line . . . and nothing much happens, it just feels good. Once, in a dream, I saw a bunch of Indians entering a high-country cave. After they left, I went over and entered the cave and found all these little springs.

"I guess water is pretty important in my life. And in my dreams.

"Other times I'm out on the mesa, just walking around, discovering things. Arrowheads. Stuff like that. All of a sudden I'm in an arroyo I've never been in before. And it becomes this great big beautiful canyon. And there's all kinds of trees and rocks and little springs, and an old old village, like that village over at Mesa Verde. . . ."

Each time we trudge out of the gorge, during The Season, his limp is worse. The ankle pains, and in his heel a bone spur is festering. It hurts. "Sometimes it's hell walking out at night, a regular damn nightmare. . . ."

When the mood hits, Charley drives over to the Moreno Valley and fishes Eagle Nest Lake, where you fling some marshmallows and corn into the water and just sit around, waiting for them to bite. Hook a big fish, and pulling it out is a bit like hauling in a dead log. But it can be fun. "And anyway," says Charley, "I got to get used to it, because someday I'll no longer be able to get in and out of the gorge."

Yet he'll always love the river, even though every step these days is paid for in agony. What he is held by is the diversity: "You never know what you'll find." Each pool and situation is different, perhaps even dangerous. "It's like walking down the long corridor of a whore-house, and looking into each room at a different situation, a different woman. 'Course, what would I know, I never even been in a whore-house. . . ."

Out of the blue, as we climb higher, he remembers how he used to cut out and paste into scrapbooks the silhouettes of enemy aircraft published in newspapers during World War II.

Or he stops to elucidate on this subject: "You know the recipe for how to cook a carp? Well, I'll tell you. First, you arrange your carp on a sugar-pine plank, and sprinkle seasoning on it, to taste. Then you place the plank in the oven and leave it in at 350 until the carp is brown, and baked all the way through. That means it's done, so you remove the works, throw away the carp . . . and eat the plank."

Maybe on the way we bump into another fisherman, like Alex Quintana from Arroyo Seco, a river devotee who works at the Moly mine, and broke his leg not long ago. He and Charley philosophize about aging, about the infirmities that one day may keep them from the river. Alex says, "Comes the time when I can't hunt and fish around here, well, I guess I'll just pack it in."

Up top, gathered at the front fender of a pickup, we trade stories, guzzle canteen water, and analyze flies. Alex remembers he used to buy a blue quill at old Doc James's place, east of the Taos Plaza—but that establishment is long gone.

The consensus is that in the old days many more big fish were caught. Alex remembers an afternoon ten years ago on The Riffles below Los Cordovas in the Rio Pueblo when he captured a thirty-two-inch brown on a Black Gnat.

And his dad once killed five fish all over twenty inches in a single pool above Ox Trail.

At long last we are slumped in Big Red, dog-tired, munching on apples, heading home. Kangaroo rats zip lickety-split back and forth across the road. The usual jackrabbit jumps out and scampers for a hundred yards in front of us before darting back into the sage.

At Charley's house, his dogs—the big shepherd and the mala-mute, Puddles and Lobo—dance gleefully on the end of their chains as their master limps over. He releases the yawpy friendly beasts, and they bound off happily into the darkened sage.

It would be easier if we started out while some daylight remained. But an unwritten angler's axiom insists that we always fish until dark. Or at least until that sweeping luminous twilight when stars begin to appear, and trees and boulders lose dimension, becoming silhouettes.

Usually, I'm burned out at the start up. On rougher trails, the trip can become a poetic nightmare. On Suicide Slide, for example, there's nothing to do except claw my way straight up. It's dark, visi-bility is near zero. One hand is occupied with my rod case; my other hand grapples for plants, which often tear loose from the steep bank.

Heavy fish in the gunnysack looped around a backpack shoulder-strap bash against my ankle. A bush has so much sticky resin on it that my fingers are quickly glued together. Traversing helps little: rocks constantly rumble from under my feet. Half a dozen times I trigger slow avalanches and pitch rocks ahead to warn rattlers of my approach. Tonight, several of those rocks bounce back at me, and I have to duck quick to avoid a braining by my own missile. Shaken, I figure it's better to probe ahead with the rod case—tap, tap, tap . . . you there, snakes? Please don't strike. I promise not to hurt you. . . .

Drenched in sweat, I stop often to wipe off my glasses. At the top, I am trembling, nearly prostrate. Dully, gasping, I stare west where a thin strip of horizon is vitriolic blue, a posh color as surreal as lapis lazuli. To the southeast, heat lightning garishly friezes Picuris Peak.

My keys are under a rusty, flattened tin can; I open the car and guzzle half a canteen of water, then pour the rest into my sack to keep the fish cool and fresh.

The route home lies north on a dirt road that follows the contours of the rim. Rocks force a slow pace; the stones in the road seem like hundreds of petrified turtles. As the bus bucks along, my bones feel as if they are disintegrating. I'm so pooped I could howl at every joggling outrage. Headlights across the sage lend to the plants a bizarre frosted look, like calcified underworld stalagmites. Black-and-white sheep moths act as pilot fish.

Gaining speed on the highway a half hour later, I slam into a storm of bugs—desperate moths, grasshoppers, and little beetles—which spatter like a hailstorm against the car.

Though Sheep Corral is much easier than Suicide Slide, it is on that trail I witnessed—and even took part in—one of the most outrageous pratfalls ever to occur in the gorge.

The classic, painfully cartoon incident featured my good friend Doug Terry, and was the crowning gaffe to a faena of comical faux pas Doug had been fashioning on the river for two years.

Like all of us, Doug is something of a klutz on the river. He clatters among the rocks until his black-and-blue shins are gruesomely swollen, periodically misjudges his leaps and cannonballs into foaming whirlpools, and has smashed to smithereens every bit as many reels as the next snakebit person.

Doug long has claimed that such ineptness is a new act in his life. Raised in Crosby and Galena Park, Texas, near the Houston shipping channel, Doug was a standout high-school football player in the Lone Star State. He spent his childhood learning how to be tough and coordinated. A weight program made him awesomely strong for his size. Fourteen eggs a day—consumed in milkshakes—rounded out his superb teen-age physique. At five-eight he could bench-press four hundred pounds; and, age eighteen, he battered his way to a local Golden Gloves heavyweight championship. Then he earned a football scholarship to SMU, where he played starting noseguard under defensive coordinator Bum Phillips, who later went on to NFL head-coach jobs at Houston and New Orleans.

A disenchantment with football set in, however, and Doug bagged the sport a year before his eligibility expired. He turned to literature, and, upon graduation, earned a scholarship to the Wallace Stegner graduate writer's program at Stanford. After a year in Palo Alto, he moved to Taos, founded a ski-shop enterprise, and shortly thereafter sold a fine first novel to Doubleday: it was published in January 1982.

In short, Doug moved through life like an agile (if ferocious) golden boy, until he met his Waterloo on the Rio Grande.

I could see it coming for almost a year, yet I never had an inkling it would be so horrible.

The evening was placid. Eagerly, we descended Sheep Corral

Trail. Although the river was muddy, we had gone too long without wetting a line, and looked forward to the exercise. But on the last steep slope just above the water, it happened. Doug lost his footing, twisted sideways, and landed flat on his back—in a wide nest of prickly-pear cactus!

He screamed. And, on that steep slant, he could not move. I whirled, almost crash-landed, took one look at his spread-eagled body held a few inches off the ground by his straining arms, hollered "*Oh no!*," and burst out laughing.

At that instant, Doug was one of the more ridiculous and terrifying sights I have ever seen. I had thought that only in comic books were clumsy cowboys ever pitched into the embrace of those painful succulents. The sympathetic anguish I immediately experienced triggered goosebumps from my toes to my gullet, though I kept on laughing even as I shed my pack and maneuvered into a position to grab his arms and heave him upright.

What can you say about a balding, thirty-year-old literate football player who almost died?

From his broad shoulders to his big buttocks, Doug was riddled with a thousand needles. Some were as large as porcupine quills; others were tiny and feathery, excruciatingly painful, and almost invisible. He nearly passed out from the hurt.

I plucked the largest spears. Then, wailing together, we removed his fishing vest, his shirt, his shorts. Rarely have I witnessed such naked distress as—cursing and whimpering—Doug bent over a rock and begged me to extract those spines.

I spent an hour with my nose in his butt, trying to remove the vicious needles with my chewed-down fingernails. We guffawed the whole time, even as tears fell from his eyes. But when I had excised as many spikes as I could see, and suggested we head back up, either to find tweezers or drive to the hospital, he drew up sharply—winced!—and growled, "Oh no, I came to go fishing, let's head on

out. I'm gonna beat you today, Nichols, you wimpy little mother-effer."

Well, Doug is a man who hates to lose. And in disbelief I watched him head upriver, naked but for a T-shirt and sneakers, and so covered by red welts he looked to have been peppered by a half-dozen shotgun blasts.

In the muddy river, on that particular evening, few trout were biting; we fished in vain. Right about dark, however, the river gods added insult to Doug's injury by allowing me to catch a single chunky fifteen-inch rainbow—our only trophy.

Banging his head in dismay, Doug charged up the trail ahead of me in the dying light. Toward the top of Sheep Corral we took a breather, turned around, and faced back down into the gorge, leaning reflectively on our rod cases. Of a sudden, the lonely outpost we momentarily inhabited was a beautiful place on earth. As our breathing calmed down, we settled gratefully into the silence and that majestic view. Cliffsides were nearly obliterated in darkness. But silvery lemon moonlight rippled along the narrow curving streak of river. And far away the distant southern mountains were half shrouded in mist. The clear sky bristled with stars.

"God, I love moments like this," Doug murmured, unabashedly and affectingly sentimental. "When all of a sudden everything is perfect, and you can share it with a friend, and you'll never forget how lovely it was."

His wonderful capacity for rejuvenation has always awed me.

Once I am on a trail, particularly a highway like the Big Arsenic bajada, I like to walk out in the dark, without a flashlight (if I happened to bring one). No need to see the ground beneath my feet, I can feel it. And any artificial light would eradicate the universe. Better to plod instinctively through a friendly gloom defined by pines silhouetted against the starry sky and far cliffs sending mooncast shadows down steep talus slopes. At autumn Arsenic, the Big Dipper is always north, balanced on the canyon rim, our brightest constellation. Sometimes a wispy diaphanous veil seeps across the clean cold heavens, barely affecting the luster of wintry star configurations.

Arsenic is a long, carefully groomed trail that rises from the most spectacular part of the gorge. I enjoy taking my time on the way out. At a little bench a mile above the spring-fed pools, I usually rest and take stock of infinity. The roar of the river is remote, dull and peaceable. My heart quiets down. There's no more violence to the phantasmic meanderings of the tiny river far below. For five or ten minutes something spiritual burgeons inside me. I have a marvelous sense of *being*. I feel happy and wish to laugh. I congratulate myself for having such a full life and feel no guilt about my creative triumphs. Glad I am to be alive. Sometimes, I feel ingeniously detached from earth, ensconced far out in the galaxies somewhere, peering at our puny planet upon which miracles fester. The mysteries are funny and important and worth it, though not very articulated. My time on the bench engenders a powerfully *active* relaxation.

Let's say that on a rare occasion I desert the river before dark. Perhaps the fishing is slow or nonexistent. Maybe a dreamy laziness clobbers my limbs, and—full of lotus blossoms—I can't concentrate or punish myself. Then I'll leave in full daylight, and that's often revealing. Landscape I never notice on the way down suddenly makes itself available.

Rope Trail, on a nondescript day, gave me a treat. Troutless after an hour beside the murky river, I hiked out early, and soon began to notice the personality traits of the trail. Mottled blue-gray sagebrush, pastel-green lichens, gouche gray-and-russet boulders. Halfhearted storm clouds emitted guttural rumbles. In the narrow couloir halfway up, I noticed piles of birdshit on ledges above me, and detoured to investigate. Obviously, large raptors had occupied the aeries earlier in the season. Scattered about were bones—of mice, lizards, small birds. White, calcified, splintered by fierce beaks, some bones seemed large enough for rabbits. I weighed them in my palm—light, hollow, and feathery—and put them back.

For a while I sat on the ledge, playing hawk, vulture, eagle, staring sleepily past boulder outcroppings toward the river. I could almost feel an alien pulse in my body, the active energy of the life-and-death dramas that took place on my ledge; I am soul brother to eagles . . . and their victims.

Higher on the trail I found a hawk feather, and the dried-out carcass of a dung beetle. Holding them both in hand, I tried to imagine the experience of being a hawk, of being a dung beetle.

December. Snowflakes are falling. I'm alone on the river. I ease a rainbow onto the sand, where it lies panting quietly. I am reluctant to touch it, because the skin like ice will instantly hurt my fingers. It will be like touching a diamond fresh from a powerful deepfreeze.

I stare at the trout, puzzled by the fact that something alive and energetic can survive in such a terribly arctic environment.

Shel Hershorn is both a stubborn man and a mellow human being. A former news photographer, he was the best at his trade. A picture he took of Billie Sol Estes became immortal. His coverage of the Texas Tower Massacre, which appeared in the pages and on the cover of *Life*, is a classic. But Shel tired of life in a fast lane and moved to Taos. Here he now lives with Sonja de la Parra on a very small farm. He spends much time in a warm, wood-heated shop painstakingly creating custom furniture. In a 1954 Chevy 6 pickup, model 3100, with a sheep skull bolted onto the front hood, he delivers the furniture to people scattered about the Southwest. His gadding-about-town car is a 1953 four-door Chevy deluxe Bel-Air sedan, lovingly preserved. In his early fifties, Shel has deliberately slowed down life in order to enjoy it.

As I mentioned, his fatal flaw is that he's a dry-fly fisherman who insists in plying his trade on a wet-fly river. Using his father's ancient, custom-made, three-piece bamboo fly rod, there is nobody better at catching trout than Shel . . . *if* the trout happen to be hitting dry flies. But in the Rio Grande the trout do not often go berserk surface feeding. And the best fly water is white and roiling, not exactly your classical dry-fly territory.

I am learning, however, that dry-fly fishermen are not easily converted into wet-fly enthusiasts.

No matter. Shel is fairly rational in most other categories. He has a laid-back sense of humor, and a mischievous pixie gleam on his bearded warmly human fizzog. The man boasts a carefully crafted equanimity in life, and is no longer in a hurry to get somewhere else than where he's at.

The exception, of course, is an occasional sortie into the gorge, where he stubbornly persists in his arcane and precious angling oddities. But I enjoy his company anyway.

Especially it's a pleasure to rap with Shel on our return journeys, absorbing a bit of his sly and gentle philosophy. I can see us seated at a picnic table at the top of Arsenic Trail, downing beers after a moderately unsuccessful day among the boulders and the white water. We are laughing about life's foibles. Shel remembers the start of his career, up north on the *Casper Tribune-Herald*. His first big coup was a picture of a woman who had killed her husband. As she emerged from the courtroom, he jumped in front of her, aimed his old Speed Graphic, and snapped a picture. He felt terrible afterward for being so obnoxious, but that brazenness launched a brilliant career.

Shel and Sonja raise goats, which they slaughter for food. "I don't like to kill them," he says, taking a sip of beer at our picnic table. Moonlight reflects off his wire-rim glasses. "Still, it's something I have to do. So I down a shot of bourbon, and walk out to the pen. I spread a little grain, and while they're all calm and eating it, either I shoot them, or clobber them on the head with a five-pound axhammer . . . and that's it."

He kills turkeys, too, although never his seed stud, a large tom who goes by the absurd moniker of Turkey-Lurkey. One day last year, Shel tells me, Turkey-Lurkey had an accident. "Kicked by a goat, maybe—nobody knows for sure." But his neck was kinked over, the bird was half paralyzed. Shel had an idea, though, on how to save him. A Taos doctor named Robert Lupowitz, a practitioner of the Toftness technique, had been treating Shel for a bad back. So Shel transported the turkey to Lupowitz, who saw nothing unusual in applying his expertise to the bird. Presto!—his bones realigned, Turkey-Lurkey strutted out into the barnyard all puffed up and thumping, providentially cured.

The story doesn't end here. Shel's neighbor Mike Mabry had a large black dog named Bear, who grew old, slipped a disc, and developed paralyzed hindquarters. Frozen into a sitting position, Bear seemed doomed until Shel and Mike rolled the dog onto an old door and carted him off to Lupowitz, who applied his art in all the relevant areas. Pretty soon Bear was up and about, feeling almost frisky. Then a neighboring bitch went into heat, and Bear joined the gangbang. By the time the dust cleared, he was a cripple again.

Back to Lupowitz journeyed the intrepid altruists, and once more the doctor's benign fingers worked their magic. On his feet, though, during the mating season, Bear's brains were all beneath his belt, and this time he emerged from the sexual brouhaha looking like something that had been vivisected by an express load of Winchester buckshot. Eventually, Mike figured the law at play here was one of diminishing returns, and so he led his Old Shep into the privacy of the piñon forest and gently sent him on to the Other Side.

The rollicking saga of Bear's last days triggered a discussion of mortality, and Spence Saunders's name surfaced—a friend of Shel's, acquaintance of mine . . . recently he died. Spence went to the doctor feeling poorly, and emerged with a diagnosis of acute leukemia. Chemotherapy might have helped a little—but Spence said, "No deal."

My photographer friend Bill Davis heard from Shel that Spence was dying, so he went over to visit a few times. Spence was fairly upbeat about his terminal adventure. Once, on departing, Bill said, "Well, I'll see you later, Spence." And Spence replied with a twinkle, "You're pretty optimistic, aren't you?" The last time Bill saw Spence, he was seated on his daybed, watching color TV. They started rapping about death, and finally Bill asked, "Well, Spence, how much time do you have left?"

Spence replied: "What time is it now?"

Shel liked Spence, even though he tended to be caustic and vicious when drunk. And on the edge of the gorge he had a few clear comments to sum up the man's life:

"He was a genuine iconoclast, sure, and he didn't tolerate any bullshit. He ran away from home in Oklahoma, I think, when he was only eleven. And he was a bona fide hustler all his life. He lived big when he could, and he had some high times when he made a lot of money. He specialized in aluminum-siding scams for a while. When he died, there was no ceremony, none of that. He was just cremated, and gone."

Beer bottles empty, we hoisted our aching bones into the car, and headed home. On the way, Shel talked about his early life, a marriage that ended, a Dallas friend who taught him how to be giving in a relationship. We stopped at a Questa bar so he could telephone Sonja. Later, in the car, I asked about Sonja: I am always grilling people about their lives and relationships. Especially it is a treat to hear Shel on himself and Sonja. They have a straightforward and genuine air about them. Their love seems to exist without a bunch of erudite complications. "I'm her best friend," Shel said easily. "We enjoy doing just about everything together."

And during our return voyage the world is momentarily calm, with no traumatic overtones whatsoever.

I am with Doug Terry in November. The sky is absolutely unblemished, cobalt blue, almost phony, an acrylic pretension by some meticulous guru of pop art. Sunshine oozes like syrup over warm boulders. The river is as clear as glycerin.

A hundred yards above Brown Trout Alley, I say, "Whoa, walk quietly, let's sneak up and see if the monster is feeding."

Hunched over, we approach cautiously. The river runs narrow and deep. In midstream is a large boulder. Twice before I have noticed a huge torpedo-shaped shadow in front of the rock, two feet below the surface, placidly sucking in tidbits, a wild and wily brown in at least the ten-pound range. A dozen different artificial offerings dropped delicately before its toro-sized nostrils have never produced a nibble. We are dealing, here, with a survivor.

We creep within range and sure enough, the torpedo is up and exposed, quietly noshing. Nearby, several smaller obsequious fish are munching on waterborn delicacies. A three-pound eighteen-incher repeatedly dimples for tiny yellow insects, an emaciated sardine compared to the *capo di tutti capo* beneath it. A few one-pound minnows are merely finning lazily, deferring to their elders.

For a while we observe, spellbound. The scene is bucolic, the trout as lazy as grazing cattle.

But as we try to sneak closer, they evaporate. Only the monster retreats slowly, backing into the rock shadows where no doubt it has lived for many a season.

I have no plans to catch that trout. So few must survive to such heroic size. In other pools I have seen them tailing. Mike Kimmel once baited a hook with salami for a trout we estimated at over thirty inches long, that lived in the aerated foam beneath a waterfall—but the fish paid no attention.

A few of them remain, then, murderous and untouchable in the blue depths of certain pools, golems of the Rio Grande, evolved beyond vulnerability . . . the legends that keep us going.

The river giveth: the river also taketh away. Sometimes it does so in the same breath. My friend Sylvia Landfair is a case in point.

Born and raised in Mississippi, as a child Sylvia often went fishing with her father. On the banks of lethargic mud-colored streams, they baited up hooks with God knows what—cornmeal and molasses, chicken gizzards and vanilla extract—and plopped them into the sludge. After a while they hauled ugly prehistoric bullheads and other assorted blightfish up out of the muck.

When Sylvia arrived in New Mexico, she expressed an interest in trout fishing. I explained that toiling on the Rio Grande was not exactly like lolling on muggy banks in Mississippi Barcaloungers, grappling for channel cats. Jutting her jaw, she gave me a fierce look, and growled, "Just take me with you one of these days."

Okay. We dug up some worms in my front field near the ditch, and I handed her a fly rod: "Let's go."

For our maiden excursion, I chose Sheep Corral Trail. When Sylvia, who is deathly afraid of both heights and rattlesnakes, got her first look at it, she gulped, almost vomited, then gave me another fierce look and snapped: "Well, what are we waiting for?"

Magnanimously, I said, "You can always change your mind. You can wait up here, if you want. I'll only go down for a little while."

Eyes narrowing into slits, she hissed, "Get goin', Nichols. This don't look like much of a hill for a stepper."

We descended to the river. Sylvia reached the bottom ashen-faced and trembling, and also determined to catch a fish. I explained the habits of trout, deposited her at a likely pool, and hurried off to rape the river. I landed a bunch on a routine day—nothing spectacular—and kept one eye on Sylvia. She caught a miniature trout on a worm, and tossed it back into the water. Other than that?—zee-ro.

But I noticed something. All afternoon she continually rebaited her hook and kept that line in the water. "Well I'll be damned," I muttered, slinging a heavy gunnysack over my shoulder. "Maybe this one is a live one."

As we started out, Sylvia said, "I think I'd like you to teach me how to catch a trout on flies."

"It ain't easy to catch a trout on flies."

"Nichols, I didn't ask if it was easy or not; I just asked you to teach me how to do it, that's all."

"Well, I don't know if I'm a very good teacher."

"Then we'll work out just fine because I'm probably a very lousy pupil."

As we probed forward in the dying light, she shuddered, envisioning a rattlesnake behind every rock. So graphic was her terror of being whacked by a sullen reptile, that the anxiety once caused her to break into tears.

At the top, I pegged her for a complete breakdown: she would beg me never to take her again. Instead, she cuddled up against me in the car and announced sprightly: "That was *wonderful!* I can't wait until we go again."

Then she adjusted the rearview mirror and rearranged a false eyelash that had tilted slightly awry.

Each weekend, over the next month, we clambered down Rockslide and Gutierrez, Sheep Corral and Arsenic and Francisco Antonio. Sylvia began to attack the river with flies as I attempted to teach her The Charles H. Reynolds Skitterin' Method of Trout Harvesting.

A novice to fly rods, Sylvia did not immediately adapt. Often we had what has come to be known as a "failure to communicate." We reached a nadir on the rainy, overcast afternoon of September 15, 1980, when Sylvia became hysterical. Hog-tied by an unsuccessfully cast line, screaming at the top of her lungs *"I'm so fucking stupid I should be shot!"* she burst into tears. A bit rattled myself, I ordered her to cool it. She screamed a salty "*Screw you, Nichols!*" untangled herself, and furiously piston-pumped her arm, whipping the water insanely with her line. What could I do but hee-haw dementedly?

She hollered, "Don't you make fun of *me!*"

I yelled right back, "You know what your problem is?—you're full of self-pity! You'll *never* catch a trout like that!"

"You're damn right I'm full of self-pity!" she bleated. "And I don't care if I never catch a trout like this!"

Distracted by the hullabaloo, I promptly snarled my three-fly trotline, clipped it off, and fashioned a two-fly trotline. I cast it across the river, snagged the tail fly on a rock, and lost the entire leader. At which point *I* slumped onto a rock, lavish with self-pity, and began to sob!

In between these daffy contretemps, we made progress. Sylvia learned to cast, raise the rod, mend her line, skitter her dropper, work a retrieve. In time, she learned to read the river, and cast to a specific trout.

Not long thereafter, she goaded a sluggish lunker into her first actively solicited strike. The fish was long gone before she reacted, but the action was exhilarating.

At night, trooping out behind me, she still shivered at each step, convinced that man-eating rattlers lurked beneath each rock and behind all the little bushes. I scoffed, ridiculed, and tried to cajole this terror from her. But the more I sought to allay her fears, the more she pooh-poohed my indifference.

"Hey, look at me," I wheedled obnoxiously. "I've hiked in and out of the gorge a hundred times, and *never* met a snake."

"You're not afraid, Nichols, because you're so stupid you just pretend they don't exist. That's absurd."

"Look," I insisted, "I love this country. And I'll be damned if I'll walk around paranoid on my own turf."

The statement reminded me of Mike Kimmel. Years ago, he waited on tables in high-class Philly restaurants. Off work at 2:00 A.M.,

he always walked home, wearing his tux. People said, "You're crazy! You'll get mugged, robbed, raped!" Mike sneered haughtily, "Oh no, not me. I ain't gonna walk around with my tail between my legs. This is *my* city, *my* home, and I won't pander to such chickenshit paranoia."

Fear, he figured, breeds misadventures. Try to play it safe, and they'll come after you in droves.

Well, one night he gamboled home in the tux, carrying his briefcase—no problem. He opened his door with the key and entered the house. His dog, a golden retriever named Bashion, jumped into his arms before he could close the door. Mike gave the dog a loving ruffle, then turned and met a 12-gauge shotgun—over-under style—in the hands of a beefy sixteen-year-old, entering his domicile. Mike slammed the door hard, and a brief shoving match ensued. Mike lost, his ample nose wound up stuck into the snout of the gun, and the hyped-up kid snarled, "Gimme the briefcase, mister, or I'll blow your fuckin' head off!"

Mike surrendered the briefcase.

But he continued walking the nighttime streets of Philadelphia, because nobody but *nobody* was going to usurp the freedom of his turf.

Now we arrive at the grand finale: Saturday, October 11, 1980.

A nicer day hasn't been invented. We selected Big Arsenic, planning to camp in the gorge overnight. All the beautiful mauve cornflowers lining the gorge road had died and turned sere. Sunflowers had shriveled, rabbitbrush was gone to seed. Obviously, the halcyon days of The Season were over.

We strapped on food-laden backpacks, sleeping bags, cooking utensils, fishing rods, warm clothes and coats, a million other odds and ends (including a brandy bottle), and staggered down the trail like overloaded Sahara camels. A mile north of Big Arsenic, we made camp at the next-to-last cabin set among tall pines beside a gurgling spring. And at 3:00 P.M. we scrambled down to the river.

Abstaining from fishing, I followed Sylvia, commenting on her technique. The river was extra low, clear, and tempting. Abnormally exposed rocks were powdered with white dust. Half the river's normally underwater structures were visible, providing a fascinating glimpse into the nature of trout habitat.

My constant advice caused a minor tension, but soon we established a rhythm. At the first pool, near the island at Brown Trout Alley, Sylvia had a hit, but missed the strike. A moment later she tied into a chunky twelve-inch-brown—I shouted an order, she jumped, and the fish splashed free. Sylvia glared in my direction; I agreed that I should keep my mouth shut. I also suggested that when a fish hit, and was hooked, she should first reel in her extra line, then let the trout swim about on its tether until she had her bearings straight. She nodded, and returned her fierce concentration to the river.

West of the island, she soon hooked a fifteen-inch rainbow that danced through the air like a vigorous little porpoise. Calmly, Sylvia reeled in her extra line, and I maneuvered to thrust our net into the water. But the rainbow tarponed skyward again, and this time the hook popped free, twanging back onto shore.

Our groans echoed down canyon above the river's roar.

Nevertheless, we both sensed that the ultimate triumph was achingly imminent.

Five drama-laden minutes ticked by. Sylvia cast over a rock into a small whirlpool, mended her line jerkily, and a hefty brown trout missed the tail fly, bashing itself against a barely submerged rock before slithering back into the turbulent drink.

Sylvia rolled her eyes, gnashed her teeth, and stalked up to the next likely pool. Immediately, in fast water above the island, she hooked a chunky foot-long brown. This time she sucked in a deep breath, refusing to panic, and I kept my mouth shut. The fish struggled, but she worked it over to shore and into the net I was holding. Whereupon both of us started hooting and dancing and almost slipped, cracked our craniums, and rolled into the river. I shrieked joyfully, Sylvia giggled jubilantly; and our odyssey, begun but a few short trips ago, had ended in success!

We paused for the obligatory photographs, then pushed on, fishing the last half hour before dark. Abruptly, the trout ceased feeding. I picked up a few browns in a foamy pool, then we headed downstream in the twilight, easily traversing about a half-mile of boulders. Soon, we reached the alley, and had but fifty yards to cover before the trail. A small spring empties into the river there, creating a narrow grassy mat at its mouth.

As we crossed through the innocuous patch of grass, Sylvia slipped on a hidden stone, gave a cry, and sat down abruptly. I turned; her face was white and frightened. "Oh shit," she muttered, "I did it, I felt something snap."

It couldn't be: we were so *close*. The day had been *perfect*. I convinced Sylvia she could make it, and bravely she hobbled up the last steep hillside to a pine-tree plateau. We hiked down to the camp, guzzled some brandy, started a fire, and cooked the fresh trout. After a lovely dinner spent gawking at the stars, we prepared to crash. But when Sylvia arose and took a step, she collapsed in excruciating pain— and vomited.

We tried to sleep. But Sylvia's foot had swelled; it throbbed painfully. Finally, inevitably, we decided to pack out right then, in the cool dark, instead of waiting for daylight. She would lean on my shoulder and use a rod case for a crutch. We'd take our time. I heaved one pack onto my back.

But every time her foot touched the ground, a sharp pain made her cry out. The arrangement was hideously awkward, and had to be abandoned fifty feet from the campsite. I jettisoned the pack, kept only a canteen, and hoisted Sylvia piggy-back style. We had two miles of trail, rising approximately eight hundred feet, between us and the rim of the gorge.

Sylvia is five-foot-two, and at that time weighed 115 pounds.

Carefully, I felt my way along in the dark. The sky held stars, but no moon: I could barely see my feet. We neither talked nor joked—it was hard work, and we had a long way to go. Actually, I couldn't talk, I was puffing too hard. Sylvia couldn't speak because she feared that the strain on my fibrillation-prone ticker might cause it to occlude, leaving her abandoned in the wilderness, and without a lover to boot.

The trail back to Arsenic Springs is downhill, and we covered it easily. But then the task began. We started to rise. In minutes, I was sopping-wet from sweat. Taking one careful step at a time, I tried to predict when my heart would start pounding from the strain, and usually halted just before it launched a rampage.

But we couldn't stop for long: the air was icy, and my drenched shirt grew clammy fast. So on I plodded, no doubt blue in the face, setting my feet down in a cautious, jerky rhythm like a child's windup toy. Inch by inch we progressed, and I tried not to think of the distance remaining. I don't believe I have ever traveled that slowly; yet we usually managed almost a quarter-mile between breaks. After a while Sylvia's foot no longer hurt; we figured my arm must have been cutting off her circulation.

We had started to climb at 3:00 A.M. . . . and reached the top at 4:30. Had I not been exhausted, I might have babbled "Hallelujah!" Instead, I tumbled Sylvia into the car, about-faced, and headed back into the gorge for our gear. Without a burden, I found myself eager to run and leap in the dark. A euphoria captured my dazed and giddy body. Even though I couldn't see the trail, I seemed to have a perfect instinct for moving in the dark. A few times I almost tripped on wooden erosion barriers set into the path by government trailmakers. Other than that, I flew effortlessly down the mountain into the pitch-black gorge, invulnerable and acutely adjusted to the darkness.

At the bottom, all pumped up with adrenaline, I raced too quickly toward the campsite, almost dancing up the last hill light-headed and barely puffing; sensing danger in my speed I forced myself to slow down, take it easy, be reasonable.

At the campsite it took awhile to break everything down, stuff sleeping bags into their cases, fill the packs, jettison all nonessentials, and hit the road again. I must have resembled some absurd street peddler from immigrant days on New York's Lower East Side. A regular nylon backpack was stuffed full of equipment; cooking pots and pans attached to various thongs and straps clanked against each other. My left arm carried the photography knapsack, a fishing net, and two rod cases. Wedged under my right arm were two sleeping bags and all our clothes.

This time I used a flashlight. Near the Arsenic Springs a bumblebee-sized mouse floated ahead of me for a ways, then stopped. I nudged it with my toe, amazed at its full-grown tininess.

At dawn, I reached the top. Sylvia was cold, but bravely cheerful. Driving home, I could barely keep my eyes open, more fatigued than ever before in my life. I toppled into bed feeling discombobulated and fragile inside, and lay awake for minutes, in terror, convinced a heart attack was imminent.

But then I passed out.

For Sylvia, The Season was over. The river spirits had given her a sprained ankle, also a broken metatarsal bone.

But they had also allowed her a first trout caught expertly on a fly.

Are you runnin' with me, darlin'?

Remember that smoky evening of the big lazy snowflakes? When the gorge walls almost faded away into the winter mists . . . then the storm lifted, and the cliffs returned? Only to disappear again as the snowy vapor intensified? And light, filtered through the warm chummy weather, burnished the landscape with a wonderful mysterious shine, as if all rocks, leaves, and earth had accepted a sacred radiation? And remember how snow lay in dainty fan-shaped sprinkles exuding an eerie luminous quality like some sort of beautiful but perhaps poisonous sugar? And rocks had that marvelous subdued shimmer as if made out of gray flesh instead of hard, inert molecules? And all colors—all the gray and green and yellow lichens, and the tawny strawberry-ocher vanilla-fragrant ponderosa bark—all those colors were intensified with a poetic dampness? And the blooms on mere weeds were a voluptuous beigey-pink, or soft russety salmon colors, or pale apricot? And little grasses seemed as delicate as fairy-tale webs of mist? And all the smells—of damp sage, juniper berries, cedar bark, blue boulders, and burgundy stones—assaulted our well-being, making us even happier? And we left footprints across layers of pine needles arranged on the ground in a design as perfect as that of the countless joined barbs in a feather? And at the top I wandered into the sage and stood there taking a leak absolutely absorbed in the muffling active silence? And we picked sprigs of dry grasses to make into table arrangements? Then finally drove out through swirling snow along the deserted road at twilight feeling absurdly contented? And just west of Cerro came upon three big deer beside the road, a muscular twelve-point buck and two powerful does, who held their ground in the snow-capped sagebrush as we marveled over them, and the sky lowered, and the mountains dissolved, until only you and I and three quiet deer existed in that serene bauble at the eye of a gathering blizzard. . . .

Remember that?

PART FOUR

We may be about to rediscover that dying
is not such a bad thing to do after all.

—Lewis Thomas
The Lives of a Cell

EIGHT

One spring day Andrés Martínez and I drove over to Carson in search of a blowhole.

We stopped at Verde Shupe's house for directions, and got to talking with Verde and his wife. Naturally, our conversation ambled into the Old Days.

Age ten, Verde came down from Colorado with his dad. That was in 1912, four years before my own father was born. Verde's dad was a strong swimmer, and he remembers how the old man once swam them all across the Rio Grande at the Manby Hot Springs not far from Arroyo Hondo.

Next, we talked about the reservoir that could never hold water. It had filled up once, though, and the Shupes had loved to picnic on the shores of the lake. Even then, you could place your hand over small blowholes, and feel the cold air rising out of underground caverns. "It reminded you of the sea," said Mrs. Shupe. "The grasses near the blowholes were always waving."

The blowholes were a phenomenon and a mystery that intrigued the Carson residents, until all their water, and with it much of their land, disappeared into the nether regions, and the dream of a self-sufficient agricultural community dissolved.

Up until recently, even without irrigation water the Shupes had farmed in Carson—beans, hay, some table vegetables, whatever the yearly moisture traffic, and their deep well, would bear. But then (a sign of these hard times): "One day we went off for a while and the machinery up and walked away. And it ain't come back yet."

Mrs. Shupe is a dowser, a water witch. She told us proudly: "I witched the well that just came in over across the valley at three hundred and eighty-five feet."

Finally, outside in the front yard, Verde pointed to an arroyo below the eastern slope of Tres Orejas: therein lay the elusive blowhole. The history of the hole is intriguing. First, according to Verde, it was just a crack in the ground, expelling cold air. Over the years, various people dug it out, making the entrance wider. But not until some enterprising wag lit into it with dynamite could a person actually crawl inside.

The last fellows Verde sent over there "wound up killing rattlesnakes as fast as they could shoot 'em, until they had killed twenty or more. That was enough for them. They just got the hell out and never went back."

Hah, thinks I. Just listen to them tall tales rolling off that silver tongue!

Verde squatted, drawing a map in the dust of how to enter the arroyo, how far up it to go, and where to turn west—at some limestone cliffs—and start climbing.

We shook hands, got in our VW bus, and headed north.

Dirt roads in Carson don't appear to go anywhere—they just meander. It was an overcast day with an occasional rumble of high thunder. Rain sprinkled intermittently, each large drop making a puff as it hit the dusty ruts. In shallow gullies on either side of us, hundreds of old round tumbleweeds thrice the size of basketballs had come to rest. A luminous silvery-gray color, their skeletons were wonderfully intricate.

Sagebrush land turned into piñon-juniper foothills. Heading up the canyon, the road deteriorated until I had to stop. Andrés found a dead juniper branch to use for a walking stick, and we proceeded on foot. At the cliff Verde had mentioned, we split up and began canvassing the steep hillside, searching for the blowhole.

Ay, such heat! The search seemed hopeless. Rare in Taos is a muggy day like that one. Sunshine kept breaking through the overcast; a few heavy raindrops clattered against the rocks, evaporating immediately. Too rarely a streak of ice, on an errant breeze, zipped past like an arrow, a last message from winter.

Andrés disappeared. Desultorily I probed every depression, each gathering of boulders. I hollered for Andrés. He hollered back, I thought from down in the draw. So I hiked there and yelled again; but now his voice reached me from high on the slope. I worried about him; the day was heavy, a trifle menacing. Verde Shupe had not been real precise; our search seemed hopelessly quixotic.

Heading toward the dim echo of my friend's voice, I arrived at the foot of a small cliff, right at the entrance to a cave! Incredibly, I had found the blowhole. Andrés was nowhere in sight. In front of the entrance lay a foot-thick carpet of dry animal droppings, I thought at first from deer; but later Andrés attributed the musty excretions to porcupines.

Crouching at the entrance, I peered inside. A person would have to crawl on all fours into the darkness. Cold air hissed softly from the cave, carrying a disturbing stench of peculiarly threatening, almost prehistoric animal decay.

Again, I called for Andrés. His voice came back from not fifty yards away. Jubilantly, I announced my discovery.

Looking pale and tired, he walked through the junipers, the cholla cactus, and the rocks, mopping his brow with a handkerchief. His eyes, however, were alight with an impish excitement.

"Come here, Juanito. I've got some animals to show you."

"Deer?"

"Even bigger than that."

"*Elk!*"

He nodded, grinning, and I fell in step behind him, scarcely daring to breathe; I had never seen an elk in the wild. "Walk carefully," Andrés cautioned. "We don't want them to run away."

I walked *very* carefully, made no sound, and peered through the scrub forest, anxious for a glimpse of the majestic animals.

Abruptly, a rattlesnake buzzed; I froze, and grabbed Andrés's shoulder, ordering him to stop. When he turned to me, his eyes brimmed over mischievously, and he giggled.

"*That's* what I wanted to show you."

With malice aforethought, the man had led me into a nest of rattlers!

Coiled beside a rock, cooled by a sagebrush shadow, one snake buzzed alarmingly. Previously, Andrés had chased another under a rock, and now asked me to help him lift the flat slab and expose the snake. I refused and urged more caution. He seemed to have no fear whatsoever.

"I've learned," he said, "that snakes almost always travel in pairs. Same as coyotes. One hunts, while the other stands guard."

I had left my camera bag back at the cave. He followed me there to retrieve it. Stooping, he peered into the darkness, sniffing the billows of cold air, and remarked, "It smells like snakes."

When I asked "Why all the porcupine droppings?" he said that porcupines and snakes didn't bother each other. I tried to picture the cave full of snoozing porcupines and rattlesnakes, while winter snows piled up outside. . . .

I found a rock and pitched it into the cave. Instantly, the coils of a large groggy rattler twisted into action, and that warning sounded, a reverberating eerie falsetto whine. It was difficult to make out the snake clearly: it writhed grotesquely, confused by the intrusion. Light glinted off the coils of a snake that had to be at least five feet long.

Though I was not about to crawl in and measure.

Eager for some photographs, we returned to the other snakes. From about five feet I focused on the lovely, cinnamon-green reptile under the chamisa bush, coiled and buzzing alertly, ready to strike.

I know little about rattlesnakes, but have always understood they can't strike more than half the length of their bodies—and this one looked to be but two and a half feet long.

Closer would have been better, though. So I clicked on a zoom lens, and swung downhill a few feet to a rock upon which I could steady the camera, enabling me to zoom right up to the serpent's eyeball. I set down the camera, spread my legs wide, and was settling down when I noticed another snake coiled at the base of the rock, between my legs, its head a foot and a half from my crotch.

I *jumped!* Five feet up and five feet sideways in a single terrified motion! The snake never buzzed, never bothered to strike. Grabbing a stick, I returned and poked at it a bit. Sluggish, still sleepy, not quite "thawed," I suppose, the rattler still refused to issue a warning.

We concluded they had spent the winter denning in the blowhole, and were just now emerging. *"Salen al primer trueno,"* Andrés told me. When the first spring thunderstorms hit, they awaken.

Returning to the car, we walked carefully, almost on tiptoes. But no further snakes gave us a start. As always, deer tracks abounded—but we saw no deer. An unusual number of wrens flitted about. Mountain bluebirds, shining like bursts of aluminum-turquoise fire, disappeared behind juniper trees. A few jays chattered raucously in the tops of taller piñons.

We also saw a sage thrasher, a sparrow hawk, and the proverbial lone buzzard circling overhead, more to the west, near the three peaks of Tres Orejas, receding behind us.

Only a handful of men now earn their living from herding sheep in the Taos Valley. Pacomio Mondragón is one of them, a cheerful, taciturn man from Llano Quemado who lives by the seasons, struggles hard to stay afloat, and is a staunch defender of the land. For years he was a major force in the Tres Rios Association during a struggle to keep a conservancy district and a Bureau of Reclamation dam from entering, and hastening the agricultural destruction of, the Taos Valley.

In the spring he drives his herd of ewes to a campsite on the Carson mesa a few miles southwest of Tres Orejas. And after our adventure at the blowhole, Andrés and I headed for Pacomio's camp.

West of the mountain, last year's crested wheat was high, a warm yellowy color—it hadn't been grazed. Around the clusters of dry stalks, new green leaves were pushing up. The overcast remained high, distantly threatening. From wispy, slate-blue rain clouds big drops still spattered down irregularly. The dusty smell they released was wonderfully evocative. A single raindrop touches a sage leaf, and a rare perfume is created! For me, the odor is nostalgic, rich, beautiful, and lonely: it evokes memories of things I have never experienced . . . history, the Old Days, hard times, a spare and precious freedom.

We passed an old tank truck full of water parked beside circular metal watering basins for lambs. Rain, finally, gathered heavily overhead; the air turned ominous. The sheep in a nearby herd were lying down, unperturbed. Fat ewes, not yet sheared, were flanked by newborn lambs. Andrés said this flock belonged to Bonifacio Martínez. In the distance, a man on horseback galloped through the crested wheat to reach an old aluminum trailer before the deluge.

It hit, so powerful and thick I couldn't see to drive—and I stopped. Water drummed against the roof; wild streams against the windows obliterated the landscape. I worried that rain would quickly make the roads impassable.

But the downpour ended in two minutes. We pushed on, and within a hundred yards the road was almost dry.

A large dying ewe blocked our route. I braked, took her by the hind legs, and pulled her into the grass. She was bloated, who knows from what? Her mouth was full of green grassy flecks of foam. Her eyes rolled, staring at me, scared. Sheep eyes always seem timid and alarmed and ready to die at the slightest provocation.

Andrés said that sometimes a healthy sheep will enter a green alfalfa field and start grazing—and fifteen minutes later it will die from the accumulated gases.

I had an experience with that once. I was spending the winter in Albuquerque's South Valley. My neighbor John Leyba had a fat ewe and a lamb. On his birthday I gave him several bales of dry alfalfa. He broke off a flake, and fed it to his ewe. Twenty minutes later, when he entered the corral to check on his rabbits and collect chicken eggs, the ewe was dead.

He had thought the alfalfa dry enough for sheep to eat. Instead, it was still green enough to be a murderer.

Farther along, a different horseman galloped toward us. Three cocky dogs raced beside the horse, noisy and exhilarated. Dogs, horse, rider, the entire landscape seemed charged by the excitement of natural flux in that wide environment.

The horseman reared in; Andrés and I descended from the bus. The horse pranced anxiously, the dogs yapped heartily at us, and then at the rider, impatient to be after sheep.

Jaime Gonzales is a Mexican national, and we spoke in Spanish. He had worked for Pacomio for several months. Layers of baggy ragged clothes made his body seem puffy. He wore a red hat that buttoned under his chin and resembled a shabby hockey helmet: he seemed like an apparition from the windswept steppes, from the lonely isolated prairies of Mongolia.

According to Jaime, Pacomio was not at the campsite. Instead, he could be found farther west, herding his flock toward water in the Petaca Arroyo.

Then he left, galloping across the empty vistas with the frolicking dogs, speed-for-the-sake-of-speed silhouetted against distant thunder and thin stuttering streaks of quicksilver lightning.

First we saw the blue pickup—Pacomio's—parked in an empty territory. Then Pacomio's distant figure, and his helper, another Mexican national, rounding up the sheep.

Pacomio never says too much to me. He smiles, brown and chapped from the wind, comfortable and almost absentminded with his sheep. They flow, he flows—the large herd presents little problem for a couple of men on foot. Pacomio carries a tall herder's crook, but I never see him use it.

He works hard, earning a living against the odds, and seems most comfortable among men, out in the open, although recently, late in his life, he married, and now has a beautiful daughter. I like best to hear him joking and bantering among his helpers and visitors like Andrés. There's a bawdy and lighthearted register to all that is said.

For a man, it's a lonely life, with few surprises. Danger is always present—mostly to the sheep, although I am constantly cautioned to "watch out for víboras." Coyotes are a royal pain in the ass. The scare guns surrounding the camp are always booming—like cannons going off at deliberate intervals in the distance.

I love coyotes. I love the idea of them on the mesa. I love to hear them barking and cackling, causing their busy furors at dusk. But Pacomio loses dozens of lambs and thousands of dollars to the predators every year.

Hence, I sympathize with Pacomio. And openly root for his survival, against all the odds, including coyotes. Nevertheless, in my secret soul I pray for coyotes.

To me, no animal has a more attractive myth or reality. I identify completely with coyotes. Funky, down-to-earth, and clever, all the wonderful, whacky lusts and perversions that make my own life rich and worthwhile are also attributed to coyotes.

According to J. Frank Dobie in his classic book *The Voice of The Coyote*, they are often called "the Charlie Chaplin of the plains." Though unable to speak English, they are fluent in many Indian dialects and converse perfectly in Spanish. They have been known to play dead at midday in order to draw a buzzard to their carcass, then leap up and grab the startled bird. Crow Indians believe Old Man

Coyote was entrusted by God to carry out much of the creation chores, and most of the mistakes among earthly things happened because he blew it. In much tribal lore, according to Dobie, Coyote assumes three characters: as mythological creator he is revered; as cunning trickster, often exercising magical power, he is admired; as the dupe of all other animals, the master trickster in reverse (and utterly fallen from his original estate), he is mocked.

The image I carry in my head is of a ribald, oversexed ghetto survivor with a marvelous sense of humor. That coyotes have survived at all is certainly one of our twentieth-century miracles. Here's how John N. Cole, writing in the May 1973 *Harper's* magazine, put it:

> Wolf, fox, weasel, crow, hawk, owl, eagle, mountain lion, bear, badger, and coyote—every animal that posed a danger to buffalo, cow, sheep, or chicken was deemed an enemy to be killed. And of these the coyote seemed the most immortal, therefore the most threatening and super-natural. So resilient was the creature's foothold on existence that it began to seem as if the settlers sought to exterminate a phantom.
>
> From the mid–nineteenth century to the mid-twentieth, the coyote was killed in greater numbers than any other four-legged animal in the known history of the continent. Millions of coyotes were shot, trapped, drugged, poisoned, gassed, clubbed, electrocuted, and suffocated. The animal's extinction became federal policy, worthy of an Act of Congress, yet the varmint refused to vanish. The hundred-year effort to control it simply produced more coyotes. In response to mass murder, the coyote increased its numbers and its range. It was the only wild animal in North America to do so, with or without man's persecution.

To be truthful, I have had little actual contact with the animals. I saw one trot nonchalantly across a meadow near an alpine body of water called Heart Lake a dozen years ago. A few more have darted across highways and dirt roads in front of my car. Last autumn I saw two varmints in the Carson area: one leaped from my headlight glare into wild sunflowers at the bottom of the reservoir; another I watched for five minutes, in broad daylight, trotting casually along a shallow arroyo near the rim of the Rio Grande Gorge.

Still, their voices loom large in my legend. Picture this: It is dusk, in December. The sky is high and spottily overcast. No wind is blowing. You can see the half-moon, bathed in haze. Dozens of dim stars are not lost behind the gray mist of winter clouds. Suddenly, it starts snowing; big dry unhurried flakes. Yet the moon is clear, the stars are bright. . . .

Then, near the Tres Orejas foothills several miles away, the coyotes unleash a noisy, urgent racket of yelps, barks, funny crackling whines.

It lasts for a minute, then stops as abruptly as it began. Is the rabbit dead? Has the bitch been properly fucked? Or can nobody else think of a coyote joke with quite as hilarious a punch line . . . ?

From a distance, back again at Pacomio Mondragón's sheep camp, I watched Pacomio and Andrés herd sheep across the mesa toward the Petaca Arroyo. The ewes knew exactly where to go, but sometimes the lambs strayed. When I was close to the herd, the noise was deafening: such unrelenting sheep babble, shrill baa-ing, frantic wailing. But when I retreated the cacophony almost subsided completely, swallowed up by the muffling omnipotence of rainy sky.

Andrés stooped over and shooed the animals ahead, guiding little lambs back into the flock. Sometimes he and Pacomio walked together, talking, almost oblivious to the sheep. But when animals strayed off, the two friends split apart, circled out, and chased the borregas back into the fold.

In this manner, they soon reached a trail descending into a gully that arrived at grassy banks near the bottom of the arroyo, a cleft miraculously full of water, a river almost half the width of the Rio Grande!

I was stunned. Normally, the Carson arroyos were empty. Usually, Pacomio had to ferry water in a tank truck over terrible roads from the Rio Grande to his campsite. But on this day, water draining from the porous reservoir after a heavy winter runoff was plentiful, and saved untold time and wear and tear on the vehicles.

From above, I watched the sheep clustered on the banks, drinking. Hummingbirds scissored noisily through the air. The entire scene had the quality of a mirage.

Seated on rocks, I overlooked that biblical illusion. Then I noticed at my feet, nestled on a slim ledge, four delicate mauve pasqueflowers . . . wild crocuses, I think they are also called.

A pure blossom in that dry territory—so delicate and out of place. When I looked up, most of the sheep were back on the trail, leaving the arroyo single-file, returning toward the camp.

In the distance shafts of sunlight that had broken through encircling webs of rain landed upon the sagebrush in theatrical colorful bursts, like fantasies of powdered gold.

We headed home, tired and satisfied. Andrés was sleepy. He muttered, "I overdid it." I acted surprised. Why shouldn't a man of eighty be able to trudge miles up and down the side of a mountain, play with rattlesnakes, herd sheep to water, climb in and out of the Petaca Arroyo on steep trails, and proceed another mile or two back to the car?

Eh?

Horned larks scattered ahead, flying low over the road. I stopped at the dying sheep and confirmed its death. Stiff and cold, its lifeless icy eyes still looked timid and frightened, forever frozen in weird chickenshit apprehension.

In the Pueblo Gorge I pointed to several mammoth rockslides, asking Andrés, "Can you remember when those happened?"

He knew one had occurred during the last ten years, but had no recollection of a date for the other.

At the Martínez trailer, a neighbor, Enrique Mascareñas, stood on the haycock beyond Andrés's garden, sawing off a chunk of straw with a hay knife. I'd never seen a tool like that. Andrés said he used to have one, and used it all the time before the days of hay balers.

A memory: When first I came to Taos in 1969, a farmer five miles south of my home, near Los Cordovas, gathered his hay on an old wooden wagon with rubber tires, pulled by two massive white workhorses. Driving slowly by in the evenings, I watched the horses plod along, while men walked beside them, pitching up forkfuls of hay.

No more . . . that's gone.

Andrés offered me a glass of homemade chokecherry wine. I let the first sip loll on my tongue, and, although I know nothing about wines, my guess is that his stuff is what the cult of the vines is all about.

A meadowlark call bubbled out of the dark with astonishing melodic clarity. And, as the moon rose, I had a dream. . . .

I was sitting on the portal of an old adobe house, built in the simple classical manner. It had a tin roof. The outside walls were of carefully rubbed mud instead of hard plaster. Windows were small, the walls very thick. Faded turquoise paint flaked off posts supporting the portal roof. I sat on a bench, my back against the wall, facing a pretty field. Springtime grass was not very high. You could smell germination in the air.

Andrés Martínez and a few other old-timers also sat on the portal: on my bench, on another bench, in an old straight-back chair. Everybody gazed imperturbably at the field. It was a gathering without tension, very serene. A few wingèd insects floated mutely through the dying daylight moments.

I felt a yearning closeness with Andrés. I wanted to reach out and touch him, giving assurance that I believed in and accepted his legacy. I wanted these dignified old people to feel comfortable bequeathing the future to me. I very much hoped that they knew the beauty and worth of their lives had been passed on successfully.

I did not want their spirits to die.

What a sweet unnerving anguish! I know it had to do with mortality and gratitude, the tragedy of our lives, and the joy of being here.

Nobody said a word. The field simmered peacefully as the twilight thickened. Instinctively, we all realized that the field had experienced its last haying season. Next year, a house or a little development would obliterate the tired grass.

Very clearly I remember the old-timers' faces—composed and relaxed, but not complacent, or smug, or self-satisfied. Rather a kind of intelligent sadness was in their eyes, and something else I found reassuring—they were at ease with the prospect of eternity.

It was growing darker. Some bats began their dances above the field. They multiplied, and the dim crepuscular light grew nervous with their irregular flight patterns and sonar squeaks.

Now I could see only soft highlights on the weathered cheeks of my old friends. Their eyes were fixed on a line of thickly bunched willows across the field where a phantom shape began to assume familiar characteristics. I leaned forward and peered intently. A remote ivory gleam shimmered along the forearms of an elderly skinny man walking toward us. Underneath a dark beret he had wavy gray hair, and wore glasses: several days' stubble on his face made him look tired. He wore a clean denim shirt and pressed khaki pants, and moved forward with a fragile gait.

It was my friend Craig Vincent from San Cristobal, another true keeper of the flame.

He raised his hand in a friendly greeting, said "Hello," and settled on the edge of the porch. A Chinese red star was pinned to his beret. Reaching into his shirt pocket, he removed a pack of cigarettes, tapped one out, and paused a moment, coughing; the cough rattled deep in his throat, tears appeared in his eyes. When he fixed the cigarette in his mouth and lit it, I said, "Craig, why do you keep on smoking?"

He shook his head, smiling gently: "I just can't stop."

Then he began to talk and his eyes lit up; he has a sly sense of humor, an easy laugh. He spoke of Kiko Martínez, a Chicano-movement lawyer under suspiciously political indictment in Colorado—Craig was raising money for his defense. . . .

That has been Craig's role, these struggles: he has given his life to the wretched of the earth, to underdogs, to working-class people. He dreams of a more equitable society; he has actively supported the courageous idealists and revolutionaries of our time. He is a rare American with an international historical perspective.

I met Craig twelve years ago; we were opposed to the Vietnam war, we supported a people's clinic, cooperative farm, and graphics *taller* in Tierra Amarilla, west of Taos. Over the years we have worked together on different projects. Craig founded the Taos branch of the U.S.–China Peoples' Friendship Committee and kept it going for years until our country finally recognized the People's Republic. Because of Craig, I met men like Joshua Horn, author of *Away with All Pests*, a doctor who spent much of his life in China and received a hero's burial there when he died. Thanks to Craig's hard work and dedication, many citizens from the Taos area, including Chicano and native people, have had an opportunity to visit China and gain important insights into societies other than our own.

Craig is a patient and loving long-distance runner; he has never lost his sense of humor, he has never wavered. Called before the Senate Internal Security Subcommittee in the fifties, he stood his ground and sold out to nobody, least of all himself. Moving back and forth across America in the name of one good cause or another, he has not given up hope, or lost his compassion.

I have been in valuable study groups organized by Craig. We have attended meetings called to protest the oppressive tactics of grand juries. We have met at benefits to raise money for the legal fees of local New Mexicans trying to protect their land from corporate developers. Most recently, at a small gathering to protest the U.S.–El Salvador intervention, together we watched a powerful film called *Revolucion o Muerte*, made by the World Council of Churches.

I know that Craig is tired, but he keeps on, dreaming of a more humanitarian world. His friends cross all political boundaries because his integrity has never been suspect.

Like Andrés Martínez, Craig is an old-timer who one day will be sorely missed. The man has a vision and a world view all of us need to acknowledge; his skills have supported and enriched us all. Caring about people and the land, he has tirelessly defended the rights of both. Though we are far from intimates, his presence and his work have always inspired me to feel hopeful about the future of humankind.

Now he is in my dream, on the edge of that porch, smoking a cigarette, coughing. His eyes seem almost cruelly fatigued. But then he laughs, and his entire face softens. We even make jokes to dull the pains of daily holocausts. He brings me up to date on the defense of Kiko Martínez; we also speak about Cuba and China. I ask after his wife Jenny, a fine musician and important folklorest. Then we talk about El Salvador . . . and the Velasquez family's land battle . . . and an upcoming demonstration against the draft.

I have nothing but admiration for old-timers whose lives have encompassed these battles, whose decency and unfaltering vitality make everybody around them more whole.

I awoke alone at 5:00 A.M. on a dark November morning fulfilled by falling snow. Groggily, I sat up. A funny light infused the bedroom; I had forgotten to close the curtains. The room pulsed in a faint luminosity, as if an incarnation waited just around the corner.

At the window my breath misted the cold glass. The snow absorbed a provocative radiance from the air out of mercury-vapor lamps and artificial town lights reflected off the claustrophobic atmosphere.

At the front door, a plump mouse in his jaws, Duke gave a half-strangled meow. I shuffled to the kitchen and ushered him inside. He entered proudly, emitting growly egotistical purrs. In the middle of the kitchen floor he sat down and gazed at me quizzically, his prey still fast between his teeth. Snowflakes dangled off his whiskers like angelic dandruff. Though alive, why struggle? The beady mouse eyes roamed helplessly, assessing doom.

"Duke," I muttered hoarsely, "you're a murderer."

Carefully, he set down the mouse between his paws, and without fanfare drove his teeth through the teeny brain—*crunch*. Then he devoured the little fella.

I listened to teeth crunching minuscule bones. Soon, not much remained. Duke demolished the tail, paws, ears, nose and teeth. But he left a little green bag, shaped like a stomach. Or was it a gall bladder, full of mousey bile? Then he licked up a drop of blood, and preened his gleaming fur. Finally, he sauntered into my bedroom to make a nest in the puffy folds of my sleeping bag.

Alone in the cold kitchen, I stared at a tiny green mouse organ in the middle of the floor, and pondered my dream, and had thoughts about the dying of old-timers, the end of a way of life.

NINE

I have written elsewhere about my friend Justin Locke, in *If Mountains Die*. Justin never lived to see the publication of that book. He died alone, in one of his Taos houses, in the spring of 1979.

An overpowering person, riddled with a manic gusto, he turned out to be a fragile human being. The last two years of his life we drifted apart. This happened when I realized he was killing himself, and there was nothing I could do to save him. A stubborn man, he became locked on a tragic course, and I suppose lacked either the desire or the confidence to save himself.

For much of the time that I knew him, I cherished his idiosyncrasies. A lunatic?—sure . . . but a creative lunatic who made me happy, and lived with a marvelous giddy intensity. For years I envied Justin. He seemed to have an indefatigable ebullience. I ignored the dark side of his nature and tolerated the fact that he was a totally self-centered individual. The innocence of his rambunctious winning naïveté appealed to me. He had a talent for whacky living: he had a rich, convoluted, sexy, and bawdy style.

Justin was a rake and a rambling man. He had been all over the world. French and Spanish he spoke with arrogant fluency. English popped from his lips like a cross between a British duke and Damon Runyon. He was obstreperous, pushy, gung-ho, noisy. I loved his insatiable curiosity about bizarre manifestations of humanity. In a branch of the Secret Service during World War II, he had slept with women who were spies and double agents, and he had reveled in what sounded, when he recounted them, like James Bond intrigues. After the war, he was a top-notch photographer for the *National Geographic*: all his pictures that survive are beautiful.

He went back a ways, too, having arrived in Taos not long after World War II. Hence he was a bona fide town character: a true Taos original.

Functioning with a careless, ribald ease, he had many women. Each new affair he approached as the first of its kind on earth. Justin in love was a heady and bombastic adventure. He exhausted women with the joy and intensity he brought to the game. Each time out of the gate, I think he saw himself as a devil-may-care lothario at play in the fields of Eden. The man took his pleasure, gave it, and had a lot of fun. He enjoyed leaping out back bedroom windows while husbands turned keys in the locks of front doors. I personally invested him with the notoriety of a latter-day Canterbury Tales character. With one eye closed, I could always see Justin as a goat man, a real honest-to-God satyr—one of those perky letches designed by Picasso or William Steig, innocent and relentless, a man who truly loved women with all his soul, and renewed himself in every body. I listened at length to his escapades and forgave him his irresponsibility. Up into the hills he danced with his girls, and photographed them as nymphets surrounded by the lush foliage of autumn leaves; he kissed their thighs pressed into tufts of soft green moss. Or wheedled them into closets at cocktail parties and screwed them with laughter in the suffocating dark.

He was a madman, he had flair and a brash cockeyed delivery. He fashioned bonsai trees. And dashed through the woods in a frenzy of greed for trilobites. He had no fear of tarantulas and played with them gleefully. Black widows ran across his arms. Once he chased me and Mike Kimmel down a country road, a little squeaking bat in his hands, threatening to make it bite us. He returned from expeditions with bags and boxes full of stones, classified them, learned all about them, indulged his fascination for archeology, land forms and structures, weather, fossils, and mystical happenings.

All things were pregnant with significance. Justin had to tinker with the straightforward meaning of objects and ideas. In his later life he could not take a straight photograph, he was always double-exposing, fiddling with negatives, creating hidden meanings, placing water in the desert, moons in midday skies, mountains in the middle of valleys. He inverted dual photos of erotic flowers to make black-magic symbols. And took profound experiences *seriously*. He only smoked pot a few times, and then all alone—it was a truly mystical trip. In Mexico, he had eaten mushrooms. He loved to float down rivers full of crocodiles. He had no fear of the jungle, nor of the occult.

The later symbolic pictures he painted seemed Tinkertoy to me, but they arose from visions he had in dreams. Today, I believe the polyurethane poisons he used to create them were killing his brain as he worked, even if momentarily the fumes prolonged his euphorias.

One winter day, while Justin was off in Mexico, I paid a visit to his house on the ridge in Llano Quemado, just checking on things. An old friend of Justin's was on the ridge, rekindling memories. "The trouble with Justin, poor man," she said, "is that he was ruined by money."

A trust fund decreed he need never work in his life. Had he not had that freedom, perhaps he would have stayed at the *Geographic*. Instead, he bounced around and never truly focused. Photography gave way to painting. For a while he enjoyed a vogue, and had shows in Mexico of voluptuous jungle watercolors. Just when he seemed to have it made, he lost interest. During the decade of the seventies in Taos, he wanted to be a teacher; the high school hired him as a substitute. But the novelty soon wore off, and he became a door-to-door huckster, selling Amway products. He loved it. And regaled me with

stories of himself on his hands and knees, scrubbing the kitchen linoleum of Ranchos housewives to make them buy his biodegradable wares.

But when he discovered that the phosphate substitutes weren't necessarily the environmental answer, he dropped the business in alarm. He thought of attending school in Española to become a male nurse—but that never worked out. Inflation was hurting his trust-fund income and killing his Mexican investments. He spent too much time managing properties, in Taos and Mexico, always terrified that the vagaries of current events would divest him of his meal tickets. He seriously feared an inevitable revolution would expropriate his property "for the people." In the meantime, he rented out this house, and worked on that house, and worried about the construction of a third little hacienda in Mexico.

He spent decades on rooftops, slopping down aluminum paint, repairing flashing with roofing felt and asbestos cement. For twenty-three years he created a Garden of Eden at his Llano house; then one day he up and sold it, seeking liberation from his folly. But I think he had sold an all-important part of his spirit—that place was a work of art. Orchards groaned with fruit every year; tall grasses rippled like American clichés in the winds sweeping up from the Ranchos-Talpa Valley. Elaborate vines curled around the old portal posts: plants were always flowering. His vegetable gardens produced legumes that put Rodale to shame. He always sent me home lugging bags of soft apricots. Wonderful ripe and rotten and alive smells surrounded his house. Bees congregated in the foliage of his trees and gardens. Aspens he planted along his acequia grew lush and tall. A master irrigator, he laid trenched veins throughout his property with mad disdain for the lack of exaggeration. I used to help him irrigate. We flung off our clothes and danced naked in his man-made waterfalls on the edge of the cliff, overlooking the valley.

An impetuous and spontaneous and sophisticated bumpkin, he

could also be a little old lady, guarding his properties, terrified of financial ruin. I never understood such paranoia in a man capable of ecstatic abandon. One Christmas, my gift to him was a photograph I had taken, a closeup of kids at a street fair in Santa Fe reaching up to grab candies bursting from a piñata. Over the candy I had pasted a cartoon of Justin himself, a skinny frantic little figure, falling toward all those eager, grasping fingers.

Justin cried and said I had captured the essence of his soul, and of his tragedy.

He often claimed I was the only male friend he had in Taos. Well, we got along fine, played the dozens with each other, and kidded around; he always made me laugh. I liked to be awed by his hyper-active self-centered energy. An outrageous person, he loved to shock other people with hilarious antics, he enjoyed being a buffoon and a clown in an uptight and constricted world. He had the body, at fifty, of a twenty-year-old. He ate salads and raw tartar meat. Constantly, I yelled at him to lower his voice. He worried a lot about "coming on too strong," and always came on too strong. Seeking sanity, he taped notes all over his house, urging himself to stay calm, speak in a normal voice, be *controlled.*

No matter what his shortcomings, Justin had an intense curiosity about life. He was not ashamed to make a fool of himself. One day he decided to have a vasectomy. He insisted on a local anesthetic, and observed the operation. He brought in a taping machine, and recorded the proceedings. Afterward, he played that tape with twinkling delight to anybody who would listen.

Justin could lie, thieve, scheme, and cheat in his romantic entanglements. Sometimes I trashed him for being callous. In America, he had a terror of breaking the law. Yet he thundered around Mexico like a whacky calavera, dishonest as hell, paying out the mordidas at every opportunity.

A fanatic about his body, he bought a ten-speed bicycle and ped-aled all over town. Then he became a jogging nut in his early fifties and leaped up at dawn to race off on long hauls through Llano Quemado, Ranchos, and Cordillera. He had every allergy imaginable, and took hundreds of pills. Sometimes he fell off the wagon and emptied a bottle of bourbon in a single night of writing self-consciously spiritual verse. But never an ounce of flab hung on his bones. He always looked tip-top, weathery brown, and agile.

Then one day something happened. Overnight he grew scared. His life came to be governed by panic: things were falling apart. Trapped in a profound depression, he struggled but couldn't pull out of it.

Part of the problem centered around Security, a preoccupation with his properties that sometimes he couldn't shake. He gave up all faith in his ability to earn a living should his trust fund collapse. He rented out all his Taos houses to earn more money, and for a while tried living in his VW camper van. It was crazy. One night he would park in Taos canyon; next night he'd sleep in my driveway! But I'd kick him out. I was trying to write a novel, and I had no sympathy with somebody renting out three houses who claimed he had nowhere to crash.

Sometimes he wailed that he had done nothing useful with his life. He accused himself of being a grasshopper who had fiddled while everyone else took care of business. That major depression was always right around the corner, ready to wipe him out. Something in his personality, heretofore dormant, manifested itself, a quality the legendary 1929 stockbrokers who sailed out Wall Street windows must have had.

"I wish there'd be a revolution," he whimpered. "Then the government would take my properties and order me to do some kind of useful work, and I wouldn't feel bad anymore."

His act disintegrated. The merriment died. The childish ebullience deserted the man, and only a shell remained. Days and weeks he spent entombed in a dark house, unable to sally forth, staring at

TV, disinterested in the world. He repaired his houses, figured and refigured his net worth, moaned about inflation and his heavy losses in his bitched Mexican financial finaglings.

What to do with his life? He tried writing poetry. And sat up all night thinking . . . unable to sleep for long. Now I visited a different person. He pissed and moaned, always about the same thing, trapped and pathetic. I tried to talk him out of it, but he couldn't be swayed. I begged him to make decisions, but he waffled and promoted a stupor. He was torn. He traveled back and forth between his family in Mexico and Taos on exhausting, destructive journeys.

After a while I couldn't bear his house. Such a mess. Curtains always drawn. No life pulsed in his body. Dejected, demoralized, depressed, he moped around, laying down the same repetitive rap. Halfheartedly he played with old photo negatives, limply trying to get back into pictures. But nothing worked. The depression deepened. We saw each other irregularly and had little to say to each other. He became bitter, sharp, and desperate. We avoided each other. A shrink put him on antidepressants. He took all kinds of pills. And drank a lot.

In the end, when an old friend found him, he had been dead for several days. And he wasn't even sixty.

It is late springtime. I am with Justin's wife, Luz, and his stepson, Arturo; they have come up from Mexico to arrange his affairs, and want to scatter the ashes. In my bus, we drive east of Ranchos de Taos, on Route 3. The road circles over the Sangre de Cristos to Peñasco and Mora. It is a lovely day; the aspen leaves are new and green, and the creamy white bark is as rich as an ermine fur. Clouds are like puffs of gigantic inessential popcorn in the pale green sky; winds are persistent, full of energy, but not belligerent.

We turn off on the road to Picuris Peak, a primitive dirt track eight miles long, leading to the very top of the mountain. Shortly after I arrived in Taos, Justin took us to the end of that road. It was his kind of outing. He loved to perch above it all, gazing down at humanity. Often I have thought he should have been a large noisy bird, a cross between a raven, a peacock, and a magpie, capable of soaring.

So we turn off, drive a ways, and then park on the grass. An overgrown logging road leads to a pretty spruce-tree-and-aspen glen. Big dead logs crisscross the rich ground overgrown with little bushes— mountain oaks and laurel, grasses and weeds, picturesque clumps of holly.

At first, we can't figure out how to open the canister. We dig at the carton with keys, with a pocketknife—finally something gives. We slide off an outer, plastic sheath, and remove a Twiston from the mouth of a Baggie-like sack.

Luz is a beautiful cinnamon-skinned woman with black hair, not even five feet tall. Her eyes smile, but always sadly. Her hands and feet are doll-sized and perfect. Arturo is a melancholy, gentle person. They feel awkward.

Luz slips her hand into the plastic sack and removes a handful of ashes. She is puzzled by the hard, pebble-like fragments, and asks, "What are these?"

"Pieces of his bones. Not everything burns. They crush them up in a mortar and add them to the ashes."

She lays her other hand atop the fragments, saying, "Oh, poor Justin . . ." touching them with great care as if she were commenting on his fragile life. In her melancholy eyes is the intimate knowledge of how we lost him.

They divide the ashes between them and walk off into the bushes. I sit down. They drift away between the scrub oaks and the sapling aspens and the rotting logs, sowing the ashes across generations of old leaves, and among the rising green grasses.

That is the ceremony, done in private: Luz and Arturo remain out of sight for a while. When they return, all the ashes are gone. We make a little fire and burn the canister. It takes forever, and from the plastic rises a frighteningly poisonous smoke that the breezes disperse immediately.

It is almost quiet in the forest. Chickadees are flitting in the spruce trees. And we tarry a little, remembering Justin. After a while, I tell this story to them:

On picnics, he always brought along hard-boiled eggs. To peel them, he first cracked them with gusto against his forehead. So one day I brought along a raw egg, and I guarded it carefully. Time came for us to eat, and I handed him a hard-boiled egg. He cracked it against his forehead, peeled it, and handed it to one of the children. Then I gave him the raw egg. Without a pause, he whacked it exuberantly against his forehead, and it splattered in his hair and back into his ears, yolk and albumen blinded his eyes and dribbled off his nose. And, shrieking *You son of a bitch!* he fell on the ground, roaring with laughter.

T E N

In the autumn of 1979, in his mid-seventies, my friend Louis Ribak entered the hospital. He was full of pep and sassy and had no intention of dying. He also knew that he had lived a long and fruitful life. He was an artist of national dimension, who had turned his back on New York in the mid-forties and moved to the lonely high country of northern New Mexico. The move cost him a lot in fame and fortune; it also may have saved his life. In New York he had suffered from crippling asthma. Even after moving, he would spend the rest of his life in and out of hospitals, gasping for breath, popping pills and sucking on Alupent inhalers and embracing oddball diets of soya bread (and vodka), in hopes of surviving "just another year." In between, he painted his heart out, traveled extensively, opened an art school that was shut down by red-baiting McCarthyites, and stayed curious about, and involved in, the struggles of his time.

Louis and his wife, Bea Mandelman (a highly respected painter in her own right), arrived in Taos with almost nothing. Yet they had each other and, despite large and abrasive egos, they lived together for almost four decades, dedicated to their work, and to each other.

Louis entered the hospital that autumn after a rich and traumatic year. It began for the Ribaks in Asia. They traveled on rickety trains through jungles and across rain-swollen rivers, downing all sorts of suspect comestibles and exposing themselves to an onslaught of beetles, bugs, and assorted insect manifestations, in order to gawk at the ruins, the statues, the artwork and temples of Sri Lanka and India, and, homeward bound, Egypt. For years Louis had dreamed about those temples. That he was an aging man with a cantankerous body,

nonexistent lungs, and crippling bursitis made no difference. Louis was a tough and whimsical adventurer willing to knock down mighty elephants with a single swipe of his arthritic palm, if need be.

Off they traipsed to view those wonders of a foreign world. Louis gaped, sketched, kvetched. They traveled with friends, took photographs, and absorbed the spirit of those ancient Eastern marvels. It rained, it poured, droves of insects penetrated their mosquito netting. Louis visited a local hospital along the way, threatening to put his checks back into the rack. Near the end of the trip, Alexandria, in Egypt, welcomed them with open arms. The February sunshine was strained through a membrane of pearly white Mediterranean allure. They were happy, and satiated to the bursting point.

Meanwhile, back at their home on the hill, a Taos disaster was fomenting. Nobody had drained a water tank in the upstairs bathroom. The upstairs had been locked off so the renter would not intrude there. In November, temperatures dove and the water in the tank froze. The ice expanded, cracking the tank; it stayed frozen for a month while the thermometer registered twenty below. In February, a sudden thaw hit. The ice melted, and water leaked out the fissure in the pressure tank. The renter had departed for a weekend in Albuquerque. When he returned, Louis and Bea's beautiful house on the hill looked like a version of *Towering Inferno* meets *The Poseidon Adventure*. Walls had dissolved in the flood, ceiling vigas had warped and cracked open, tons of mud inundated the living room. Cherished paintings were ruined, wooden floors had buckled, the entire house tottered near collapse.

Fortunately both a carpenter and a fast thinker, the renter bought vigas and planks, raised and nailed them together to brace the roof in each room, and hollered for plumbers to stop the water. His quick work prevented a cave-in.

At first, nobody could locate Louis and Bea in Egypt. Meantime, decisions had to be made. Insurance companies arrived with their cameras, and art appraisers shuddered when they entered Louis's mildewed studio. My good friend Stephanie Sonora and I rolled up our sleeves and catalogued every painting in the house so that the collection could be moved into storage.

It was a difficult two-week job; also fascinating and moving. One by one we measured, numbered, and described the paintings of Louis Ribak: some went back forty and fifty years. In the process, the man's vulnerability, his conscience, his compassion, his shortcomings, his politics, and his triumphs and failures were revealed.

Louis was born in Russia. During his youth, the family tired of pogroms and emigrated to the United States. But he never forgot his roots, and loved to tell stories brimming over with rabbis, zaftig yentas, terrible cossacks, desperate night-flights across the steppes in rattletrap potato wagons, reeking weeks in the steerages of dilapidated freighters, and, finally, the teeming Lower East Side of immigrant New York.

Fearlessly, the young artist hustled and scuffled. He was handsome and strong and sly and richly curious about the human condition. Street people, urchins, and hobo camps on the city's Lower East Side wound up on his canvases: destitute and energetic humanity. His sympathies lay with the working class. His hopes and his positive creative impulses instinctively fought injustices.

Louis was gregarious, a sometime boozer, and he loved the ladies. He loved boxing, too, and was not a bad amateur himself. He hung around the gyms, had a few fights, and painted pictures of half-naked men beating each other to pulps, surrounded by hardy, ribald, turn-of-the-century characters: Irish bullyboys and hungry Jews and voracious Italians. He hung out in the Turkish baths and recorded them in sketches, on pieces of wood, or on occasional canvases. He trained up in Central Park, running miles on the dusty paths; it seemed that his energy would never die. And he prospered in the carnival of between-wars New York.

Louis's social conscience was revealed in his realistic pictures of humanity's underdogs. Later, he contributed political cartoons to magazines like *The New Masses*. It was powerful stuff, and his reputation in all areas grew throughout the thirties.

Came the second war, though, and Louis found himself in the army; he didn't like it. Who could believe in that war, or want to kill so many people? He was discharged honorably because of his asthma.

At that point, Louis had it made in Gotham. He ran with Bea, a good woman and a determined and powerful artist. People praised his work in print, and included him in the important shows. But he had grown tired of all the politics and the infighting and the tensions caused by the high stakes; he wanted to go somewhere and just paint.

So: Louis and Bea arrived in Taos during the "second-wave" postwar migration of big-time artists. They arrived almost broke, but needed little to survive in those days. I try to picture the valley as they first saw it. I see a town where all the houses are adobe, and few advertising signs announce the commercial areas. All roads are unpaved. Hitching posts surround the plaza, because the valley has two horses for every car, and numerous wagons. Houses do not extend onto the sagebrush mesa. Fields surrounding the plaza, and extending outward for miles, are irrigated and green. The communities of Ranchos, Llano Quemado, Los Cordovas, and Cañon are distinct entities. Taos itself is still a quiet village under the sun, composed and serene. The outside artists have landed in a hardscrabble, but hauntingly beautiful Shangri-La. They comport themselves in a dream, having all the usual bohemian adventures. Picnics by the rim of the gorge end up in feisty intellectual squabbles that are soon forgotten. All the usual infirmities, egos, and jealousies abound, but are softened by the locale. Local folks view the newcomers as creatures from another planet, with their odd nationalities, phony ascots, intellectual pretensions, and esthetic pursuits. Life is fairly beautiful, fairly simple, fairly good.

Three and a half decades later, Louis and Bea returned from Egypt to face a home almost destroyed by water. Stunned by the extent of the damage, all they could do was stare, momentarily at a loss for a good kvetch. Then they rented an apartment and began a six-month hassle with insurance adjusters, art appraisers, carpenters, accountants, plumbers, financial advisers, and electricians. Bea took it hard and staggered a bit; but Louis lounged back in an armchair, bemusedly smirking over vodka-and-tonics, sucking on his inhaler, and pontificating about Picasso and Sugar Ray Robinson.

We had a party: Everybody got soused. I played my guitar, we sang songs, Louis did his Yebache dances. When things got rough, we had pizzas at the House of Taos, or bloody Marys at the Sagebrush. Louis loved to drive, but nobody enjoyed riding with him. On one run of a mile, he swerved into the roadside ditch three times. On another excursion to an Arroyo Seco eatery, I actually reached over his shoulder and spun us back into the right-hand lane to avoid a head-on collision. Louis smiled, serene as you please, and asked, "What's the matter, John?" His voice could sound like a whimsical W. C. Fields.

I often wondered how Louis and Bea ever made it back and forth to Mexico. At least a handful of times I'd watched their overpacked old station wagon chug off for San Miguel de Allende. They had made the trip for thirty years, and spoke at least ten words of Spanish. Watching them depart, I always thought it was like throwing lambs to the wolves. Yet somehow Louis always maneuvered them successfully through the carnival. If, in Guatemala, they came across a human body on the paving stones of a famous ruin, they tactfully gave it a wide berth. Yes, Virginia, that wispy, wheezing, good-humored, absentminded, paint-splattered Litvak actually negotiated the Petén jungle without incident. And they always returned from the southland overloaded with canvases and sketchbooks full of good work.

Then, just as the finishing touches completed their rebuilt house, and all the paintings returned from storage, Louis reentered the hospital.

Irascible, funny, impetuous, he was eager to get out and go back to work. If nervous, he didn't let on much in my presence. He was uncomfortable and had some trouble breathing—though what else was new? One tube entered his arm; another his nose. At first, doctors suspected tuberculosis, and we wore masks whenever we visited.

Louis kidded with all the nurses: the elfinly wicked male chauvinism made women laugh along with that white-haired man so full of teasing pep. Observing him, I thought that a really sweet attribute of my worldly friend was a certain innocence, and a sense of renewal he brought to the times we hung out together.

They did chest biopsies in Santa Fe, and brought him back alive. He told risqué stories about the effects of the morphine. I caught some trout and laid them on Bea to cook for Louis. Occasionally, I focused on the worry in his eyes. Then he allayed my fears by being energetic, feisty, funny. He talked about boxing. We made a deal to watch an upcoming Sugar Ray Leonard fight together. He reminisced about the old boxers, the punches they used to throw, and the best he ever fought in New York. He remembered the Turkish baths, the hobo jungles, and his friends—the famous, the anonymous—who were gone. Andrew Dasburg, a long-time Taos resident and artist, had recently died. That death left Louis feeling like one of the last leaves upon the Old-Timers' tree.

He swore a lot: Louis liked bawdy language. And that twinkle never died. Flat on his back, he pontificated about art, and criticized almost everybody; Louis handed out no gratuitous compliments. For a half hour, one evening, he analyzed the career of Clifford Still, admiring the fox in that man, which had enabled him to maneuver through the New York jungle onto the cover of *Time* magazine.

On the day of the Leonard fight, they rushed Louis to the Bernalillo County Medical Center in Albuquerque. The biopsies showed he had squamous cell cancer of the lungs. At BCMC, while under a CAT scanner, he suffered a massive heart attack and stopped breathing. A minute later they revived his heartbeat, but he had suffered extensive brain damage, and lay in a coma.

Stephanie and I drove down to meet Bea in Albuquerque. We spoke with a gentle and realistic doctor. Then we entered the ICU to see Louis. He was hooked up to an incredible array of machines. A respirator breathed for him through tubes inserted into his throat. I.V.s in either hand pumped in aminophylline, glucose, and other liquids, also vitamins and drugs stimulating his blood pressure. A tube inserted in his side drained liquid off his lungs—on top of everything else, he had pneumonia. A penis catheter handled urine. A beeping monitor had his heartbeat at 122. Later, they would insert a Swan gas line into his heart. And though his lower brainstem functioned normally, there was no evidence of the higher functions governing thought processes, speech, and sight. The prognosis? "Wait and see."

Bea thought if we talked to Louis, it might help; perhaps he would hear us and be stimulated. So we stood around his bed for a while, murmuring softly. His face had puffed up. The male nurse arranged a pillow at his feet so they wouldn't lock into a downturned position.

That night at the hospital we waited and wondered. People drifted around in the hallways, similarly anguished, awaiting developments. Smoke befogged the waiting room; Navajos occupied the couches, trying to sleep. Bewilderedly, Bea said, "Only this morning Louis was talking to me. He was reading the newspaper. . . ." The doctor returned and explained everything in detail. He could offer no hope, not even a guarantee that Louis would make it through the night.

But he survived the night, and the next day. In the evening, Stephanie and I drove back to Taos. We stopped in a restaurant for a beer and supper, and talked about Louis. About his life and his spirit, his mischievous and pixie eyes, his arrogance, his joie de vivre, his confidence and his sense of humor. Steph remembered a night long ago, with Louis and Bea down in San Miguel de Allende. They had been drinking at a fiesta. A local yokel decided to kidnap Stephanie, and began carting her off on his donkey. But Louis galloped out of the cantina, snatched her off the donkey, and carried her back into the party on his shoulder.

He died without ever regaining consciousness, on the last beautiful day of autumn. I spent that afternoon in Santa Fe, having a dental operation. Late in the day I returned to Taos. The sky was ugly, the radio repeated storm warnings. At the top of the gorge, where the entire Taos Valley lay before me, the sky was turbulent and angry; sagebrush glowed feistily, as if charged with malevolent electricity.

As I bounced up my potholed driveway, first snowflakes began to fall. A note on the door from Stephanie said, "Louis died this A.M. Please call Bea—mucho amor."

In the kitchen, I started to cry. I had not bawled like that in a long time, and it took me by surprise. For two weeks I had known that my friend was gone, and I had made peace with that understanding. But the tears gave needed relief, and I sat in the icy kitchen sobbing for about ten minutes, while the cats rubbed against my legs, loudly purring.

When I drove over to Bea's, we held each other, and I cried some more. Then we pulled out the liquor bottles and the eats, downed a few stiff drinks, grew calmer, and began to talk. Bea asked me to empty the mousetraps in her kitchen. While she had been in Albuquerque, the house had been invaded by rodents. I carried a couple of bodies outside and flung them over the cliff into a snowstorm, then reset the traps.

Now a bizarre and hilarious time occurred. Audacious little mice raced forth from their secret bivouacs and got nailed in broad lamplight, while Bea and myself and some other friends sat around, our faces soaking-wet from tears, noshing and boozing, and remembering Louis. First one mousetrap, then another snapped, making us all jump. The little critters squeaked and thumped in their tiny death throes. I hurried outside and cast two more victims into the white whirling snowflakes.

A few minutes later I saw a mouse dart into a hole beneath the doorjamb, and I set a trap beside the fissure. A minute later, while six of us sat nearby noisily conversing, the greedy mouse emerged from the hole, reached for the cheese . . . and entered eternity!

We made a memorial for Louis, an informal and fairly lighthearted wake. We had lots of wine and good food. People stood up and talked about Louis, remembering how he was good and how he was bad, what he accomplished, and how funny he could be. Some of us cried, and we laughed, too, and got loaded, and felt at ease. We considered it the celebration of a damn good life. We played some classical piano music, also a few guitar songs. For my friend I sang a Spanish tune called "Yo Soy un Hombre del Campo," and "The Midnight Cowboy Song," and finally the first verse and the chorus of "Cielito Lindo." What I felt about Louis is contained in the mood of those three songs.

I also wrote a eulogy, and read it aloud. The first part went like this:

Years ago, I was afraid of death. I especially had a deep and nagging fear of those times, somewhere in the future, where I would begin to lose people that I cherished: my mother, my father, perhaps my children, close friends. We live in a society, I think, which tries to cover up death, hide it, pretend it barely exists. In a nation so obsessed with security, good looks, and youth, we are robbed from understanding the experience, from feeling comfortable with it. We have a tough time opening up our hearts: sometimes we don't really know how to mourn.

And we are left bewildered, at loose ends, and frightened. We are embarrassed by deep losses, and our rituals in saying good-bye are all too often kind of morbid.

So I had a fear in me, an apprehension over the losses I knew were certain one day to come. Yet I have discovered in the past decade that I was frightened for no good reason. I have learned that sorrow and loss is nothing to be ashamed of or to fear. I have discovered that I feel almost the same emotion when a close friend dies as I felt when I witnessed the birth of my two children. I have learned for real, finally, that life truly is unutterably precious because it is so ephemeral. And I have discovered, each time someone I love has died, that somehow that experience teaches me to care more about my daily life, spend less time beshrying all the daily torments that threaten to murder us all, and more actively appreciate everything from my mundane little daily rituals to all the electric currents of these vital and traumatic times in which we live.

John Donne wrote long ago that "Any man's death diminishes me." I know that is true. And each death I experience personally makes me that much more aware of my own mortality. Yet in an interesting way this knowledge makes me stronger, more at peace with myself. It's kind of like when you're a kid and a friend dares you to jump across some narrow but frightening river. "You go first," you say timidly. And when he or she does, and successfully makes it, you feel this great relief: if they could do it, you can too. And so now I know I can die, and what's more, I really *am* going to die, sooner or later. And, curiously, that somehow means that I'm not worried about it anymore. I'm no longer wrapped up, inhibited, and made miserable by a childish lust for immortality.

I suppose one reason I don't have that fear anymore is that I've come to appreciate what a good time I have had on this earth, what a rich and productive life I have already been privileged to live. And Louis Ribak was one of those people who helped give me the gift of learning how to enjoy my days. I'm sure we traded off this gift to each other: he got a chuckle out of my shenanigans, and I got a kick out of his. But for me, the following is what was so especially important about Louis:

He wound up, after seven and a half decades, with as much positive energy and love of life as he must have had when he was a young boy, new to this country, an immigrant from the Old Country. Through all the good times, and all the hard times, through all the personal trauma, and all the global machinations of disaster, through two world wars, Vietnam, crippling asthma, the Great Depression, prostate operations and other assorted daily familial disasters such as having his house and many of his paintings destroyed by water last winter, the man remained positive, unbitter, creative. His sense of humor was going as strong at seventy-six as it must have been going fifty years ago. All his life he kept working, building up a body of work, growing, changing. He never allowed a shell to harden around himself, he kept trying out new things, even at the risk of falling flat on his face, which he did often enough to make his life thoroughly painful, as well as enjoyable. Yet he arrived at the year of his death spiritually intact, creative, hopeful, still changing, uncynical, and, most importantly, still curious about all the wonderful and terrifying adventures this planet has to offer. And if I were ever to ask any superior force or voodoo magician Out There to grant me one gift in my lifetime, it would be to arrive at the end of my life with that same lusting twinkle in my eye, that same devouring thirst for knowledge and experience that characterized my recently departed friend.

ELEVEN

For years I lay in bed at night, listening to the mournful cries of peacocks nearby, just across the Pueblo River. Their haunting, almost frightening calls pierced the autumn darkness. Taos superstition defines peacocks as a death symbol: at best, they are said to be harbingers of truly bad luck.

In recent years, Isabel Vigil, the lady who owns the peacocks, has become a close friend; she pooh-poohs such old wives' tales. But if you tried to find somebody in the Taos Valley who has suffered worse luck in their life, you'd have to search hard for a person or a family more snakebit than Isabel and her brood.

On all the human levels that count, Isabel and her daughter, Evelyn Mares, are two very special people. Somehow, they have endured more adversity than I could hope to combat in a dozen lifetimes. And their lives, their energies are a real inspiration to me.

Nobody's saying they have survived unscathed, or even entirely intact. Often they teeter about punch-drunk and gaga, utterly baffled by the vicissitudes of life. Yet they always muster the courage to keep on fighting. Winning battles is not their forte; but they struggle with an instinctive class I admire a whole lot. Outraged by daily injustices, they wail, beat their breasts, tear their hair, crack jokes, resurrect each day The Hope That Springs Eternal, and, even when exhausted, refuse to stay down for the count of ten.

Isabel is like a character from *The Grapes of Wrath* or *The People, Yes*. Of course, her lifelong saga is not unique: it is the story of all working-class people around our nation and the world. In her life is the poetry and hardship contained within the universal human spirit.

Summing up that spirit, as we did recently when Isabel's husband finally died after a ten-year illness, you sure can't laugh off her capacity to take it. I believe that Isabel's anger and outrage, her good humor and vitality in the face of all the little holocausts and Armageddons, dignifies us all.

Cowboy Joe Vigil was Isabel's second husband and her true love: he suffered an incapacitating stroke in 1970. Thereafter, he was an invalid. For a decade, Isabel and her daughter Evelyn cared for Joe, a legendary man in the Taos Valley who would not die. Though subsequently laid low by every disease in the book, he refused to capitulate. Unable to walk or feed himself, barely able to talk, Cowboy Joe hung on. Perhaps only the momentum of his full-tilt life kept him going after the stroke. But at long last, in the summer of 1980, he reentered the hospital for the umpteenth time, and the doctors figured by then he was probably tired enough to let go.

On July evenings, returning from the hospital, Isabel and Evelyn often stopped by my house to talk. We drank beer, tea, or coffee, and said things that people usually say when death is near. We hashed over memories, and tried to sort out feelings: we summed up Cowboy Joe's life, interpreting it by its most common sad, humorous, and poignant denominators. What seemed destined to be his final illness brought us together in a heightened intimacy from which we drew strength by ruminating on the generational heartbeat of humanity.

Even in July the nights are chilly in Taos. So I built fires in my kitchen stove, and then we tackled almost everything that came to mind at that difficult time.

Isabel's original name was Lorrita Elizabeth Sanks, and she hated it. Soon as she could do it legally, she had it changed to Isabel Rita Stanhope. "That was after a silent-movie star of those days, whose pictures I really loved. Her name was Isabel Stanhope. As I remember, she was mostly in jungle pictures. . . ."

Because her dad had difficulty maintaining a family, Isabel grew up in and out of orphanages, in Nebraska and Montana. She had a passel of brothers and sisters. Most clearly she remembers the orphanage in Lincoln, Nebraska. As a child, she lusted for solitude, impossible to find in the orphanage: kids or supervisors constantly surrounded her, except in the deserted library. Hence, Isabel spent many hours in that library, reading to be alone. The books developed her curiosity about the world and released her vivid imagination.

One day her dad took them from the orphanage and drove the entire family over to Twin Bridges, Montana, a small town south of Butte. Isabel liked it there, and for a while the family lived together. Her dad bought a house and tried to pay for it by gathering and splitting firewood.

Montana was a wild and romantic place in those days, full of cowboys. Isabel and her brothers and sisters used to sneak off and hide in the bushes, watching local ranch hands skinny-dip in the stock tanks and little streams. They also spied on the hard-boozing cowboys as they broke horses while zonked out of their thick vaquero craniums.

"For a while," Isabel said, "I worked in a place called the Owl Café. Back in the kitchen. Oh, that was a rough joint. They had fights all the time. They had male waitresses in those days—and I tell you, I just kept to my place, back in the kitchen.

"It was account of my working there that I was present when one of my brothers died in a car accident. This was around 1928, I believe—long ago. My father had cataracts in both eyes, and he couldn't see too good. He didn't even have a driver's license. But he was crazy sometimes. One night he got mad, and said he was gonna drive me and my brother to work . . . and he wouldn't let nobody else drive the car. Around nine o'clock at night, I guess, we left the house. We would work in the café, see, all night long, until the morning. The car we had was an old Model T, and it didn't have very good lights. They would sort of blink on and off when you hit bumps. So he couldn't see very good and crashed into a hay baler parked beside the road, on the shoulder. Something on the baler rammed through the windshield with such force that my brother died instantly of a broken neck. I had seven teeth busted out; my daddy didn't even get a scratch."

Not long afterward, Isabel was burning brush in their orchard, when a log caught fire and a sudden wind blew it out of hand. Flames soared off and burned the entire mountain behind their house. The fire also destroyed all the fuel wood her dad had gathered to meet house payments. So he lost the house, and pretty soon the kids were back in an orphanage again. Fact is, "My father left the country, and we never saw him again until 1965 at his funeral in Idaho."

In the middle of the Depression, age sixteen, Isabel walked away from the orphanage and hitchhiked south to Idaho Falls. She had nothing to her name except the dress on her back and a Bible. Her shoes had come apart—the soles flopped noisily, so she found baling cord in a field and tied them together. Though all alone on the road for several days, nothing bad happened. She ate berries and slept under the stars. And remembers that trip as one of the most wonderful and liberated moments of her life.

Idaho Falls was a wild town. When Isabel arrived, she asked the police for help. They offered a cell for the night, brought her some food, and next morning sent her off to a lady for a job.

"In this real rich people's house, as a maid. I'll never forget my first night there. I had my own room with a thick rug on the floor, and I just sat there for a while, curling my toes into the thick rug.

Then I took a bath. But I didn't last too long, and wound up next working as a housekeeper for a man and his wife and their two small children. The man would go on big drunks, and beat up his wife, poor thing. I stuck it out for a while, though. I got room and board and three dollars a week. Once he started bad-mouthing me when I was in the kitchen making a sandwich, but I wouldn't take none of that offen him. Then the darn fool grabbed my knife and it slashed his palm. He let out a scream, and I dropped the knife and took off out the back door and made it to a friend's house. Next day, they asked me to come back to work, but it was no fun in that place, and so I left."

Not long after, she met a fellow and got married: his name was Mares. Eventually, they settled in Gallup, New Mexico. Isabel started bearing children, and the hard times came in droves. She miscarried twice; two other babies died. For one of them, a girl, her husband wouldn't let her go to the hospital. "He got a Mexican woman to come in. She gave me warm water with pepper in it. I kept vomiting. I had been hemorrhaging off and on for nine months, because, as it turned out later, I had a couple of tumors in there. Finally, the baby came. But something was wrong. And that man didn't know what to do with it. I remember that she had blue eyes, because her eyes were open. But she expired right there in my husband's arms. Her little arms shot out straight when she died. . . ."

The marriage was rough, and Isabel worked hard, trying to raise five kids and hold down a job to keep the rent paid. Sometimes she grew real depressed. Once, around 1950, she swallowed half a bottle of sleeping pills, mostly just "for a bit of rest." Again, nobody would take her to the hospital, and she barely survived.

When the kids matured a little, they about ran her into an early grave. Isabel shudders now to think of all the pranks and downright criminal acts they performed.

"They would go out and steal all kinds of stuff from the stores in Gallup. Bob and Tom, that is—but not Larry. Larry was always sickly, he had Bright's disease, so he never actually went out and did anything. But he was the brains behind a lot of the operations. If the rest of the kids wouldn't split the take with him, he'd threaten to squeal on them—so they always gave him a dollar, or something. I couldn't keep track of them, because I was usually off at one job or another during the day, trying to make ends meet.

"Once they robbed a pastry truck, and brought back a whole lot of doughnuts and cookies, and hid them in the garage. They only brought a few inside at a time, though, telling me they'd bought them with money they earned shining shoes and selling newspapers. But Larry got mad because they weren't giving him his share, so he squealed."

Figuring the best defense is a good offense, Isabel stormed off to confront the pastry-truck man. "I told him it was all his fault for not locking up his truck when he parked it—that just invited the kids to steal. So the next time he locked the truck. He even parked it in a locked garage. And you know what happened? My kids broke into the garage . . . but they couldn't jimmy open the truck."

Evelyn said, "We used to go to residential neighborhoods where richer people lived, and sit on the curb. When a car came along, we ran out and sat down in the middle of the street, blocking it, demanding money before we'd move. The women were easier targets—they often gave us a nickel or a dime. But sometimes the men cursed and got out. Then we had to run for our lives."

"I just couldn't keep tabs," Isabel remembered ruefully. "I had to work all the time to get money. I was a maid. Then I was a caretaker in an old hotel in Gallup. One night I saw a Zuni Indian come in drunk—he was a jeweler, and he was wearing a lot of nice things he had made himself. The cops came rushing in after him, beat him up, stole his bracelets and his wallet, and then took him off to jail. The Zuni man came and asked me next day did I see the cops do anything, but I told him no, because I was afraid to go against the corrupt police. They were like that, the police, always beating up and robbing the Indians. It was terrible."

Meanwhile, her own family drove her half-bananas. One day Larry stole forty-two dollars Isabel had saved for the rent money. "It was a four-room house, but in real bad shape. It had an indoor rest room, but even that didn't work very well. Nevertheless, I had to have that money. So I went down to the school and ordered the principal to take each one of my kids out of class. Then I grilled them until I found out that Larry had done it. I took him home with me. He had changed the large bills into small ones, and had hidden little sums of money in secret places all over the house. I threatened to kill him to get him to bring it all back."

Some kids! They just never quit. One of them stole the only valuable trinket Isabel owned, a precious brooch, and sold it for fifty cents. "That like to broke my heart." Another time, Bob copped a whole bunch of tires, and unloaded them real cheap. Seems Isabel spent all her spare time trundling over to the authorities and bailing out her children. Conveniently, they lived but two blocks from the police station and jail. The first Mares to be held overnight in that jail was only eleven years old.

Jail did not deter them, however. Those half-pint pirates had a thousand get-rich-quick schemes. One involved hiding out in a movie theater after the film let out during the Gallup Ceremonial Days. Then they broke into the vending machines, grabbed the coins, and fled out a back door into an alley. With the money, one of them bought blue-jeans, boots, a cowboy shirt, and a cowboy hat.

If nothing else, "he sure looked like a real little cowboy."

They had to move from their forty-two-dollar-a-month house to a cheaper place, which had an outhouse instead of an indoor toilet. They hadn't been there long when Isabel heard screams and raced outside. Bob had dropped a toy car into the commode, and Isabel found her son dangling upside down inside the crapper, hanging on for dear life, about to plummet toward the shit.

A metaphor, indeed, for where the Mares brothers seemed headed, despite their mother's desperate efforts to stay the execution-ers. As they grew older, the kids joined in that ignoble Gallup pastime of rolling drunken Navajos who often wore valuable bracelets and other jewelry. They also came upon Navajo women passed out in the out-skirts gullies and ripped off the dimes sewn onto their purple velvet shirts.

"Everybody treated the Indians like that in Gallup. It was inhu-man."

Finally, it looked like curtains for the Mares teen-agers. The fam-ily was disintegrating. The authorities planned to ship Tom and Bob off to the Springer Boys' School. One son ran away to live with his grandmother in Costilla, an hour north of Taos near the Colorado border; but she kicked him out, paying for a return ticket to Gallup. And his bus passed another in which Isabel was riding, on her way to find him in Costilla. When Isabel got there, the grandmother groused, "Well, one fool leaves . . . and another arrives!"

In the end, on just two weeks' notice, Isabel packed up the family and fled Gallup, bringing everybody to Taos, the only way to save her boys from reform school. In Taos, she begged them to be good, and build a better life. But right off they broke into a place, and trouble started again. At that, aided by the Welfare, she had two of them sent to Boys Town in Nebraska. Later, the boys lived with their father in an Albuquerque apartment and started working. The marriage was over, and somehow the hellions discarded their wayward predilec-tions: they went straight, grew up, became respectable citizens of the community.

Isabel has no great love for her first husband. "But he taught me some good things, too. He had an upholstery shop. He taught me to build things, to use a hammer and other tools. And I'm grateful for that. I like to build now, and I got that from him. In fact, I'm building a potting shed—a place where I can get out of the house. Sometimes I get so claustrophobic in the house I just gotta head outside, even in winter, go for a walk, mess with the animals. I like to dig in the earth. I like to put seeds in the ground and watch 'em germinate."

In Taos, Isabel's luck changed. Desperate for work, she hired on with Cowboy Joe Vigil to be chief cook and bottle washer for him and seven men helping with the haying on his Ranchitos ranch. The job was supposed to last for five days. But Joe, who at the time was a footloose bachelor between marriages, kept her on for twenty-five years. They fell in love, and their first fifteen years were the halcyon days of Isabel's life. A tough time, to be sure, but also fertile, resonant, happy. It seemed as if she had fallen through a magic looking-glass into a wonderland of positive and loving endeavors.

Not that Cowboy Joe Vigil clocked in as an easy guy to live with. In his fifties when they met, fortunately he had slowed down a trifle. But he was still an adventurer, a real old-fashioned rootin'-tootin' son of a gun, with plenty of rough-hewn charm and braggadocio, and an incurable lust for life.

"When he was younger and on the rodeo circuit, he used to go to the bawdy houses up in Wyoming," Isabel told me. "He had a different woman every night. . . ." He had not lived a protected life in other ways, either. Most of his teeth and all of his bones had been broken rodeoing. He had lost the little finger on one hand roping a calf—the hemp just formed a loop, snapped tight, and chopped it off. "And I never could find that finger down in all that dust," Joe told his wife.

As Isabel and Evelyn sat at my kitchen table, reminiscing while Joe lay on his deathbed at Holy Cross Hospital a mile away, we laughed and felt privileged to have known the man.

Isabel and Joe were a team; on the Ranchitos place, and outside it. The ranch had thirty-two acres of vega land, wide pastures stretching back to the Taos mesa. Through the meadows ditches ran. Little springs beneath the surface made some areas swampy. Hundreds of killdeer populated the fields; flights of wild geese and ducks were always landing. They ran cattle back there, and horses, and a few sheep.

Corrals closer to the house held goats. They had dozens of fowl pens; for peacocks and ducks, for domestic geese and lots of chickens. The yard was inundated with dogs and cats, and most any other animal you can imagine.

Wild plum trees grew in the back pastures. Near the house an orchard bore fruit; they raised vegetables in a quarter-acre garden. In front of the house lay more small pastures, a weeping willow tree, a little pond full of trout. Beyond beehives and a thick cottonwood grove ran the Pueblo River.

It was a full-time job, caring for the land. But Isabel's recollections are happy. Seems like everybody had a fair share of fun. An old eight-millimeter film taken during branding time at the ranch shows Cowboy Joe bent over a calf, and the kids—Danny, Bob, Tommy, Larry, and Evelyn—helping out. Then everybody starts clowning around, doing magic tricks behind a blanket, jumping off the roof, dancing a whacky twist for the camera. Turkeys, horses, and dogs ham it up, pet skunks play with cats, a pet sparrow hawk gobbles goodies right off Bob's tongue.

Sometimes they had to leave the ranch to earn cash for paying bills. Once they wintered in a cabin up at Eagle Nest, an hour east of Taos, working for the Leyba brothers at a mill. Another time they hired on at the Charles Springer ranch in Eagle Nest: it eventually sold out to Angel Fire developers.

Music was part of their lives. Joe played accordion, piano, harmonica, Jew's harp. He worked hard and played hard, too. He liked his liquor, though it never made him mean. Silly and sentimental, maybe, bawdy and comical—but never nasty. Of course, he could look out for his interests if push came to shove. Everybody recalls a day when Isabel's son Tom and Joe finished the haying and drove over to Sebastian's Bar for a drink. Tom had a broken leg (in a cast), but, according to Isabel: "You couldn't keep him at home. You had to steal Tom's boots to keep him from roaming."

Well, they entered the bar, got a little looped, and then an altercation developed. A man started needling Joe and became belligerent. So Joe hauled out a knife and ended the discussion by taking a mean swipe at the son of a bitch.

"Oh, he loved his liquor," Isabel said. "Sometimes he walked around with a six-pack under one arm, and a bottle of whiskey in his boot. When I got fed up, I hid his bottles. Then he pleaded with me. He said he'd give me fifty cents for every one I'd hand over."

Stories of Joe's drunks, like stories of the man himself, are legendary. As soon as she heard him arrive home making a commotion that indicated he was in his cups, Isabel would hide, often in the same bed with Evelyn. His accordion to his chest, Joe would creep through the dark house calling, "Honey, where arrrrrrre you?" And when he found her, he would strike up his favorite Spanish song on the squeezebox: "Tu y las nubes me traen muy loco. . . ." You and the clouds are driving me crazy!

"And what could I do?" Isabel sighed, chuckling. "I just melted with love. Honestly, that man. . . ."

Then there's the night Joe came home drunk as a skunk, flopped from his pickup onto the ground, and couldn't rise. Loudly, he demanded his accordion. Dressed in her nightgown and slippers, Isabel marched out and handed it over. For hours he sat there, beneath the moon, winked at by the saintly nebulae, playing songs until the coyotes started complaining and he passed out.

According to all the noted authorities, Cowboy Joe rarely spent time in jail. Fact is, said Isabel, "Joe always tried to avoid trouble."

But came a day when they threw him into the Taos slammer for causing a traffic jam. Absorbed in listening to a song on the truck radio, Joe had forgotten to proceed when the light changed; and no amount of honking could rouse him from his reverie.

"So we had to go down and bail him out. He looked so funny behind bars with this great big grin on his face. . . ."

Medium-late one night, Joe made a wrong turn, he thought into his own driveway. But he happened to be a few driveways short. Puzzled, he stopped, quelled the engine, and rested, listening to radio music while waiting for the cobwebs to clear. By that time, however, the radio had killed his battery; he walked home to fetch Isabel, and returned with another vehicle to tow off his truck. Too late, though. For by then a neighbor had spotted the impostor in his driveway, notified the gendarmes, and they had towed off Joe's pickup.

Precipitating a blood feud between Joe and that neighbor which lasted honorably for years until the neighbor's death.

Isabel has less whacky, more gentle memories of Cowboy Joe. When calves were born in the winter, Joe brought them inside at night and set them behind the kitchen wood stove. Isabel loved to lie in bed beside her man, listening to those little calves snoring.

Although coyotes are The Enemy in Taos, Joe had a soft spot for the critters. He liked to awaken early and take up a station in the orchard with field glasses, spying on the coyotes a half-mile away, trotting along the distant acequia, or meandering along the mesa overlooking the rich vega land and small herds of Upper Ranchitos.

Each day brought another adventure. For example, Cowboy Joe narrowly missed death one night when he discovered the driveway gate closed. Prudently braking, he descended from his pickup. As he did, an enormous cottonwood tree crashed onto the driveway in front of him. Had he not stopped, the truck would have been crushed.

In the tree they discovered an owl's nest; one of the baby birds had survived. Bob took charge of raising the oddball pet. They caught mice at the haystack to feed it. Whenever Bob took a bath, the owl bathed with him, standing on one of his knees, ruffling its feathers delightedly whenever he lowered it gently into the water. The story, however, like so many Taos animal stories, ends in tragedy. Bob left his bath, set the owl on the edge of the tub, dried himself, and moseyed off somewhere, forgetting the bird. Pretty soon Isabel found it floating in the bathtub, drowned: it had tried to bathe by itself.

On various occasions Isabel traipsed outside the home to earn money for them. Among other jobs, she would clean the Baptist church. Sometimes Joe popped in unexpectedly to play the piano and sing for her while she worked.

In the beginning, they went hunting together. But when Isabel saw Joe actually aiming to kill a big buck, she shrieked and bumped her husband; the shot went awry. "I can't *bear* to see people kill things."

Did Cowboy Joe swat her for insubordination?

Nope. He laughed.

But he never took her hunting again.

Now came the hard times. Everybody except Larry, who was increasingly incapacitated by his illness, entered the Army. Evelyn included. They dispersed to army bases in the States, or overseas. Evelyn was the first to come home . . . in shock because her fiancé had just been killed in a California car accident.

In 1970 the stroke felled Cowboy Joe; and of a sudden he was helpless, totally dependent on Isabel. He couldn't think straight. Sometimes he talked funny, lost the thread. His limbs no longer functioned, and the vitality accumulated, pent up inside his body without a release valve.

Then Bob died; he was shot to death in California when he surprised a burglar in his home.

Isabel remembers a phone call from Bob shortly before his death. She sensed he too was in trouble, kind of desperate, lonely, and afraid.

He talked funny, and laughed a lot, strangely—it really broke her heart. He said, "Mom, remember what it was like when a bubble kicked out of the mud in our pond and rose toward the surface? That's the way I feel right now. . . ."

Hospitalized after an operation, Isabel learned about the killing. Evelyn, Tom, and Larry tried to say it was a car accident. But later she happened to open the coroner's report and learned the truth.

Around that time Danny returned from Vietnam, burned out, on drugs, confused, and floundering. "He was on all kinds of dope," Isabel said, "and we couldn't get him off it. He'd go out to the communes around Taos and buy marijuana. I even tried to smoke it with him once, to see what it was like, but I couldn't even inhale it. That stuff didn't do anything for me. It just seems like when he got back from Vietnam, Danny didn't care about anything anymore."

Danny suffered, and trundled in and out of hospitals. He was scared. Shortly before he died in 1973, Isabel traveled with her son in the ambulance on his final journey. The attendant asked her to hold Danny's kicking feet so they wouldn't be bruised. Tenderly, she held down her son's feet during that drive to the hospital . . . and then Danny too was gone, still in his twenties.

"When he died, I just went crazy with grief," said Isabel. "I couldn't stop crying. Tom and Evelyn finally took Joe up to Denver, and they left me alone in the house so I could go all to pieces in peace. I guess that's what I needed, and I finally got over it. Tom told me not to go upstairs to Danny's room, but I did. At first I was real frightened. I went up there with my cross and my Bible. I remember five days after Danny died I was sound asleep, when suddenly, at five to eleven, I woke up with a real chill. The whole house was cold. I knew it was Danny. It happened at five to eleven because that was the time he would often wake me up to watch a television program he liked. I believe that people you love can come back and get in touch with you up to five days after their death. Then they're gone for good."

Increasingly, Larry grew more helpless. His kidneys deteriorated.

For a spell he lived away from home, but eventually—enfeebled and failing—he had to return. Numbed by medications, he became an invalid. Evelyn had worked in Denver for a while; now she returned with a daughter named Tanya, and settled in to help her mom care for her stepfather and her brother.

The time sequence is not too clear. But one autumn Isabel developed a pain in her chest that wouldn't go away. They had enough troubles, though, and she kept quiet. The ranch had to be run, money for bills had to be drummed up somewhere. But the struggle had worn her out. And in January of the new year she had a major heart attack. After long weeks in the hospital recovering, she came home and went right back to work.

They rented out the back pastures to earn a little cash; burned off the front field and repaired all the animal pens. Selling peacock feathers earned a few dollars; chicken eggs brought in harder cash. They robbed Peter to pay Paul, managed to get Medicaid and welfare payments, bought clothes at church rummage sales, sold turkeys and geese and goats, gathered apples, put by heaps of their own garden vegetables, and tried to repair the house, which was slowly crumbling—just Evelyn and Isabel, the two invalids, and a little child. Tom had married and was living outside Denver.

Slowly, Joe headed downhill. He was still a big heavy man, though, and the two small women developed strong muscles lifting him out of bed, moving him around, taking him for walks across the lawn. Sundays, they wrestled him into the pickup and went for drives. Joe bore up, but he grew stoical and quiet. That fierce energy to live never left, but he became a different person, sleeping much of the time, gradually receding, slowly slipping away.

In tears, Isabel asked him, "Whatever happened to my Cowboy Joe?"

And he replied: "Oh, that son of a bitch went away. He's gone . . . and good riddance."

"Then who are you?" she asked unhappily.

He said, "I am just José Epifanio Vigil."

Then, in 1977, Larry gave up his prolonged struggle with Bright's disease, and died.

That left just Isabel and Evelyn on the ranch, taking care of Cowboy Joe. Within a decade, almost the entire family had been leveled prematurely.

When I first met them not long after Larry's death, I never would have guessed that so much hardship had badgered their lives. Their house seemed like a wonderful hobo castle, cluttered with a billion knicknacks and photos, children's paintings, aquariums, green plants, and rich smells from the kitchen. Outdoors they had playhouses for kids, dozens of flower planters full of snoozing kittens, a regular army of Chihuahua-sized dogs yipping about, big malamutes and gorgeous puppies in pens, herds of geese racing down the driveway to splash in the irrigation ditches. Tom turkeys strutted, posturing and thumping, and grandiloquent peacocks displayed their finery. Quail and pheasants occupied some pens, also a partridge, esoteric doves, and a dozen bantam chicklets. Goats cavorted in old jerry-rigged corrals, a horse and her colt meandered about. Lilacs bloomed, other flowers blossomed, bees congregated at hives by the little trout pond.

It was, and still is, a magical farm.

And I was being shown around by a woman telling me things like this:

"I don't know where all these aphids come from. We got 'em all over. I was going to spray this spring, but then I noticed there were ladybugs all over, so I didn't. I figured they would take care of the aphids. I used to send away for praying mantis eggs, and let them hatch. But I guess I haven't done that in a while."

She recounted an experience with the bees, to whom she often took a thin amount of sugar water. One day, out by the hives, thousands of bees congregated on her head. "They covered me entirely, my whole head, and my forehead and my cheeks, all of my face except my eyes and my lips. And nobody stung me. I just stood there feeling almost light-headed with joy. It was one of the most wonderful experiences of my life."

Immediately, I saw their spread as a positive, rambunctious farm: Evelyn and Isabel came across as indefatigable, courageous people. Each day presented them with a ludicrous trauma to overcome. One of their Chihuahuas is called Squeaky. He sickened, and they rushed him to a vet. Who cured him up and charged eighty bucks. "Ever since he got better," Evelyn complained, "he can't stop screwing." He got jammed inside a bitch three times his size, and couldn't extricate his penis. Evelyn groaned, "We spent eighty bucks to make him feel so healthy he's gonna screw himself to death!"

They laughed a lot—how else to survive the daily holocaust? Yet Isabel could fall into a funk, also, and yearn to pitch in the whole mishpocheh. Not only had her family been decimated in the past decade, but Taos had changed radically. The atmosphere was tense, neighbors alien and paranoid: a precious coherence had been lost, strayed, or stolen. A competitive and selfish mean streak had transformed the valley, and the old-timers like Isabel were befuddled.

"Canada geese always used to land in our back pasture. But they never do anymore. Because people nowadays will shoot anything that moves. I don't understand it, but folks have gotten so damn ornery. There's an Indian pasture just up the road a ways. Somebody kept opening the gate to let all their horses out. Finally the Indians put a lock on the gate. Now, you didn't used to have to do that around here. But the lock didn't deter people. They just climbed over the gate, and, instead of letting the horses out, they shot them."

Glumly, she said, "Sometimes I just give up on people. I lose all faith in them. I only got faith in my dogs and in my cats."

One of their neighbors told little Tanya Mares: "If any of your dogs come through the fence onto my property, I'll shoot them on sight." Then his dog killed one of Evelyn's goat's babies, and dragged it back onto the neighboring doorstep. When Evelyn confronted the owner, he not only refused to pay restitution, but said, "The goat's dead now, so you might as well let my dog eat it." Fiercely, Evelyn replied, "If I'm gonna raise kids for dogs to eat, it'll be my own dogs, thank you," and she lugged the carcass home.

The neighbor became an enemy. He took to firing his gun a lot, hither and yon. Isabel and Evelyn feared a ricochet might hit one of their animals—or worse, little Tanya. They begged him to stop; he refused. Evelyn exploded and told the man, "If you don't quit shooting that damn gun, you son of a bitch, I'll come over there and stick the barrel down your throat, and pull the trigger."

He blanched, holstered the shooting iron, and soon after commenced firing a powerful hunting bow and arrow all over the place.

Their poverty, the struggle to hang on to their place and keep it vital, has been real taxing.

"I'm pooped," Evelyn murmured on a sunny Saturday last year. "I'm so tired of never having any money. Of always reaching into my pocket, and finding a dollar—one lousy dollar—and knowing that's supposed to last for fifteen days. . . ."

Still, they never moped for long. Forever on the edge, they bitched and laughed, cared for Cowboy Joe, harvested apples and collected eggs, helped Melissa foal a blue-eyed colt called Pickles, worried about the thistles threatening valuable pastureland, plucked destructive foxtail by hand from the fields, cooked up hummingbird syrup for their feeders, and in general worked themselves half to death maintaining a healthy quality of life.

Always, their enterprising imaginations propelled them awkwardly through boundless crises. Somehow, they could always prestidigitate the price of groceries, or unclog the septic tank.

Even little Tanya was in on the game. When a family friend, Delfino Valerio, had a cow that birthed a two-headed calf, they strung up the oddity over a corral, and she crayoned a sign: 25¢ TO SEE THE 2-HEADED CALF!

At the heart of their lives lay the quiet heavy bulk of Cowboy Joe, whom they cared for, loved dearly, and knew one day would die. "He wants to leave me now," Isabel used to say. "I can tell he's real tired. But I don't want him to go yet. I love him so much. I can't let him get away. . . ."

No matter. During the first week of July, in 1980, Cowboy Joe Vigil, age eighty-three, finally died. Isabel said, "We sat with him while he took his final gasps. I felt so bad, because there was no way I could help him. One nurse even gave him mouth-to-mouth resuscitation. But nothing worked. He was so tired, and he just wanted to let go. Young Dr. Pond was there. And Father Mike O'Brian too. After Joe died, everybody left the room, and I just sat with him for the longest time, holding his hand."

A day before the funeral we are seated around the Vigils' kitchen table—Evelyn, Isabel, Tom, his wife Carmela, and myself. And Isabel says to Tom, "It's getting so hard to bring you back down to Taos anymore. You only come when somebody dies."

And I say, "Well, you got a problem, Isabel, because you're beginning to run out of bodies to sacrifice so Tom will come down here on a visit."

Everybody laughs. And then we conjure up a scenario of how to lure Tom back to Taos on a regular basis. We'll kill off the horses and the goats, and finally the peacocks, staging such elaborate funerals he'll feel he *has* to attend!

At the rosary, everybody sang "Amazing Grace." When the service ended, we walked up front, passed the open casket, and paid our respects to the family. My children, Luke and Tania, were afraid to approach the coffin, but I told them there was nothing to fear in a dead body. Nervously, they joined the line, reached the coffin, and stopped, staring down at Cowboy Joe. His face was so thin and chiseled, fragile, yet almost fierce like an eagle, and very pale. Afterward, the kids were bouncy and cheerful because they had come through the initiation intact. It had been an interesting and curious and not at all scary experience.

Death, it turned out, was not a malevolent mystery.

Time then, at last, for Joe to go into the ground. Isabel asked me to give a eulogy. And so I read a short piece to a gathering in the Santa Fe Veterans' Cemetery at 11:00 A.M. on a windy, sunny July morning, shouting the words to overcome the roar of the traffic on a nearby highway. And here is the way it ended:

There's no tragedy in Joe's life, nor in his death. In a sense, the man did it all. He was one of those gallant and gallivanting old-timers who were somehow larger than life. He became the stuff of myth; his kind of saga is the material that makes us nostalgic for those Good Old Days.

Mostly, I suppose, the magic of Cowboy Joe is that he loved and enjoyed it all. He loved newborn calves and colts . . . and magpies in his apple trees, irrigation acequias, pickup trucks, ranchera music, cowboy songs, borracheras, peacocks and tecolotes, hauling piñon wood, and knee-deep snow covering the wide western ranges. He loved to challenge a bucking animal, and to hold a gentle woman in his arms.

He also had a kind of grandiose humility, and never apologized for being the way he was.

In short, he really took advantage of the gift of vitality that he received at birth. He played it for all it was worth. And he exits now with head held high, and no shame; he leaves us now with a body busted half to smithereens, but with an unbroken spirit that ought to inspire us all forever.

Adios, José Epifanio Vigil. . . .

So long, Cowboy Joe from New Mexico.

TWELVE

My grandmother, Cornelia Floyd Nichols, lived to be ninety-five. She was born in 1882, and died shortly before Christmas in 1977. Her life spanned what is probably the most amazing hundred years in world history.

Only horses trod the New York City cobblestones during her youth, and she could ride sidesaddle across Long Island without worrying about fences or towns or traffic. Yet many decades later, the little girl who had pressed her forehead against Manhattan apartment windows yearning after the stallions prancing through gaslamplight in holiday snowstorms, would sit in front of her television set as people landed on the moon. Telephones, TVs, motion pictures, automobiles, and airplanes were always younger than my grandmother. Born only six years after the Battle of the Little Big Horn, she was eight years old during the massacre at Wounded Knee. What wonders and horrors must have astonished and appalled her! How incredible it must have been to enter her first motor car! I envy her the ages that she spanned.

Her husband, my grandfather (after whom I am named), was a noted naturalist; he bowed out almost twenty years before his wife. We never conversed much, but the man was an important marker in my life. He was physically very imposing at six-three, and he had wonderful bushy eyebrows, wore perfectly rumpled clothes, smoked a pipe, inhabited an office full of pickled fishes, and generously extended to me a profound curiosity about the natural world.

I like the way he died. After a few operations for his terminal cancer, my grandfather decided to call off the doctors and let nature take its course. He proceeded to tidy up his affairs. My dad attended his death. Apparently, Grandpa was working on some notebooks when he could no longer make legible corrective pencil marks. He asked my father for a softer lead pencil, and used it to finish his notations. Then he set aside the pencil, and shortly thereafter died. He was buried in the family graveyard at the old Mastic house on the south shore of Long Island, about sixty miles from New York.

Many years later, my grandmother's heart finally stopped. When it did, an era ended, the entire thrust of a family came to completion. Grammie was the last true bearer of several hundred years of historical continuity connecting the family in spiritual and physical solidarity. With her death, the Mastic house and surrounding acreage, which had been our home since the early 1700s, passed on to the trusteeship of the United States government. Grammie's body was cremated, and in the spring of 1978 the family gathered at the Mastic house to bury those ashes and say good-bye.

Dad and I drove cross-country from Colorado Springs to Long Island for the ceremony. Once before we had made that trip together, in the winter of 1951. I was eleven years old. We had a green Studebaker crammed full of junk, including a Siamese cat named Boris Caleb Cadwallader—B.C. for short—a huge airedale named Terry, and a caged parakeet called Shelly.

That voyage was one of the great adventures of my early life, just my father and me in the Studebaker, flying across America in the middle of a furious winter. In Reno, abetted by the old man, I gambled away all the money I had earned selling our household furniture in Berkeley; then my dad threw in a silver dollar of his own and struck a jackpot. Awe-stricken, I stared at real cowboys in roadside cafés, and remember clearly a strange straw-colored girl in an east Nevada diner who gambled away a bag of nickels while we munched our hamburgers. And in every town we touched, I insisted on buying a newspaper.

Two minor accidents on icy roads marred the journey. In Nevada, we skidded slowly into the rear of a pickup truck hauling lumber. In Colorado we half turned over in a ditch, and had to be towed out by a wrecker. Later, zooming along at eighty, my dad had just said, "Gee, John, going this fast makes me feel like I'm flying," when we hit a railroad trestle, and were scarily airborne for an eternity.

During a Rocky Mountain blizzard I had to scrape ice off the inside of the windshield so the old man could see to drive. Later, in prairie flatlands, we hit a hen pheasant, threw her in the trunk, and feasted on her corpulent body when we reached the East Coast.

When not gazing out the windows at America, I drew a comic strip in one of my notebooks: in those days I planned to be a cartoonist when I grew up. And I read all the newspapers. I remember particularly stopping in Wheeling, West Virginia, for breakfast. Snow was falling. A lovely deer lay in the back of a pickup parked outside the diner. As always, I derived a deep thrill from buying the Sunday papers and churning through the comics and the sports section in the steamy heat of that homey beanery.

Years later, our repeat of that trip had very few rough edges. Yet it signaled a demarcation and moved me greatly. My father, after all, is the last person born in the old Mastic house. His mother, that house, and the surrounding territory had been a powerful and at times traumatic force in his life, forging both the strength of his spirit, and its weaknesses. The journey was no easy lark for my old man. As soon as we reached the first hardwood forests he inhaled the air with anxious ecstasy; I swear he could smell the Atlantic Ocean from the east bank of the Mississippi! As the vegetation thickened, and he embraced the sights, smells, and memories, his apprehension increased. I watched him merge with courageous trepidation into the complicated origins of his existence.

My father was brought up on the land and water, out at Mastic, on the Moriches Bay. Today he is a scientist, a linguist, a zoologist, an ornithologist, an ethologist, a psychologist—in short, an intellectual with a deep curiosity about the world. He is fascinated by human minds and by the communications systems of birds and animals. He has led a rich and varied life—in business, government, academia . . . and in the outdoor landscapes of America from Alaska to the Florida Everglades. Always, his roots remained deep into land. His salvation, his most profound and instructive foundations, are built upon the natural world. He has collected bird and mammal specimens for museums, and spent a lifetime taking photographs from the dark interiors of bird blinds. All our houses were surrounded by birdfeeders; peanut butter and suet were poked into wire contraptions on tree trunks; one-way glass in special windows allowed us to observe, without intrusion, Kaibab squirrels and Steller's jays and mourning doves. Occasionally, Dad stuck a stuffed owl on a pole into the ground so that we could observe the mobbing patterns of crows or blue jays. In later years, when I traveled across America, I constantly stopped to pick up dead roadside owls for Pop to use in his experiments.

Thanks to his knowledge of the natural world, my father drew many people around him into the adventure of identifying bushtits, or peering closely at a star-nosed mole. He always had a passion for making the physical universe seem knowable and important to others. In 1939, as a recently married twenty-two-year-old Berkeley undergraduate, he might suddenly bag his studies in order to drive my mother over to the Nevada pelican rookeries. They once made a special trip to Los Angeles hoping to track down some black-necked stilts in a swamp south of the city. Dad fought to keep the California state legislature from dooming sea lions the fishermen claimed were raiding their grounds. And his little student apartment always contained many experiments, such as germinating, in damp cheesecloth, the seeds discovered in the cheek pouches of a trapped desert animal to see what kind of plants it had been eating.

The announcement of my birth, sent out to various interested parties, read like so:

```
NAME    John Treadwell Nichols 2nd
DATE    July 23rd
LOCALITY    1713 Dwight Way, Berkeley, Cal.
SEX    Male
TOTAL LENGTH    20 in.
WEIGHT    7 lbs. 5 oz.
LOCAL HABITAT    Alta Bates Hospital
COLLECTORS    Monique & David Nichols
FIELD NO.    1
```

No question about it, my father gave me the gift of the natural world. I was born in 1940. But my first real rememberable contact with Dad occurred late in World War II. I received letters from him, full of crayon drawings not of the war, but featuring the jungle trees and beautifully colored exotic birds of the Solomon Islands.

When he returned to America, I tagged behind him on some of his collecting expeditions. We gathered field mice and shrews at Mastic. I remember when he shot a rusty blackbird out of a tree in Smithtown on a state permit for the Natural History Museum. He gave me a passion to experience the natural world up close, touch it if I could, marveling over a butterfly's habits, or over an intricate spiderweb, an oriole nest, a feather. My butterfly collections, nest collections, leaf and flower collections, and eggshell collections were inspired by the old man. I built figure-four traps to catch birds, and held them in my hands for just a beat before letting them fly away.

Pop showed me how to catch bats behind the warped green shut-ters at Mastic. I sat in Channel Island blinds while he aimed his old Graflex through a little hole, photographing sandpipers, plovers, and terns. From other blinds we watched mice eat grain on a log, or observed the complex interaction between doves and jays feeding at a banquet he had spread.

A few times, we hiked together through the forests, taping bird-calls. Dad also taught me about animal signs: we melted paraffin and poured it into their tracks, then later reproduced the prints in plaster of paris.

In Berkeley's Tilden Park we caught lizards; in particular I seem to recall heroic searches for the wily blue-tailed skink. In that same town, in 1950, we made many trips to the Aquatic Park, where Pop handed over the field glasses, and identified the shore birds for me.

A distant airborne silhouette, or the simple rhythm of flight, immediately divulges a bird's identity to my old man. When I walk with him outdoors nothing is anonymous. Every sound has a real bird or a real animal behind it; all the plants have both a common and a Latin name. That way, the natural adventure is intensified. I learn that if a rabbit laden with fat ticks can survive until autumn, the ticks will fall off and it will live. I learn that the strange diving antics of woodcocks are called "towering," a mating display. And when he plays back a wood-thrush call we taped an hour earlier, I hear a dozen incredible melodic syllables I never heard in the wild.

Wherever he lived, my father always tried to finagle a little piece of land. On that score his life is a bit like a bad Yiddish joke. Because almost every time he acquired a small terrain, set up his bird blinds, and began to attract all kinds of wildlife, he promptly lost it in a divorce settlement.

During the mid-sixties, after he returned to Berkeley for his Ph.D., Pop had an old mining claim on the north fork of the Yuba River. There he spent many weekends with friends working on the rickety hillside cabin, or perhaps panning for gold. The flakes were kept in a pill bottle beside the door, and helped pay for the required yearly improvements.

Later, in Colorado Springs, he purchased twelve acres of the Black Forest. There he built the most lavish bird blind ever, an army bunker with one-way windows, hot plates, a refrigerator, even a cot for sleeping. He drilled a well, then dug by hand a very small pond, filled it with well water, planted assorted reeds, threw in a few bluegills, spread grain on a slope between the pond and the blind, and brought countless students out to take field notes on the wildlife attracted to the oasis he had created in that dry forest.

Vandals came, too, of course, and trashed the bird blind and the pond. Then it all went in yet another divorce settlement.

Reeling, but never defeated, Pop cast his attention westward to a ten-acre mountain parcel in Florissant. There he built another blind and watched things happen in the little ravine bisecting the land. One day an elk herd came through. Not for a while had he seen anything quite that breathtaking: steam misted from their nostrils as they moved quietly through a fine powdering of new snow.

One spring day in Florissant we were at the "west ten" just walking around, smelling the land, looking for signs, inspecting bushes and trees. Below the bird blind, on someone else's property, was a little spring. "Where there's water," we told each other profoundly, "there's got to be life."

Little bugs struggled to leave their larval bodies at the roots of some water stalks. A western tanager landed overhead. Pop bent over to photograph a flower with a beautiful yellow and gold and green bug on it. Then he aimed his lens at a caterpillar . . . and started hopping because ants were crawling up his legs.

Slowly, we climbed over rocks, up out of the arroyo. Both of us were puffing halfway up. "I gotta go slow, guy," he said. "I'm getting old. I'm out of shape."

Farther along, we stopped again, gasping, and looked around.

Pop said, "It makes me uncomfortable seeing something this beautiful. I get so covetous. I'm greedy for land."

Then our discussion grew truly profound. Dad commented on the philosophical difference between rabbit pellets and deer pellets. To wit: "A rabbit is only about one-fiftieth the weight of a deer, and yet its shit is about half the size of deer shit. Leading one to surmise that deer must have highly constricted assholes."

At last we reached the top. Dad stood heroically upon a rock and remarked: "You could stand right here during a rainstorm. . . ."

And we did. We stood right there in an imaginary rainstorm, gazing down into the arroyo where the rocks just sat still, and pine needles lay quietly around their gray bases, and the western tanager warbled a lovely note before it flew away. . . .

I forget the year—call it a handful ago, mid-seventies.

We leave the Mastic house, crossing the wide lawn into the front field. Dad points out a bright orange butterfly weed, and mentions that the small butterflies nearby are called little coppers.

At the corner of the field, where a sandy road enters the woods, he looks around for a Dutch spruce tree, but cannot find it. "Maybe somebody cut it down." But then he locates the tree back a ways, buried in a thicket of young locusts—"A real weed tree," he says thoughtfully. "They grow up everywhere."

We walk along the road to Indian Point. Trees tower over the road creating an almost gloomy tunnel. We can hear gulls and other seabirds squawking. Along the way Pop stops to point out old locust posts. He taps one, jiggles it a little: "Still firm, by Jesus. These posts were put in when I was a child. They kept cows in the fields around here. This was all fields—now look at it: solid forest."

I stoop, picking up feathers. Dad can't identify them. He starts a dissertation on photographing feathers. "You could lay feathers on a photographic plate and make a negative exposure—they would come out very clearly, giving an exact pattern of the barbs. Then you could shoot one feather in every series, and make blocks of different sizes, each with a certain feather on it, taking a shot of all the different feathers on a bird. That way, you could work out a really specialized identification process for those who might want it."

Glancing up in the middle of this talk, he says, with a love and admiration that have not diminished since his childhood fifty years ago: "Look at all those terns."

A wood thrush calls. Pop can only faintly hear it—his ears are shot but he refuses to wear a hearing aid. We crawl into the woods to get closer and wind up kneeling in poison ivy, trying to tape the thrush. Planes constantly flying by make this difficult.

Farther along we hear a catbird mewling. A plane passes, then another, then a helicopter thunders by. After that, during a moment of lull, Pop punches on the recorder. Immediately, crows start hollering a half-mile away, drowning the catbird.

Next, a red-eyed vireo. We go through the motions, outwait the airplanes, and manage a pretty clear rendering of the call. That's followed by a blue jay, after which Pop fiddles with the machine, slowing down the cry, and, incredibly, it sounds like a foghorn. The wood thrush, at half speed, is an amazing construction of complex and liquid bell notes.

We continue, talking but little, listening to the forest, hunting melodies. I find an acorn wrapped in feathers and ask, "Do owls eat acorns?"

"No, but a fox will. And shit 'em out afterwards."

Quail leap up from a field, followed by a young pheasant that scrawks off into the trees.

It is a beautiful, cool, sunlit day. Lightning bugs sit on twigs or float through the forest, incongruous in the daytime.

We are so quiet I can hear a noise to the side. I step off the path and find a turtle—the ultimate Mastic thrill. I turn it over, but the shell has no markings—that's a disappointment. Ever since my grandfather first arrived at Mastic, turtle records were kept. Sometimes we found turtles that were originally marked thirty or forty years earlier.

Pop turns this one over in his hands. "It's pretty old," he says. " 'Course, turtles can't think much." He smiles. "Still, it's lived as long as I have, and it must have gathered a lot of impressions."

We release the passive reptile. Motionless in the brown leaves, it awaits our departure before proceeding. With luck, it may live another fifty years.

At the end of the day, we sit on the screened front veranda in the dying light. Grammie is there, already over ninety. We have played our collected birdsongs. Now everybody is having a glass of sherry. Rabbits are grazing on the lawn as large as a football field. Fireflies float languidly through the soft darkness, blinking lazily.

Pop says, "Listen to the whippoorwill."

We stop, cock our heads, and listen. The call of that whippoorwill emerges from the idyllic years of my childhood, and from the childhood of my father, and from the childhood of my grandmother, breaking our hearts a little, because so soon, for us, this land will be over.

So: in May 1978, we left Elbert, Colorado, early on a foggy morning, and cruised along without incident, chatting about the world situation, the family, birds, and animals. Because the trip in itself was a kind of summing up, I grilled Dad about intimate things: life with my mother, Monique, and how she died down in Florida when I was only two. I asked about their love life, and he spoke frankly and gently about their sexual naïveté, and the wonderful romance they enjoyed when first they met at the American Museum of Natural History in New York. They had experienced a euphoric infatuation—carefree, energetic, silly, and truly loving. "When Monique died," Pop said, "I never really recovered, because I didn't know how to mourn." Instead, he flew the body north, buried it in the family graveyard, farmed me out to cousins, and joined the Marines. And carried a crippling wound for much of his life because he had never owned up to the loss.

On we cruised in my father's 1973 Chevy Impala, which he called The Womb. We gave each other dissertations on communism, grackles, and human sexuality. Sometimes I felt a certain frustration, because Dad would answer my grillings in a way that sounded very frank, intimate, and to the point: yet he utilized an abstract phraseology that stopped short of revealing the innermost self I was after.

Speaking of his own father, he revealed that it wasn't until much later in life, when he remembered many things Grandpa had said, that he understood, finally, what his father had been driving at so many years ago.

My dad has a habit he indulges while driving on trips of significant mileage. He carries a tape recorder and comments on the birds along the way. He plans at some future date to make a few relevant statements about the migratory habits of birds in those areas through which he has traveled.

So on this trip to my grandmother's funeral I often found it difficult to maintain the momentum of a serious discourse with the old man: his scientific observations into the tape recorder were forever sabotaging the dialogue.

Here's a typical riff from that trip (Pop speaking):

"Yessir, John, I found that the sexual relationship I had with your mother was [*click*] four redwing blackbirds, flying north by northeast, speedometer reading 87,015.6, sky overcast, wind approximately four knots [*click*]. Like I was saying, I think the most serious physical problem between your mother and me was [*click*] one *Butorides virescens* flying south, speedometer reading 87,016.1, sky overcast, wind approximately four knots [*click*]. You see, John, one thing I didn't learn until a relatively late age, in dealing with women, is that the most important thing you have to remember is [*click*] two magpies on side of road feeding on raccoon carcass, one sparrow hawk on power line above. . . ."

Frustrated by the effort to communicate, I often grabbed the microphone and inserted one of my own clever observations:

"Two scum-bellied ballcatchers flying circa three o'clock. . . ."

And more than once our scientific chatter degenerated into definitely nonscientific comments. For example, here's the old man remarking on his number one son's flatulent proclivities:

"[*Click*] Difficulty making out with accuracy roadside creatures or passing birds because of strange fog inside automobile. . . ."

When we came back to our senses, though, we analyzed Grammie at length. What a tough old bird she had been! And with what an iron fist had she governed the family all those years!

In 1951 we had barreled along narrow tooth-rattling roads. A quarter-century later, nary a bump jarred our delicate fannies, the air-conditioning controlled our climate, and we halted often to scarf down six-course meals at Nickeson Farms restaurants and other mid-American eateries. In western Kansas, the rain and fog lifted, and immediately hundreds of pheasants appeared, resplendent beside the highway; my heart surged as it had twenty-eight years earlier every time I spotted a beautiful bird. We stopped once, and I jumped out to remove the tail feathers from an exquisite ring-necked cock dispatched earlier by a speeding vehicle.

We zoomed easily up the Jersey Turnpike, onto Long Island, out to my Uncle Floyd's house in Smithtown. Pop kept squinting out the window, exclaiming, "It's so crowded, now. Everything is so small and squunched up." But salty ocean dampness in the air had his blood running. When we turned into Judge's Lane, a box turtle blocked the path, symbol of our Mastic childhoods. We put it in The Womb and released it at the old estate next day.

To avoid "embarrassment" at the Saturday service, Floyd wished to bury the ashes a day early. So we three drove out to Mastic on Friday. Suburbs now control the area that was a rural paradise in my youth: ticky-tacky houses, shopping centers, and highways dominate and gobble up the natural terrain. Then abruptly we popped into a sandy tree-shaded lane wending through a virgin forest, taking us home.

The house seemed forlorn. Paint peeled off the austere Puritan structure, shutters sagged. The syringa bushes near my grandmother's old nasturtium beds had been chopped down; so had the western lilacs. Inside, drawn shades created a depressing gloom; the old piano was hopelessly out of tune. Museum-type tags identified furniture, geegaws, and paintings. Being a visitor to our own heritage created an eerie sensation.

Down at the graveyard, in the shade of a lovely old spruce tree, Pop and Uncle Floyd took turns digging through the lush grass. I leaned against the white fence and observed those two big men in their sixties. Wearing sneakers and baggy old clothes, they self-consciously fashioned a small hole. In it, they placed a canister carrying the most symbolic ashes our family ever committed to the ground.

Being of stern Puritan stock, Nichols-Floyd descendants have been notably short on openly displayed emotions. Hence, this rather significant act was handled as a routine chore. My dad and his brother got on their knees to insert the canister, then they tamped down earth over the vessel, arranged a grass lid, and scattered the extra dirt in the surrounding grass. Blue jays scrawked, catbirds sang vociferously. Then we took a walk.

The easternmost road on the estate runs along Home Creek out to Indian Point, where the brook becomes an eastern tributary of Moriches Bay, and salt meadows begin to curve around the southern edge of the property. Not far across the water lies Tern Island. We flushed four woodcocks on our journey. And paused often to watch the terns and the gulls. Spotted towhees and catbirds maintained their cheerful ruckus. And we soon discovered the woods were crawling with ticks!

Halting, we dropped our pants and nervously plucked them off our thighs.

"My God," Uncle Floyd groaned. "Do you suppose everyone will get covered with ticks at the graveyard tomorrow?"

At the edge of the water, little minnows were thrashing. A green heron jumped, prompting Uncle Floyd and Pop to wonder why green herons always release an enormous splatter of shit when they take off.

I found the eggshell of a wood thrush and some feathers we decided belonged to either a pheasant or a marsh hawk.

Next day, we had our ceremony and our reunion. I enjoyed it, but several of the old-timers seemed distraught: after all, the rug had been yanked, the linchpin had been removed from their identities. The graveyard scene was disappointing. Nobody gave a eulogy, or summed up my grandmother's life. A Center Moriches preacher did a ten-minute service: a couple of psalms . . . over . . . and the Lord's Prayer . . . and out. I guess that's how Nicholses and Floyds and others of our ilk have always done it. But not me: in my head trumpets blared, flowery eulogies fell like rain, everybody joined hands and sang hosannas. If only my old man and his brothers had dropped to their knees over the ashes and pounded the earth, tearfully and bitterly denouncing the old tyrant, even as they wailed for all those wind-grieved ghosts who would never come back again. I wish somebody, on that dappled honeysuckle May morning, had delivered an elegy for Mastic, remembering it lovingly, romantically, historically. It wouldn't have hurt to recall the roots and knotholes, the slave pen, the Civil War, the icehouse, the Fire Island picnics, the box turtles, and the young people fucking in the spare impressionistic rooms of summertime. *I see my grandmother and grandfather in ancient bathing costumes, beside picnic baskets on the beach, surrounded by sanderlings.*

We missed the opportunity. We said good-bye in a routine service, and all-important emotional things went unsaid. A good feast followed: we drank a lot and renewed acquaintances. Children and grownups together played on the wide lawn; others gathered for the last time on the screened-in veranda. Our laughter was like the sunshine; nobody made any waves.

I walked off for a spell, eager to reconnoiter the house a final time, indulging some reminiscences. I remembered myself, the small boy, climbing across warm wooden shingles that felt queasy-strange against the soles of my bare feet. And I remembered lying alone on the evening lawn as woodcocks towered in their mating displays above me. I remembered standing at a bedroom window gazing down at my grandmother napping beside a flowering syringa bush. And I remembered a flicker picking bugs from between the flagstones on the patio outside a den and library room called the Office. Finally, I remembered sitting at a window during a hurricane as winds battered the ancient linden tree at the southwest corner of the house. Older than the Revolutionary War, that tree bent under the brutal attack by a destructive fury. Branches snapped helter-skelter from its leafy innards and whistled off ferociously like jagged bullets. Leaves exploded clear of enraged whirlwinds, and it seemed certain the decimated linden must surely disintegrate into a million tiny pieces. Yet the tree held fast until the blue lights of an exhausted dawn, when suddenly the tempest died, and, with a great sigh of foliage, all branches settled. Only then, no longer mesmerized, could I retire . . . on the brink of tears.

Lastly, I tried to recreate the moment of my father's birth at Mastic in 1916, the youngest child. I don't know who presided. My grandmother was thirty-four. No doubt my grandfather was elsewhere, probably outside listening to a vireo or carefully marking a turtle he had found on the Indian Point Road. In white porcelain pans midwives fetched cold water pumped up by hand from the pantry well. My grandmother lay on clean starched sheets. Bees were humming outside, and apples rotted in the September orchard. Little brothers and a sister ran around in sailor costumes, agitated by the excitement. And barn swallows twittered and plow horses whinnied when my little red-faced daddy unleashed his very first cries.

PART FIVE

The ancients used to like to sing about
    natural beauty:
Snows and flowers, moon and wind, mists,
    mountains, and rivers.
Today we should make poems including iron and steel,
And the poet also should know how to lead an attack.

—Ho Chi Minh

THIRTEEN

Sometimes the philosophical meanings of daily obliterations escape me. I am aware that in many ways certain death experiences enrich me. I am not speaking of some dour necromantic obsession, nor of a cynical complacency in the face of those murderous outrages that hourly stun the globe. I'm talking, instead, about the mortality of seasons, and of magpies and little water snakes: I am referring to the finales of long and useful lives.

In my younger days, all death seemed tragic and romantic. Being a hunter, I purified myself with Hemingway-esque self-consciousness each time I expertly nailed a teal. I rationalized that I understood nature better and loved it more dearly by occasionally zapping some of the wild kingdom's tastier denizens. I was adamant about killing a thing "the right way"—you know, nailing it "truly, and with love, and with no malice aforethought."

A wonderful autumn ritual was the 4:00 A.M. wake-up call in October; my cousins and I rustled hush-hush through the sleeping household, rounding up our gear. Eggs and sausages and hot coffee tasted special in the cold, dimly lit kitchen. Eager labradors squirmed impatiently, bursting with energy.

We drove east on Long Island in darkness, heading for Mastic, pleasantly groggy and bloodthirsty. The car smelled of dogs, of gunpowder, of gun oils and cleaning fluid, and of anticipation.

Duck boats we hauled along narrow canals in saltwater marshes, breaking ice as we went along. Plumes of tall fragmites weeds were frosted white like stately albino peacock feathers. Attached to frozen reeds and cattails were the bulbous lumps of marsh-wren nests, awaiting another summer.

At dawn, by the edge of a salt meadow on Moriches Bay, my cousins paddled around, removing broadbill decoys from burlap sacks, unwinding the anchors, setting up a rig.

Then we crouched against icy abrasive turf behind a row of spare raggedy weeds, waiting for rising breezes to set the birds in motion. Feet froze, knees ached, ears stung bitterly, fingers grew numb—but we hardly moved. We had the patience of killers, and were so alert we could spot them coming from a mile away.

Every nerve strained to be ready for shooting. And I experienced great exaltation within earth-shattering explosions, as graceful birds crumpled in midair, did somersaults, and abandoned forever the ecstasy of flight.

As a little boy, I felt an intense resentment and frustration because I could not fly. I dreamt often of soaring. I'm sure that is the most common human dream, also one of our most bitter disappointments.

I wonder if my delight at the violent airborne annihilation of a broadbill or a beautiful mallard was related in some vengeful way to that yearning sorrow of my childhood dreams.

It was a stern law, an absolute blood code, that we never shot any game bird except in the air.

The only death comparable in savagery, I sometimes think, is to be annihilated during the act of making love, or giving birth.

At the age of twenty-six, I laid down my guns for a while. That was the time of the terrible death ritual in Vietnam. I had recently married; Ruby was pregnant with our first child; I had published two novels.

I had no desire to give up my innocence, the infatuation of our romance, the idyll of a first child. But it was impossible to ignore the carnage. Helplessly, I veered into the oncoming headlights of Vietnam.

The war tore apart my beliefs, my daily rhythm, my fledgling writing career, leaving me momentarily nonfunctional. I participated in marches and demonstrations, supported peace candidates, wrote propaganda for SANE. But I was not terribly useful. I was incapacitated by outrage, and bewilderingly fascinated by the logistics and sensations of mass murder. I could not turn off the TV news programs; I immersed myself in the choreography of slaughter. The air I breathed seemed misty with Asian blood. Every day my soul, part of a collective American soul, grew darker.

I sat dazedly in our little apartment on East Seventh Street. Sunlight drifted through the window and spread across the carpet, snoozing and mellow. Two dozen fat transparent balloons cast colorful shadows as they stirred quietly in soft air currents. Among them, baby Luke, all fat and pink, lay on his back regarding the globes with infant wonder. His chubby fingers sent them bobbing. He laughed as they soared—enormous molecules barely affected by gravity—off his tummy.

Drenched in the Vietnam anguish, I gazed despairingly at my new son. It seemed as if all justification for babies had been destroyed by William Westmoreland, Lyndon Johnson, and Curtis LeMay. I believed the world had become an impossibly ugly place, and I was too naïve and fragile to survive the daily slaughterhouse.

At times death seems uncontrollably on the loose and the earth is a graveyard. Bodies fall from the sky in horrible pink droves, and each morning History wakes up screaming. Massacres abound. It is not at all funny when Don Rickles insults someone by telling them to gargle with razor blades. You can smell the stench of jellied gasoline in Ben Suc as far away as Chicago. Lieutenant Calleys are on the loose, poking their scalding gun barrels into the soft tummies of women and children, dealing unbelievable death behind a bevy of careless shrugs. Pinochet Uguartes hide their frozen irises behind Acapulco sunglasses. And American advisers from Bloomington and Walla Walla teach El Salvador death squads how to drop the broken bodies of assassinated bean farmers into kicked-apart mildewed anthills.

"Life's true face," once wrote Nikos Kazantzakis: "the skull."

The February 1968 Tet Offensive in Vietnam occurred during a garbage strike in New York. I staggered along Second Avenue sidewalks made surreal by six-foot-high echelons of rotting basura. Wind whistled across subzero pavements, carrying hysterical flocks of madly flapping newspapers whose bold headlines and graphic photographs vividly described the slaughter. My legs were constantly tangled in bloody events. Damp, drifting soot blackened my teeth and nostrils. Tiny blisters of machine-gun fire chased me everywhere. Dogshit and barf piled up. I always felt on the verge of crying. It seemed the entire universe was collapsing. My chest ached with the hope that this time the Vietnamese would triumph. I flinched horribly from so many Asian bodies smashed to pulps. Death spewed them out like coins in a Las Vegas jackpot, they spilled over everywhere. Wherever American shadows landed, life became a free-fire zone. Rats scampered in the mounds of New York garbage, same as in Saigon. All we lacked were quicklimed bodies sprawled atop our refuse.

After a while it seemed as if actual bodies, and not just the candid photographs beating against me, littered my domain. I felt crazy. On TV a police chief named Loan summarily executed a suspected Vietcong by discharging a pistol into the side of his head. The man fell over sideways with blood spurting in a single powerful stream out the bullet hole in his temple.

I prayed for our American Empire to give up, come home, holster those horrible shooting irons. Instead, we continued to wallow in grotesque scenarios of wholesale horror, framed by an obscene rhetoric of megadeath and kill ratios. I shut my ears, closed my eyes, and gritted my teeth, convinced that, as an American, my debt was already too great—I could never atone. I walk around today, still, with the feeling sometimes that because of my roots, the color of my skin, the nature of my country, I am a murderer all the world abhors. I know too well that when a local bum in front of a whore's stall on Seventeenth Street in Guatemala City salutes me with a grin and says, *"Hola, canchi,"* in truth he despises my guts with one of the purest hatreds smoldering on this planet. I'll never understand why total strangers, years ago in Central America, never pounced on my blond and blue-eyed symbol with honed machetes, trying to even the score.

Desperate to escape, I spent almost a month, in the autumn of 1968, alone at the Mastic house. And that was a lovely and frightening time.

My work was going badly, and I knew it. The novel was a hardass, bitter tale, and I suspected I would never ask anybody to publish it. In it, an American soldier won the Medal of Honor for murderous deeds in Vietnam, and returned a hero to his homeland. He shook hands with the president and tried to resume his former life. But he found this society paranoid, uptight, cruel, self-centered and greedy. What he had fought so gloriously to protect was nothing but a social monster. Bit by bit he went bananas, and ended by offing his friends and family with a .45 automatic at a cocktail party. Then he raced down to the beach, and flung his Medal of Honor into the ocean.

In writing, I have one irrevocable rule: once started, I never abandon a book until I have a clean first draft. Otherwise, I would despairingly desert all my books long before they reached the halfway mark.

So I retreated to Mastic and tried to finish that nihilistic novel. I had all the spare cold rooms to myself and acres of fields and forests in which to wander, hoping to make myself whole again.

Every day I ran along the narrow sandy roads bisecting the land.

I had run cross-country in college, and I loved it. During those jaunts I reentered an ordered universe. And during that Mastic sojourn I determined to leave New York.

The forest was rich with thickets and thorny tangles, dead logs and layered leaves, pine trees and oaks and maples, and wild grape vines. At dusk the scent of ripe wild grapes seemed to manifest itself as delicate streams of mauve-green mist through which my face broke like the prow of a soft white boat.

In the evenings rabbits sat on the sandy, grassy paths; they scampered off as I approached. Doves burst noisily out of treetops, wings whistling loudly as I trotted by underneath. Fluffy storms of white dandelion seeds floated across the road.

At intervals, the forest opened up; I ran past patches of barley and rye planted by my Uncle David for pheasants and quail. But I had no interest in hunting that season. And never even quartered the fields for fun, to see if anything might jump.

I just ran by myself for miles at dusk. A squirrel zipped out of the brush, almost hitting my legs—I stuttered my steps to avoid it. Migratory warblers popped out of dry goldenrod stalks; acorns crunched under my sneakered feet.

The woods teemed with monarch butterflies. Orange wings frayed and faded, they wandered absentmindedly, seeking shadows in which to die. Often my face burst through an invisible fragile web spun across the path.

In a sandy area I stopped to check out the animal tracks: of little birds, and mice . . . of rabbits and quail. Crickets marched through the sand: I nudged them with my toe; frantically they hopped away. A few big spiders had hundreds of tiny offspring clutched around their abdomens. When startled, all the little spiders sprang off and scampered around in dizzying hysterical circles—then they rushed back onto mama's bandwagon.

At 2:00 A.M., exhausted and able to work no longer, I took walks along those same roads accompanied by my cat, Swoboda. Occasionally, the moon shone brightly; more often the midnight sky was simply littered with stars. Overshadowed by towering trees, the paths were pitch-black.

I could only follow my cat's progress by catching reflections off white patches on her hind legs when she scampered forward.

Smells were much stronger at night: oak leaves rotting . . . the wild grapes . . . the scent of juniper . . . a velvet musk of damp moss . . . the white odor of sand . . . the raunchy skunklike stink of a fox.

I walked through warm air currents, the cooler air, then warm air again. I passed through ribbons and scarves of mist. Off to the side, Swoboda rustled, then froze—I held my breath . . . she pounced.

Maybe a shallow layer of mist unfurled along the road, no higher than my waist. While above me the treetops were clearly etched against the hazy velvet of a damp ocean atmosphere.

By October, only a few crickets were singing: presentiments of winter were birthing a lull. A lonely owl called; but fewer small critters scuttled in the brittle leaves; only a handful of birds shifted on their nocturnal perches in protective brier tangles, nature growing calmer as November approached.

I heard geese high overhead, aiming south, invisible among the stars. I listened for wings up there. Who said migrating birds fly mostly at night? Is that true? I suppose so. Guiding themselves somehow, in a process we do not yet understand, by the stars . . . ?

Indoors, I was reading a John Hersey novel, *The Wall*, about Jewish resistance in the Warsaw ghetto during World War II. Our astronauts up in space were laying the groundwork for a moon landing less than a year later. In my journal I wrote:

> Up in space Walter Shirra refuses to flip a switch so all we panting earthlings can see them eat Cheerios on our TVs, our reward for exorbitant taxes . . . revolutions begin with such small insults!

The Wall. One thinks of a Revolutionary situation in New York. Sewer plans and subways. How do you survive? Will it come to that . . . ?

I have daydreams of Resistance, killing cops, hiding, running, I beg not to be drawn into that. Will it happen? What if Wallace is elected President?

Wallace never became president, of course. But right now in 1981 it appears that Ronald Reagan is preparing to emasculate El Salvador, multiplying its misery by the square root of conservative cruelty. The Archbishop of Santa Fe has pleaded with the administration not to indulge this particular genocide—but 1981's "Tonkin Gulf Resolution" White Paper has already been prepared. Does this mean that in four years they'll hand my now fourteen-year-old son an M-16, and set him to killing brown-skinned people and taking R&R with emaciated teen-aged whores whose brutalized Latin bodies will introduce him to the mysteries of female intimacy?

I can hardly wait.

In Central America all the children are licking skull-shaped lollipops with their feverish filariated eyes cast northward. I've often wondered: How many bullets does it take to bring me my daily bananas? And how should I deal with the stamp—on the back of my assorted fishing flies in a box—that says *Made in Guatemala*?

On his gloomy days, my father has said the globe would be better off without the human race. Years ago, a man I used to work with lay in a coffin at a political funeral, riddled with police bullets; his morbid features seemed sculpted of cardboard or Play-Doh. One of my neighbors blew away his neighbor with a shotgun because that fellow had fired an arrow into his dog—thus concluded a long feud. A good friend, arrested for being drunk, awoke in his cell with flaming toilet paper on his chest. And I awoke at 4:00 A.M. suffocating from asthma, wondering when the disease would kill me.

Meanwhile, the Ku Klux Klan has a ball in Greensboro, killing Communists with impunity. It is growing closer to open season upon Marxists. El Salvador death squads are listening to the Voice of Reagan. A nobody killed Che Guevara. Another nobody touched a machine gun to the head of Salvador Allende, already dead, and pulled the trigger. A third nobody assassinated Victor Jara.

The family of Pablo Neruda began to carry his coffin through the streets to the graveyard. Congregations of people were forbidden, under threat of death. But the word went out, at first in whispers: "Who is that down there? Who is passing?"

And the answer: "Comrade Pablo Neruda."

Doors opened, the people emerged. Soldiers frowned and gestured with their rifles. But nobody would be intimidated, because Pablo Neruda was passing.

A man cried out, calling the roll: "Comrade Pablo Neruda!"

And a woman answered: "I am here, I am present, for now, and for always."

They left the buildings, they emerged from shadows, they closed their shops, they descended from their automobiles to walk behind the coffin of Comrade Pablo Neruda. They risked death to do this. They created immortal poetry by doing this. They gave courage to the entire world by their fearless homage.

A child, another woman, another man answered: "I am here, I am present and accounted for! Now and forever!"

Hundreds joined the solemn and defiant march through the city to the graveyard. At the risk of death. Under the eyes of Fascists. They did that for the Communist poet who said:

> I continue to work with the materials I have, the materials I am made of. With feelings, beings, books, events, and battles, I am om-nivorous. I would like to swallow the whole earth. I would like to drink the whole sea.

Me too.
Now and forever.

In life we occasionally complete full circles. Not long ago, I took up a gun and went hunting again. On my own I doubt I would have made such a decision. Nevertheless, when my friend Doug Terry and his father, Jim, invited me to go dove hunting near Costilla, I went, and fired a gun for the first time in about twelve years. It felt uncomfortable, but I chose not to belabor the sensation. The world has not greatly changed, but I think I have. And I can deal better with the paradoxes.

Now, every autumn I usually head north with Doug and his dad at least once during the season. I am a lousy shot, but always kill a few birds. I enjoy the camaraderie we share, traveling to the grainfields, making plans, and afterward, on the lazy return journeys, commenting on each other's luck or lack of expertise. Mostly, though, I enjoy getting away in that country, walking through waist-high barley, or proceeding alertly and quietly through hushed, pebbly arroyos, superattuned to the world, delicately tensed to kill.

It's a different countryside from the Taos Valley: wide open, flatter, fewer trees. Grainfields cover hundreds of unbroken acres, ranch houses are far apart, the scale is grander. Long lines of metal irrigation pipes on wheels cross some fields; the mountains seem more distant and lower. Harvesting combines work well into the evening. Only a few shallow arroyos in which cottonwoods grow bisect the land. A prairie mood prevails, casting real intimations of Nebraska or Kansas.

We arrive in the late afternoon, hunt together for perhaps an hour, then split up, heading into different areas. Away from their guns, I can savor the experience. Then the placid evening becomes the most peaceful I have ever known. Far away the combines are chugging remotely. Closer by, dozens of hawks and owls populate the landscape. Their presence is eerie and haunting. They drift by overhead, curiously following my progress. Perched severely in the topmost branches of dead trees, they are absolutely unafraid. Even when I fire they hardly flinch. Eager to pick up a free meal, they are waiting for me to lose a cripple.

Their arrogance is unbelievable. I was circling a dense thicket at the edge of a sandy arroyo when a dove jumped. I fired quickly and the bird plummeted into the thicket. But even before I could mark exactly where it had entered the foliage, a great horned owl flapped out of nowhere, diving after the dove. I ran forward, shouting *"Hey, scram!"* and practically had to beat away the owl to claim my dove.

I gather nobody has ever fired at the raptors of that area. Repeatedly, as I cross fields at twilight, owls hover overhead, flapping their big wings slowly, intrigued by my moves. Once, stalking a dove, I heard massive wings above me—I could practically feel the turbulence of feather-stroked air. An enormous great horned owl was fifteen feet away, etched in a clarity I shall never forget, its big yellow eyes peering down intently, every feather on its chest standing out in perfect relief.

I halt, set down my gun, remove the Nikon from my backpack, and photograph the birds. All the impressive big buteos, the medium-sized Coopers and sharp-shinned varieties, and the little sparrow hawks. They treat me as a fellow hunter, entitled to a piece of the territory. I presume they pluck mice, gophers, and rabbits from the freshly mowed fields; and also feast on the doves.

Silent, they seldom utter a croak. And I pause repeatedly to marvel at the sight of so many legendary birds looming nonchalantly across the uneventful horizons.

Doves spring out of their cover suddenly, usually at a distance, and wing quickly away from me, flying low. I knock one down wounded in the tall grasses, and curse myself for taking the shot. Slowly, I quarter the area, stopping every few feet to listen for a rustle—but all I hear are grasshoppers rattling among the beige stalks.

With the wind, doves take to the air and are swept out of sight instantly. But later, as I retrace my steps back up the arroyo, they come flying against the wind, always high and not very fast, easy targets for even a mediocre gunner like myself.

I don't like to sit in one place, at a stand, waiting for them to pass by as they begin moving at dusk to their roosting areas. I'm too impatient. My motion is more important than bagging a dove. The real point is to cover terrain, inspect trees and land formations, always change the angle at which light strikes my immediate universe.

I am quartering a cottonwood grove, slowly reducing a small flock of birds that keep to the outer edge of twisted trees, reluctant to abandon their cover. Intermittently, I have a brief glimpse and a quick shot through gaps in the foliage. Usually, I miss. It is dark, and they are very skittish and fast. Yet I persist in sneaking through the trees, spotting the birds, and chasing after them. In the end I add four to my sack. I have been doing this for twenty minutes, when I look up after missing a bird and notice a fat porcupine sound asleep in the V of two branches, undisturbed by the shotgun blasts persistently shattering the quietude. For some reason, every animal *not* a dove seems instinctively to realize it is in no danger.

I am plodding along a dry riverbed. It is almost dark. Everywhere, the big hawks are laconically hunting. The stream bed has camouflaged potholes; my feet continually crunch through a fragile crust into shallow pockets of dry loam, and I stagger, almost sprawling. My only shots are at birds in silhouette against the sky—the rest of the landscape is ebony. The doves are winging toward me, no higher than my head, and I never see them until the last instant. Then I must swivel abruptly, catching but a glimpse of their quicksilver bodies against the rosy sky, before they zip into the safety of darkness; I never get off a shot.

Suddenly, by my right shoulder, a luminous barn owl flaps off a branch, almost brushing my head in passing, and lumbers a few yards down the arroyo.

Then it is dark. The hawks melt away, and the shooting is over. Combines continue to labor in the distance, their multiple lights shining across the barley. A rabbit—a little cottontail—leaps out from under my feet and scoots across the sandy arroyo, only its white tail visible and frantically bobbing.

Heading home through a field of stubble, I come across a scattering of rabbit bones shining in the dark. The air smells tangy, crisp, cool. To the south the soft breast-shaped mound of Ute Mountain shimmers against a dim burnished aureole, the final remnants of daylight.

The killer in me is honed again: I have my reasons.

PART SIX

You must recognize
    the importance of the earth,
you must believe
    that the earth is eternal
Distinguish not between your mother
and your mother Earth.
You must love it
    as much as you love her.

—Nazim Hikmet
Advice to Our Children

FOURTEEN

Two years before writing this book I decided to buy some useless land, and set out to discover the country within a twenty-mile radius west of Taos. I bought U.S. Geological Survey Maps and studied them intently. I asked different Taos realtors for listings of land parcels west of the Rio Grande Gorge. Then I launched an odyssey that lasted for months, radically changed my life in Taos, injected a new myth into my experience, and without which this book would not have been written.

It was like suddenly falling in love with somebody you have known for a long time and always taken for granted. I have mentioned in other writings how the mountains east of Taos easily fulfill for me the psychological need to be near an ocean. Carson, on the other hand, I constantly describe to people as an actual ocean. Above miles of monocolored sagebrush hang skies much clearer than those above Taos. In the vast emptiness, even the smallest bird or butterfly in flight is openly exposed. A single automobile miles away feels like an intruder. And for long stretches only a lone cow or a horse surfaces briefly, like a dolphin, to break the monotony, and then it is lost to view.

Everything that touches the senses there is absolute. I love the un-paralleled panorama, and the anonymity. The sky curving over the wide bowl has an unreal dimension. Wandering through the waste-land, I revel in a universe larger than life.

Given the desert atmosphere, small quirks in the terrain take on exaggerated importance; insignificant details stand out with alarming vigor. Because the area remains largely undisturbed, its history has a comforting continuity. Each moment feels as close to the 1600s as to the twenty-first century. Human beings have not yet buggered the fragile territory, and the cliché of "timelessness" aptly applies.

Alone and aloof, Carson's added poignancy is that, like the rest of the valley, it is also on the block. A few sheepherders and ranchers long situated there probably cannot hang on much longer. The economics, politics, and sensibilities of a rapidly growing middle-class transformation work against them. Old homesteaders clinging to the lonely life may become disgruntled as newcomers like myself put down their eclectic roots. And they'll leave, or simply die off, fragmenting on the restless winds.

Dreading the thought, I wonder how *not* to aid the demolition. By writing with such love of an area, perhaps I attract the killers, or become one myself. Should I censor my feelings, queer all this heart-felt rhetoric? It's an important question, and one I intend to address later in this book.

For the moment, however, I only wish to transmit the lure of a deserted mesa.

With maps under my arms, with directions and notations scribbled on old envelopes, I traversed the sagebrush plain. Sometimes the sky held me spellbound; more often my eyes stayed glued to the ground. Until the cold weather set in, I paid special attention to the earth, always alert for rattlesnakes. The saving grace of Carson may be its rattlers. I'm not fool enough to claim they aren't dangerous, but I do not consider the snakes hostile. Most people I know are afraid of them, though, and beat the serpents to a pulp whenever possible. Yet as we all know, rattlers provide food for hawks, badgers, eagles, roadrunners, and coyotes, to name but a few. They are also invaluable in keeping down varmints such as mice, rats, and prairie dogs. But my most fervent hope is that the Carson rattlers' biggest coup will be to keep down the invasion of human beings onto their turf. With this in mind, I ask the avid (but perhaps slightly timorous) reader to refer back to my blowhole adventure with Andrés Martínez. And to reflect that Nichols once came within a foot of being whacked in the crotch by a baby diamondback, over there in Carson.

Despite the rattlers, it is difficult to keep my eyes off the Carson sky for long. Just today I spent two hours over there, taking photographs. A hundred clear shades of ultramarine blues were modulated by dark amethyst variations. Puffy expanding white clouds engulfed the entire range of air. Invisible winds played with the vapor formations. Utterly fascinated, I watched a cloud tear apart, undergoing mitosis I suppose, until it had dispersed into shapeless wisps about to evaporate. But then the winds reversed direction, and all those dissolving filaments, as if in a film being run backward, rebunched together, forming nearly the same-shaped cloud that I had seen disintegrate.

I marveled, took my eyes away for a moment . . . and when I looked back the entire cloud had evaporated!

Today, also, wind was attacking the distant mountaintops. Fuzzy plumes of white spindrift curled off the Truchas Peaks behind Picuris. And the plumes seemed to pour into the underbellies of horizon clouds, feeding their misty fibers.

A cloudy sky never stagnates for a moment. Everything in nature is always moving. Nothing stays the same shape for long, no matter how forceful its impression of immutability. There can be little wind in my hair, while thirty thousand feet above, on an absolutely clear and cloudless day, great gales are fomenting the turbulence of a gigantic washing machine.

Light, too, is impossibly evanescent. Against clouds, or across foothills, or delineating the veins of a leaf, it seems always to pulse through a jumble of colorful registers. I've learned to hurry all my photographs, setting an almost frantic pace for capturing brief bursts of luminescence.

The bold saga of clouds is so exhilarating. The space they occupy recreates the human imagination. Pablo Neruda once looked up and observed, "The clouds travel like white handkerchiefs of goodbye. . . ."

Then it is night on the mesa: grand thunderheads have mysteriously dissipated, revealing constellations and galaxies of indifferent spangles backdropping the perfectly round harvest moon.

I like to cast myself into that infinity, wallowing indulgently in awe. I luxuriate in my insignificance. My smallness puts my heart at ease, and I relax. I welcome the respite from self-importance. Although I understand little about the stars, they seem very simple, twinkling in their inhuman beauty, beyond the reach of astronomers and warriors.

Darkness on a damp road: it rained earlier. The air is dead still. I smell stones, sagebrush, and bones. Taos and Picuris mountains are dark silhouettes. Faintly, from deep in the gorge, I hear white waters muttering. The sky lowers, and a sense of distance between me and all those tiny lights disappears. If I concentrate hard, I succumb to a star-created vertigo.

Look Ma, my feet have left the earth—*I'm floating!*

Taos twinkles across the gorge. It seems as if any minute a mischievous wind might come along and fling all those pretty streetlights into astrological patterns across the sky.

The star-speckled space above Carson awakens childlike pleasures inside. I laugh as a tremor of innocence stutters through my body. I can travel no farther from despair.

Another of Carson's saving graces may be the weather. Winter winds sweeping across the treeless sagebrush create a murderous chill factor. When snow melts on the dirt roads, they soften into gooey slop, becoming impassable. The summertime sun, on the other hand, is relentless: there's no escaping it, the heat is a butcher. Close to sunstroke several times in September, I had to terminate my hikes prematurely, staggering back to the car with blistered lips and a thudding headache.

Hopefully, such drawbacks will further discourage the civilizing of Carson. It is a territory that becomes supportable only in autumn.

Water is also real hard to obtain. Around the mesa about ten earthen dams have been bulldozed in selected arroyos, creating stock ponds. After a good winter, the little ponds can hold water well into summer. If rain falls, the moisture may last into September. Otherwise, to get water you have to drill for it. And that ain't cheap. Where I live in Taos, I can hit water three feet below the grass. In Carson, the wells come in at three hundred and fifty feet if you're lucky. The current drilling price per foot, with casing, runs about—what—thirteen-fifty a foot? Meaning close to a five-grand investment, just for the well.

Throw together the cruel winters, endless hordes of belligerent rapacious rattlers, the impassable roads in all seasons, possible death due to heat prostration four months out of the year, frostbite conditions in winter, plus the dearth of water . . . and maybe, just maybe all the conditions are favorable to Carson's survival.

With my maps, and the realtors' directions, I quartered the desolate country. Cattle eyed me from protective redoubts in the arroyos. I kept running across a herd of skittish horses I assumed were wild, until I learned they belonged to Delfino Valerio, who has corrals, a water pump, and two stock tanks near Carson.

I walked: everywhere I spied deer tracks. Yet to this day I have not budged a Carson buck from its daytime hideout, nor have I ever seen one traipsing along in the distance.

Pawprints I always inspected—of coyotes, and of smaller creatures. Any size hole in the ground drew my attention. The smallest excavations were made by wasps and lizards. Larger burrows might have belonged to owls. And of course in some areas the sage had been leveled by prairie-dog villages.

All kinds of animal trails bisected the sagebrush. Of deer, horses, cattle, and sheep. Curiously, although it is an expansive landscape without barriers, animals tend to walk single-file along the same narrow route, day in and day out, to get from here to there.

Carson anthills are large cone-shaped mounds, some almost two feet high, constructed of perfect pebbles. Around the anthills I always looked for horned toads. It was easy to catch the toads. They aren't as quick as small spiny and sagebrush lizards; certainly they cannot race with the large collared lizards that resemble miniature dinosaurs as they skitter off on their hind legs only.

Abruptly, hundreds of caterpillars lay on the puffy cracked earth between sage plants. Sheer numbers suggested they could have been dumped from an airplane in some bizarre government seeding operation. I pocketed one to take home for identification. In the car, the wee beastie crawled onto my neck and stung me fiercely. Until that moment, I had never realized some caterpillars are protected by poisonous spines.

Later, I figured the caterpillars changed into a medium-large black-and-white insect known as a hera moth (or sheep moth) that flip-flops in semispastic slow motion over the daytime sage.

Between thumb and forefinger I assessed the jawbone of a mouse, also a perfect little lizard skull. Bones—big and little—turned up all across the mesa. From cattle and horses and coyotes, from birds and snakes and rabbits. Only rarely did I find an entire skeleton. Usually nothing remained but a white femur lying jewellike in a pancake of native grasses. Or several vertebrae of a sheep. Or maybe rodent bones wrapped in hair, regurgitated by an owl. All of them clean and bleached, like driftwood. Once in a while I collected them like shells and carried them home. More often I left them there as talismans belonging to the wild world.

I return often to certain bones: a horse skeleton on the south Los Cordovas mesa, a virtual ossuary of coyote skulls in the bottom of an arroyo—perhaps a rancher dumped the carcasses years ago.

A thousand stories await me in the sagebrush if I stop and try to interpret signs. Tiny animal violence in the spurts and scratches of lizard feet. Pitch-black dung beetles lie dead in sandy hollows—why did nothing eat them? Too, the bones of civilization outline histories—those weathered timbers of old homesteads, shanties, sheds. By itself a concrete foundation . . . nothing else. A cache of rusting garbage melting into the earth—tin cans, and old, interesting bottles. Or an ancient cistern, clogged with sand and piles of tumbleweeds. A cedar fence post may still be erect after a hundred years; nearby, several strands of old-fashioned barbwire date from a hardier epoch.

A few miles south of the old stone schoolhouse in Carson a quarter-section of land was for sale. I walked across it to the rim of the Petaca Arroyo, at that point—not far from its Rio Grande confluence—a fairly deep little gorge, cluttered by elms and alamos and scratchy bushes, and patches of thick yellow grass. Among the smooth layered rocks I spotted several pools of stagnant water.

On a slab near a bajada I stopped to check out some coyote shit. Like all the other mesa animals, I am curious about my cohort's defecations. Especially, I wonder what my fellow bi- and quadri-peds have been eating.

In this case it was apricot pits. I glanced around, aware that no orchard existed for miles. But that's coyotes for you. I definitely think their turds always tell the most interesting stories.

I dropped off the mesa into a nearly subterranean world full of plants, songbirds, and strange animals. Over the years, spring runoffs have deposited tons of sediment along the floor of the basalt and volcanic riprap. Two months earlier I'm sure all the vegetation had been green—now it was growing brittle and sere, except around that series of stagnant pools. As always, deer tracks made intriguing the damp sand. And in the water, the newt stages of ugly brown tiger salamanders periodically surfaced for air, then sank back out of sight into the dirty water.

Imagine discovering such creatures in Carson! How had they arrived in those isolated pools? Known locally as juajalotes, the grotesque prehistoric beasts usually appear in sedentary shallow springs of the foothills and higher country. The reader may remember that they also inhabit Bernardin Lake.

My kids are juajalote connoisseurs. Every summer they make at least one Bernardin Lake expedition to catch and bring back alive the ugly gillbreathers. They dip them from the water with butterfly nets, sluice 'em into Tree Top Apple Cider jars, and, once back home, plop them into aquariums.

For a while we had a juajalote aquarium for a kitchen-table centerpiece. Voracious little predators, the nasty animals had to be fed constantly. In the back field we swished butterfly nets through the alfalfa, capturing grasshoppers, which went straight into the covered aquarium. (A comparable ritual is that of throwing mice or baby chicks to somebody's pet boa constrictor.) We spent most of our mealtimes, that summer, watching juajalotes attack and dismember hapless grass-hoppers. Drops of rancid water propelled by thrashing little alligator tails splashed over the sides, sprinkling our food.

I tolerated it as long as the kids were fascinated by juajalotes. But soon I found myself catching all of the Christian grasshoppers, and when that happened I ordered the slimy newts dumped into the front irrigation ditch.

With its trees, grasses, and shading foliage, the Petaca Arroyo was fifteen degrees cooler than the mesa. It felt offbeat, like a huge terrarium or a secret garden. When I climbed out after an hour, to be engulfed again by limitless spaces, I had trouble getting oriented.

Heading back toward the car I found a small, perfectly shaped Indian arrowhead, notched on either side, so clean and unflawed it seemed to have been fashioned only moments ago. It lay completely exposed atop powdery dirt sculpted with sinuously curving veins made by coursing rainwater.

My first arrowhead! Immediately, I thought *that* land was the most beautiful I had looked at, a quarter-section of sagebrush terrain with a few small knolls rising but twenty feet above the rest of the plain. Three juniper trees in the section broke the monotony.

I had first been there on an August evening, weeks earlier. I had stood on a knoll, calmed by the serenity. The moment before dark was unreal. A powerful and luminous light unfurled over the land like a wave onto the beach. Everything had a damp, totally vivid glow. Gray chamisa bark seemed infused with liquid silver; green rabbitbrush stalks shimmered vibrantly. The sky was pink, mauve, burgundy. Early snowcaps on distant mountains gleamed like fire instead of ice.

Soaking up that breathtaking serenity, I felt almost as if I was having a religious experience. The stillness was so damn *exorbitant*. My only thoughts were: This is where I want to die. This is where I'll ask them to scatter my ashes.

Nighthawks circled above me, inquisitive and unobtrusive. White bands under their wings glowed brightly. Then coyotes started barking, way beyond the Petaca Arroyo, at the edge of the piñon trees.

That night I lay in bed, thinking about the land. I had started my search with the idea that eventually I might purchase some land. I had no idea if it would be ten or a hundred and sixty acres (a quarter-section). It had soon become obvious that in Carson a person bought a quarter-section the same way, and for the same price, that they bought one or two acres in Taos. Out in the open like that, even a quarter-section seemed like a small plot. People or cars began intruding the moment you spotted them miles away.

Prices of land varied radically. The piece near the Petaca Arroyo was listed at $56,000; it belonged to an Oklahoma couple. North of their quarter-section another hundred and sixty acres owned by an Ohio man was advertised for $24,000. Most of the sagebrush was land I had seen listed at anywhere from $150 to $350 an acre. I had no idea what I would pay for land, nor how much the sellers could be bargained down. I was terrified of being in debt and determined to pay cash for whatever I chose.

Realtors said, "You're crazy!" They explained capitalism with gusto. For starters, apparently it was to the sellers' advantage to take a low down payment—for tax reasons. Meaning that some people would not accept cash from me.

"If you got the cash," one realtor explained, "negotiate for the lowest down payment you can get, then invest the rest in a money fund. From them you'll pick up at least, I think it's about 9.8 percent right now. While you're only paying 8 or 9 percent to the landowner. 'Course, with a money fund, if you want to cash a check, it has to be for five hundred bucks or more. Still, listen to this: you're earning interest from the moment you sign the check until it clears through the other guy's bank. During that time you could pick up an extra twenty dollars."

They explained how a time purchase worked. The buyer would supply a warranty deed, to be held by First Northern Savings and Loan in Taos. I would pay a fifty-dollar escrow fee. The bank would charge two bucks a month for the service. I would pay the bank, the bank would pay the owner, and keep all the records. When I finished the payments, I would get the deed. If my down payment was really low, I would probably be required by the seller to pay for title insurance; otherwise, he'd take care of it. The broker recommended that I put the minimum down, and stretch out my payments. After all, I could deduct the interest, as well as put my cash in a better place where the interest I earned might even be enough to meet the land payments.

As to variations on a specific deal: if I was willing to put half the cash down, the owner might come off his price by 10 percent. The owner, apparently, was a wealthy investor, selling for tax purposes. If I put half down on a $20,000 purchase price, I would pay $126 a month for ten years. There would be no penalty for prepayment in whole. If prepayment was in parts, we would simply renegotiate the contract. The earnest money, if I made an offer, would be 10 percent of the offered price.

If I wanted a well, he said, I could find people to do it for eleven bucks a foot, without casing, and they might hit water within four hundred feet. Because the piece was only a half-mile south of the power line along Route 96 through Carson, bringing in electricity would only cost about $3,500. I could negotiate on that construction contract, which required that I put down 25 percent of the cost, and pay off in five years at approximately $41 per month.

I lay in bed, fiddling with all those figures, clammy and cold. Still, I had a dream of retreating from Taos one day, being alone. I could build an isolated one-room house on the mesa out of wood, with a peaked roof, and large windows. Inside?—a wood stove for heat, a bed, a table to work on. White walls, a single bookcase, simple rag rugs on the floor. One painting—a landscape, pastoral, pastel, im-

pressionistic. And a sage branch in a milk bottle. Little else. Spare and clean, with perhaps a white bone on a window ledge.

No electricity, no water.

I could haul water in a jerry can, read by kerosene lamplight. And sit on a wooden stoop in the evening, listening to coyotes, watching nighthawks. Del Valerio's horses might pass by in the dark. Across the plain, at the foot of the Sangre de Cristos, Taos lights would twinkle.

What would it be like in that one-room house during a snowstorm?

Maybe I would put up a gutter and have a drainpipe descending into a large water tub.

But how long could I survive without a newspaper? Would I crouch eagerly over a transistor radio at night? It all seemed terribly impractical. Would my asthma get better? I was filled with an aching, poetic despair, a romantic melancholy I disliked. Buying and selling is a rough business.

In the morning, blindly, I decided to make an offer. I suggested $21,600 to the Oklahoma people who wanted $56,000. They gave a counteroffer of $40,000. I upped my nut to $27,000, and they came down to $34,000. I put all the money I had into it, $30,000. They settled at $32,000. At which point I got cold feet, bowed out, went up the road, and bought the same amount of sagebrush for $22,000 cash.

I had no feeling about it, no sense of triumph, nothing. The land was no different from the rest of the mesa out there. It had no fences, no water, no electricity, no trees. Perhaps someday I will build that little one-room house, who knows? In the meantime, I seldom visit that land specifically; instead, I wander freely, everywhere.

And climb Tres Orejas and survey the arid domain that should belong to everyone, and to nobody at all.

Such a blowsy, happy day: sunny, windy, chilly. Thin clouds curve over the sky like shreds of diaphanous mucus. You are so soft, sexy, cute, and erotic. All the gooshy clichés apply. Your lovely nipples seem about to jump through that thin blue jersey fabric. I hug you and melt inside, soft and powdery, corny and loving. We strut through the sagebrush, whistling Dixie. The air is dry, dusty, pungent. At the grassy space on the slope we set down a blanket and the sleeping bag. I show you the little pile of bones—sheep vertebrae?—that I had put on the spot where someday I'll build a little house. Wind, like arctic kisses, ruffles your hair.

We spread out the blanket, unzip the puffy sleeping bag, shed our clothes and snuggle. A champagne cork rockets into the sage. Your tongue tip curls into the green mouth of the bottle and emerges dappled with foam. Here's a toast to empty spaces, the forever sky, white bodies, and the wonderful lust to fornicate.

Wind presses like masseuse hands against the puffy goose down. It sneaks in through the cracks and tickles up a mess of goose bumps. "Your hands are cold," I say. "Cold hands, warm heart," you reply.

Love that loving, darlin'. Wind batters our faces. The sun shines with a thin, delicious warmth. Tugging the cocoon around us, we savor the erotic experience.

Toward the end, we hurl off the sleeping bag and make love in the wild playful commotion of air. Finally, facing across the mesa, we climax together with happy shouts. Emptying into you I feel as if I am joyfully lambasting this panorama!

Then I'm up, dancing, naked and cornball, beating my chest with comical exuberance, howling like Tarzan, feeling wonderful and obnoxious. Jumping into my sneakers, I prance through the sagebrush, emitting hokey war cries.

"Hey Nichols! Get back here! You'll catch pneumonia!"

Not me, not today, not ever. I give you the finger and my dervish grin, grab up a little bone, return, and yank off the sleeping bag and consecrate the bone with your funky juices, then replace it in the little pile, blessed by the sticky white vitality of our bodies.

Lingering for a while, we lie still, safe in our puffy cocoon, drowsing. Wind clatters against the lightweight nylon. Then a lull as all of a sudden the mesa is quiet.

You speak: "I don't mean to sound corny, but if a rock were to fall on top of me right now and kill me it'd be all right, because I feel perfect."

So we repose there a little longer, gloating.

FIFTEEN

One day, my father came to Taos. We drove out to the Los Cordovas mesa close to sunset time. I set up my tripod and camera, and we waited to see what would happen. All around the horizon rain was falling. Bits of lightning flickered nervously like bright snake tongues out of a serpentine vapor.

Overhead, nighthawks were hunting insects, beeping in their funny basso way—*peeent!*—fluttering their wings each time they uttered the bizarre cries. Then they dived toward earth in their courtship plunges, making an odd sound with their wing feathers—like lips blowing against a tissue-wrapped comb—that is called "booming."

The light died. I don't remember what prompted it, but Dad told me a story about something that had happened to him at eighteen:

For some reason he could no longer recollect, my teen-age father shot a great horned owl. He thought it was dead. But when he went to pick it up, the bird drove a talon straight through his hand, and he couldn't pry it loose.

"Finally, in incredible pain, I managed to open my pocketknife and cut the tendon in the leg to make it let go. . . . "

Next day, with assorted children in tow, we drove over to the Carson land. The kids scattered in the sagebrush, looking for horned toads. Hera moths patrolled the sage, orange heads vibrantly new, black-and-white wings freshly minted. Calling my attention to a rock wren, Pop remarked dryly, "There's a *Salpinctes obsoletus.*"

A moment later, plucking a sprig of sage, he added (as he sniffed it): "*Artemesia trifida.*"

Whereupon I pointed across the mesa to the power line that travels through Carson, and sardonically remarked: "Over there—look at the *Powerlinum electrensis.*"

And when I spotted a small beetle scurrying ahead of me, I quickly announced: "Come quick, everybody: looks like we got us a *Scarabensis vitessum!*"

Once the furor had died down, Pop picked up a green rock: "Hey, look at this, guy, you got copper on your land."

"Oh-mi-gosh! Then we'd better mine it! We'll bring bulldozers in here first thing tomorrow and level all the sage. When we've taken out all the copper, I'll cover the land with Astroturf. Jesus, do you realize what we could *do* with this land?"

"Well, you could concretize that arroyo over there, and build a dam, and make yourself a recreation lake."

"Perfect. We'll build the lake, then install a permanent carnival. We'll even have a whorehouse. And a BB-gun shooting gallery where kids get to fire at horned toads. We'll stretch a neon fence all around the place. . . . "

We walked through the arroyos, picking up and inspecting little stones, throwing them back. Pop located coyote tracks in a gully; farther on we discovered where the animal had dug into a hole in the bank.

A single thistle plant shriveled in a sageless, grassy area. A small yellow insect rooted in the still purple flower. A ladybug rested on a leaf. On the ground beneath the thistle lay a large dead bumblebee.

No other flowers adorned the land. Pop contemplated the crooked drooping plant, then allowed as how, "That's a hell of a lonely thistle."

We continued searching for signs. I picked up a little bone, held it between my fingers, then let go: lighter than a feather the bone drifted to earth, landing weightlessly.

We ate lunch in an arroyo at the base of Tres Orejas; thick sticky pitch dripped from the porcupine-caused wounds of a piñon tree onto nearby rocks. The turpentine smell was overpowering. Then we climbed the mountain, and on the summit basked in hot windy sunshine while I gave my rap about the surrounding landmarks. After descending, we bounced down a rocky road toward the infamous Carson reservoir. Cresting a hill, I braked; horses galloped through acres of blossoming sunflowers on the floor of the reservoir. From a distance they appeared wild. But they sprinted right up to us and began to nuzzle the kids—beautiful sleek quarter horses, completely tame.

When they retreated, we checked out the sunflowers. They stretched north for at least a half-mile. Hummingbirds buzzed among the blossoms, lavishly feeding. Large black wasps with vibrant russet wings slalomed between the hummers. Monarch butterflies strutted their stuff alongside dozens of dragonflies; then six ducks and a sanderling jumped from the shallow waterhole and circled the area, awaiting our departure.

An hour later we left, plowing slowly through thickets of gaudy sunflowers reaching almost up to the front windshield.

During the next few weeks, I often revisited the reservoir: with the children, with my friend Sylvia. The sunflowers began to droop, lost their petals, and died. The shallow puddles evaporated, leaving behind damp areas of cracked mud that soon hardened, were worked by the winds, and became dusty. Gradually, the hummingbird population expired, until it too, like the water, dissolved.

But for a while that was a serene and special place that I approached with reverence, and enjoyed as much as I have ever enjoyed anything.

September mosquitoes are out. I'll never understand how so many can emerge from these puddles in an arid country. Hummingbirds are busily zipping across the reservoir, wiggling at high speeds through the happy yellow flowers. The sanderling is nibbling at tidbits in the shallow water. I wonder: Do other shorebirds spend their entire lives this far from an ocean? Don't they miss the surging waves and puddles rimed with salty foam?

At twilight, light hesitates boldly. Clouds dissolve, absorbed by voracious, placid infinity. Even the air halts. The earth seems embarrassed to be so evocative and romantic.

Time for the nighthawks, who appear suddenly as if flicked out of thin air by invisible fingers. I spot them initially in the distance, high above the earth. They cleave toward me with a streamlined and absolute self-assurance. Shortly, they are flying by my face, only a few feet away, unafraid. I hear the air whoosh away from their wings. I extend an arm and the birds veer slightly, without breaking rhythm.

Soon, the nighthawks are mowing a lawn of bugs congregating above the puddle. They dip gracefully to pluck morsels off the water, causing delicate ripples. Their hunting seems a leisurely, dreamlike pursuit, even though they must harvest a thousand bugs each evening to survive.

A bewitching solitude defines the twilight moment. The sky is inanimate, captured within a mauve beige amber. Tres Orejas is a single triangular peak from this angle, silhouetted tranquilly against the lilac drowse. Bats enter the hesitant airwaves. Circles on the water seem caused by rain, but I know the "raindrops" are actually mos-quitoes hatching: they pop free with inaudible *pings!* then rise ten feet on damp new wings to become fodder for the bats and nighthawks.

Sylvia and I sit there, watching the twilight hunt. Between the bats, bullbats, mosquitoes, and hummingbirds, a lot of activity is going on, yet an overwhelming calmness reigns. I suppose it's not much fun for the bugs, but otherwise nature has carelessly fashioned a perfect moment. Above the sound of wingstrokes and squeaking bats, we can almost tune into the delicate deaf-and-dumb rustle of the universe.

As stars begin to shine those old coyotes unleash some friendly bloodcurdling yells.

At dark we split. Little owls hog the road, feasting on sunflower insects. I stop; they blink stupidly into the headlights, small nocturnal birds hardly bigger than my fist. At times I must lean out the window shooing them verbally.

Sunflowers recede, so do the owls, bats, hummingbirds. The usual jackrabbits and kangaroo rats make an appearance, and I am constantly braking to avoid squashing them. But I never mind put-tering home across the mesa; I only clench up as I approach Taos on unruffling macadam, going sixty.

By mid-September, the reservoir's ponds were gone; two circular metal water tanks for the quarter horses replaced them.

While I was stopped in the van, photographing the horses, a man and a woman rode over and reined in beside me. The lean and nearly toothless good old boy had a barely audible raspy voice that had trou-ble cutting through the wind. His daughter in the background might have been thirty, looked tough, and didn't say much. They both packed pistols. Strands of baling wire hung in loops on their saddles. He had a pair of wire pliers in his back pocket. They had been riding fences, making repairs.

His name was Jack Bradley; she never revealed hers.

We talked a few minutes; about rattlesnakes, Carson, the reser-voir disaster in the thirties. Bradley came into the area in 1928. He remembered there used to be more moisture; with luck you could grow gardens dry-farming. But no more. Now the dust piled up, the grass shriveled early. And the rattlers proliferated. Bradley himself had killed at least thirty that summer. A neighbor on the other side of the mountain had lost two horses to snakebites. An artist building a house southeast of Tres Orejas had killed a dozen already. . . .

They rode off. We parked beside the water tanks and worked south to the dam. The sunflowers had dried up into a trillion brittle stalks. Though only mid-September, a sense of loss and of imminent winter rode the air. Sylvia was nervous about unseen snakes, and as usual I pooh-poohed her concerns.

Angrily, she replied, "Well, right now is when they are most dangerous. They're denning, and their senses are all screwed up—they're kind of blind and confused and liable to strike out if they hear you coming. . . . "

We climbed to the road over the dam. On the other side still-flowering rabbitbrush livened up the Petaca Arroyo.

The Bradleys drove up in their pickup hauling a horse trailer, parked, and led their saddled animals from the trailer, mounted up, waved, and descended into the arroyo.

All of a sudden the sunset was incredible. Great spumes of yel-lowy-pink clouds whooshed up over Tres Orejas like mammoth Japa-nese waves. Sweeping smudges of pink surrounded us. Brilliant layers of fire to the west suggested spectacular world-ending disasters. It left us momentarily breathless . . . and then it dissolved into a routine dusk.

The Bradleys rode out of the arroyo, led their horses into the trailer, and drove south into the reservoir. Nighthawks, owls, and bats appeared: the calm air was again active with their predatory antics as we dropped off the dam and followed the tire tracks back to our car.

"Watch it!" Sylvia grabbed my arm.

My heart lurched. Ten feet in front of us a large rattlesnake twitched and writhed in agony: the Bradleys' pickup had crushed it. If Sylvia had not warned me, I would have sauntered right into it.

I poked at the dying snake with my tripod. It was a light yellow color, glowing phosphorescently in the twilight, startlingly vivid as if electrified. We laughed nervously, for I had been more frightened than Sylvia. Because I never expect to run into them, this one caught me completely by surprise.

The moon rose, a silver sliver half hidden in pink mist through which scattered stars were shining. Over the Sangre de Cristos, lightning zipped intermittently out of ponderous white thunderheads.

As we started home, a coyote jumped off the road into sunflower stalks. Owls, nestled in the tire ruts, challenged us fearlessly. Beyond the reservoir fence the Bradleys had built a campfire; their horses grazed next to the pickup. We told them they had now killed thirty-one snakes that summer. They nodded and stayed taciturn in the soft glare of their fire.

After that, as we slalomed through the kangaroo rats, thunderheads inched out over the Taos Valley, lightning was like a fantasy of distant threatening guns. Sylvia laughed happily, peppy and on top of the world. Then she coughed, and lit up another cigarette; I couldn't face her.

The rattlesnake I almost stepped on had given me an icy nudge from a bony hand. And smoke drifted out of her sensual mouth, sexy and deathlike.

I don't much like airplanes: I am afraid of flying. Yet on the deserted mesas surrounding Taos I must experience that freedom people so often connect to being airborne. Absolutely nothing hems me in. And as I traverse that panorama, the sensation is of floating, of a marvelous loneliness and aloneness, of a buoyancy akin to flying. No obstructions exist between me and "over there." Not a bird flies, nor a drop of rain falls, but that I take notice. The world is simple and limitless: everything is openly connected to the total ecosystem. I am unaware of private property, and thus the landscape seems very whole.

Behind my camera I wait to capture the moods of this country. Rain falls north of San Antonio Mountain. A huge fluffy puffball hovers over Picuris Peak. Mauve, yellow, and gray smoke does slow-motion dances in the sky. Horned larks twitter melodiously. My friend Sylvia appears waiflike and sexy in a way that breaks my heart: she is chipper, funny and sad, and I am scared for her health; sun setting south of Tres Orejas glows with radiant simplicity off her cheeks.

Daffodil yellows drench the valley: dinosaur-gray clouds boil turbulently out of the horizon, spitting tiny charges of fire that zap distant hilltops. Elsewhere, gleaming electric threads sputter jaggedly from the scalloped rusty-orange undersides of clouds determined to engulf Tres Orejas.

The valley is mesmerized by its own show. Air is charged with twinkling particles that imbue sagebrush with electric luminosity. Below Picuris, the Stakeout Restaurant glimmers. Up north the multiple diamonds of Taos begin to pulsate. Northwest of town, red blinking lights warn planes of power lines near the airport runway. In Carson, a single artificial bulb dimly violates the darkening solitude.

Six cows lumber past, heading somewhere. Car headlights proceed along a faraway dirt road, down by the Pueblo River Gorge . . . and I think it must be Alfred Peralta—owner of the Valco Laundromat next to Wackers—driving home after an evening fishing on the river, his creel full of fat browns.

The stock ponds hold little water in September, October, November. But I am drawn to those oases where no trees grow. A favorite is near the Martínez sheep corral, north of Tres Orejas. Two lie near Del Valerio's corrals directly east of the peak. Another lies hidden in western foothills. I am attracted by their isolated beauty, and their power to sustain the lives of cattle, small rodents, invisible insects.

Rabbits and mice, drawn to the water, are killed by other predators—weasels and coyotes. Cattle drink in the late afternoon, but some mysterious twilight signal sends them packing before dark: in single-file they head off through the sage to bed down in a distant arroyo. Always, flowers spring up near the stock tanks; a few survive, others are quickly devoured by ruminants. Near the sheep-corral tank nobody touches clumps of slender bone-beige flowers. One of Del Valerio's tanks is surrounded by nasty buffalo bur bushes whose intricate yellowy branches are full of spiky thorns. Cattle won't touch them because they are also very toxic.

An almost cruel irony, that army of hostile plants surrounding such a rare body of water.

When evening breezes relent, and all the dust has settled, pieces of sky are captured in stock-tank mirrors and held prisoner by the mundane earth. The smooth surfaces of muddy water become impossible-looking glasses that frame eternity like a master's painting. I don't understand fully the appeal of such reflections. Call them fabulous clichés, or wishy-washy metaphors, they still tickle me pink. A cloud, captured in limited mercurial liquidity, even if hackneyed becomes more beautiful. The mood grows surreal and potent. When violent clouds rage above the earth, and a storm blackens the sagebrush terrain, there is something hauntingly emphatic about a teardrop no bigger than a dime casting back a framed silvery echo of that turbulence, like a clear dispassionate eye on the universe . . . like a stupid self-conscious work of art.

Luke is learning to drive. At the controls of the VW bus he shifts, lets out the clutch, and tightly grips the jouncing steering wheel. I'm projecting myself high above the mesa, looking down at the insignif-

icant shape we must be against the land. Lazily, I track the progress of our red-and-white corpuscle as it travels the dusty veins, a child at the controls. The event is frightening. After all, Luke is only fourteen, yet there's no turning back the clock.

The little vehicle trailing a brown mist proceeds at thirty miles an hour along the middle road, turns off at Del Valerio's corrals, inches slowly into a rocky arroyo and up the other side, turns left by a broken fence post, arrives at a deserted house a half-mile west of the corrals, stops, tries to back up, and stalls.

Dead trees surround the collapsing house. Tilted sheds are rotting. Junk is scattered about—rusty cans, old coffee pots, an old-fashioned iron, bedsprings, pages from twenty-year-old magazines, the weathered timbers of a lost corral. Wind fluffs the dry grasses; a ghost-town forlornness prevails. Blind windows reflect a monotonous landscape, an impervious sky. An old cultivator will never be used again.

The rotted hoof and shiny legbone of a deer bound in baling wire hangs from an isolated crossbeam, twisting in the icy autumn winds.

The house stands alone, isolated and impersonal. What was it like when people lived there? How did they farm? Where did water for the trees come from? A well—or is it a cistern—was hand-dug, no doubt, and lined with rocks. It is almost filled to the brim with sand.

We return to the car. I float back up into the sky, and resume watch over that tin cocoon slowly maneuvering across the mesa; inside, a child is groping nervously toward the most dangerous skill of his life.

Luke and I stood on the earthen dam above a stock pond. Tina, the baby bulldog, snuffled nearby, rooting through fecund cowpies and mountainous piles of horseshit. The day had grown somber, intermittent snowflakes fell. The sky was eighteen shades of gray, the color of mouse fur and velveteen cats, junco feathers and degrees of wood smoke: it seemed eerily lucid and sorrowful. Nothing moved, or made a sound. A threatening calmness dominated the landscape. Prairie-dog mounds, on the dam and in the surrounding area, seemed without inhabitants, totally lifeless.

We heard a rumbling in the south—distant thunder? No, moments later a dustball rose against the misty ridges, approaching us. I first thought, A car. Soon, within the dust we could define the vague shapes of galloping animals—horses, bunched tightly, and racing forward at full speed.

From a mile away we watched them come, aimed directly for the stock tank. Their pounding hoofbeats grew louder, their dustball, grabbing rays of stormy sunlight, gleamed noisily.

Hell-bent-for-election, the horses pounded across the last hundred yards to the stock tank, where they reared in dramatically just inches from the water. Some pranced nervously, while others drank, ears pricked up, eyes glaring haughtily, resenting our intrusion. Skittishly, the colts drank, then the mares hurriedly took a few sips. Lips drawn back, the lead stallion trotted apprehensively among his charges, bumping them into line, dominating with his fierce moves and guttural noises.

As soon as they had drunk, the leader reared back and galloped once around the herd to assemble everybody, then took off at a full-tilt gallop; all the others broke into a run behind him. Soon they were swallowed by darkness and by the wild cloud of thick dust kicked up by their heels.

They disappeared. But we could hear their hoofbeats for minutes and for miles afterward. Then only a few snowflakes disturbed the quiet. Tina sniffed at a prairie-dog hole, wondering who slept down there in the rocky bowels of the cold earth.

I visited Los Angeles for three days just before Christmas 1980. During my stay, thirty-two people were murdered in the city. A seven-year-old girl walking home from her school bus stop was kidnapped and strangled. All the Christmas presents had been stolen from a father and son found killed in their southeast Los Angeles dwelling. Two shotgun-wielding robbers herded eleven patrons of a Bob's Big Boy restaurant into a tiny meatlocker and opened fire, killing three and wounding the others. The *Los Angeles Herald-Examiner* quoted a TV writer named Dick Pierce as saying: "I spent two tours of duty in Vietnam and I'm more scared on the streets of Los Angeles. My daughter has been threatened on the street, my wife has been mugged twice, and I'm getting ready to carry a gun on the street." I had lunch with old friends who nonchalantly explained they slept within reach of loaded .357 Magnums.

When I returned to Taos I desperately wanted to make love, and also indulge myself in that unruffled dusty ambience of the sage. I went to the stock ponds and found them frozen. Snow had fallen and on one pond wind had sculpted it into shapes like relief maps—snow manipulated to resemble renderings of Italy or of Japan. On the other less exposed tank, wind had not touched the surface, and the ice was perfectly layered with a misty film of fine white powder as clean and serene as confectioners' sugar.

Sylvia and I climbed a hill behind Del Valerio's corrals. Below us the children used old magazines and pieces of splintered wood from a derelict sheep trailer to build a fire. Their laughter carried faintly up to me. The evening was placid, uneventful. An hour ago wild clouds had cast shadows over Taos Mountain. But, as often happened, they had shrunk rapidly to an insignificant size, then disappeared, leaving the sky blushing softly in pink-iris tones that seemed like an extension of erotic flesh.

Ay, such a poignant smirrh of violets and pinks! Transcribed by a silence so total it was almost like being submerged underwater in a world without oxygen, the fragile light diffused by oceanic amber.

Suddenly, an enormous full moon emerged from behind Taos Mountain, taking us completely by surprise. Huge and voluptuous, it dominated the landscape for a moment. Sagebrush flared up under the polishing rays of reflected light, glowing as if faintly frosted, resembling a sea of brittle intriguing coral.

We tarried on the hill. Dark silhouettes of dervish children danced around the flames below. Corral timbers behind them appeared as delicate as jewelry made of intricately worked silver.

So easy to slide from there into memories of long and elaborate loving. . . .

I remember.

I remember you under the apple tree when Allende was killed, and also Victor Jara, and you gave me the collected poems of Neruda, with the inscription "And still persuade us to rejoice?" When your lips parted under the pressure of my mouth I felt dizzy and heartbroken from the facts of current history, even as I rejoiced at the gift of your white body in the grasses beneath the leaves, among the soft pulps of all the rotten apples. A magpie gave an odd uncomfortable squawk in the darkness, and the cats were out prowling, slinking without noise through crinkling leaves. Gazing past the black curve of your shoulder at the stars overhead, I could see reflected in the sky the atrocities of a Chilean primavera.

I remember.

I remember you against clean wrinkled sheets on an old tin bed in the city: the window was open, and drops of soot-darkened rain clung to the gauze curtains. In the autumn, when the yellow ginkgo leaves created an evocative mosaic across sidewalk cement, your flesh was as cinnamon-shadowed and sensual as wet sycamore trees, and your abundant hair fluffed around my fingers like the most intimate gauze on earth.

I remember.

I remember loving you on a carpeting of beige pine needles in a thick forest of evergreen trees where the sun couldn't penetrate. We ignored mosquitoes that sucked blood from our young bodies. Hundreds of small white moths drifted through the warm gloomy air,

going nowhere. In the mornings we hugged each other and listened to gulls dropping mussels onto the rocks of the inlet, while raindrops dripped off spruce branches, and the salty air curling through our windows seemed so heavy it was almost furry.

I remember.

I remember you on the ground in brilliant sunshine protected from view by flapping white sheets on the clothesline. Your brown skin provoked Mediterranean reveries as we made love among those billowing spinnakers. And I remember that last beautiful day of autumn when we knew our friend was dying, and, driving home, tried to accept that fact. When we did, we pulled off the highway onto a hill overlooking the distant twinkling city and made love.

I remember.

I remember you trailing after me in the sunflower fields as I marched to a bloodthirsty drummer, shooting sleek frightened doves out of the air. You said nothing when I quickly ripped the heads off cripples. I wiped my bloody hands on my trousers. Still, you followed me, your sensual lips pursed, your deep beautiful eyes refusing to comment. The day was lovely—sunny, warm, and archetypically autumnal. All afternoon I killed with a hardon, anticipating your body. Finally, we went home, and I cupped your breasts with my bloody fingers, I gripped your hips with my killer hands, and smelled the heady mixture of death, sunshine, and harvest as we played teasing erotic games in front of the fire, and later loved in blood.

I remember.

I remember dreams of Tina Modotti and Marilyn Monroe, the seacurves of anonymous women, long webs of soft hair, and Rio Grande boulders shaped like bold thighs, bellies, breasts, and tensed buttocks. I remember the harsh odor of a parking lot, the frozen rubbled earth beneath a night club's neon sign, streams of automobile headlights on the nearby highway as you crouched with your flimsy skirt up over your shoulders and your white panties shining: cruel and no-nonsense and irreproachably sexy.

I remember.

I remember flesh the color of seashells and river stones, smoothed by the flow of millenniums. Dim highlights repose on your shoulders like smudges of powdered sage. Your hair smells like dust with dainty deer tracks through it. Your vagina is sheep corrals in the late autumn, months after the animals depart, and all the dung is dry, and only the wind is alive, polishing weather-beaten driftwood-colored timbers. When I lower my face between your white thighs, it's like touching the killing tenderness of smooth basalt in a sandy arroyo, sculpted by a thousand years of rain. I suck on the muscles in your strong arms, separating ligaments and sinews with my tongue. I lick the smooth little hollows above your collarbones, at the base of your spine. I slide my cheeks across your voluptuous body and crush your breasts bulgingly together between your bent legs. I welcome your moist lips parted in a defiant snarl. I see the tracks of coyotes and sidewinders across your sandy belly, and picture you captured in a nest of argentine bones under the juniper trees, with a hundred tiny blue gin-smelling berries sprinkled across puddles of semen on your skin.

Coyotes are barking.

Snow is falling.

The mountain wears a halo of crimson vapor.

Frightened sheep have merged for safety under regal fire-spitting thunderheads.

Skeletons squirm impatiently.

Snakes are hunting for warm little victims.

Nighthawks are flaunting the esthetics of flight for seduction purposes.

You approach me with a crafty leer, tits dangling above my face, fulfilling old adolescent fantasies.

I remember that time in the back of the rollicking van: in the heat of our funky hijinks, you burst out giggling. When I asked why, you sputtered merrily, "I felt it!"

"You felt what?"

"I felt the earth move!"

We cracked up laughing!

SIXTEEN

One day in early December, I was stationed at the edge of a gully behind my tripod, waiting for shadows to elongate on a serpentine curve in a snow-covered dirt road. It was a cold sunny day, rather bland and hazy. No wind stirred through the sage. The mountains seemed far away and uninteresting. There was a lull in the panorama.

Suddenly, I heard a clatter of hooves, and turned. A black-and-white yearling cow raced through the sage, pursued by a dog and a man on horseback swinging a lariat. But the clever cow zigzagged, the horse stumbled and almost lost its footing. The scrufty dog barked plaintively as the cow sprinted out of sight into an arroyo.

The man reined in; gratefully, the dog halted, gasping. Lathered in foam, the horse snorted, and walked toward me. The man tipped his cowboy hat and said, "You see another rider around here?"

"Nope. You're the first live thing I saw all day."

"Well, my partner should be out here somewhere, looking for that damn other calf. We bought four of 'em yesterday and they all escaped last night from the corral. God damn milk-pan calves. I can't head 'em for love nor money, not even when I bump them."

Removing his hat he scratched his head, looking frustrated and sorely tired.

"Hell, I'm going home," he finished. "This is a green horse, and I'll kill her if I chase them anymore. Nice to meet you. . . ."

Turning, the horse limped off, followed by the droopy hound. In a minute they were gone, and my isolation was as pronounced as if no interruption had ever occurred.

I waited, but nothing happened. The day remained passive, hazy, and uninteresting. Icy sunshine neither warmed me nor allowed me to feel cold. Everything seemed dull and undemonstrative. A disintegrating shack across the road from my land creaked mutely. I sensed a kind of listless pain in the atmosphere.

In time, I knew, the light would change, a wind would rise, clouds would materialize. But not that afternoon, apparently. For nothing happened to capture my imagination.

I felt good, though slightly disappointed. And concluded I was spoiled. Or perhaps a trifle lazy?

I waited, irritated because Carson had sunk to the realm of everyday landscape. Or perhaps it was simply me who had sunk to the realm of an everyday human being.

No poetry, no bloodlust, no murder. Just an ordinary shlub with a camera, plodding through an ordinary landscape like a tourist, waiting to be coddled by easy sensations.

When all else fails, I invent adventures.

I pretend that all summer long I have built a small wooden house in Carson. Luke and Tania helped, and now it is finished. The one-room house faces northeast and southwest. Large plate-glass windows flank the only door; other windows let in the abundant southwest sun. Approximately twenty by thirty-five feet, the house has a peaked roof covered with ninety-pound green granulated paper. The walls are painted a sagebrush color. Window frames are white. The inside walls are also white and decorated with several pictures. One is a black-and-white silk screen of the four northern New Mexico seasons by Rini Templeton. Another is a bucolic print by Charles Reynolds, given to me by his son, Charley (of Rio Grande, trout-fishing fame): behind two Ranchitos adobes, cottonwoods are turning yellow; in the far background is Tres Orejas; big white clouds ride a cool wind across the soft blue sky.

I have a table, some papers, a kerosene lamp. A gas cookstove is connected to a portable twenty-five-gallon butane bottle outside the house. Inside a cupboard near the stove is a jar of instant coffee, two sardine tins, and a box of Uncle Ben's converted rice in which mice have nibbled holes. Mouse droppings litter the shelf paper, which is old pages from the *Albuquerque Journal*, taken from the sports section, no doubt.

Inside the cupboard there's also a small oblong gold-and-silver gift box containing a couple of pock-marked volcanic nuggets covered with a fine gray lichenous growth, a perfect staurolite I found east of the Pilar Arroyo Hondo many years ago, an arrowhead Andrés Martínez tells me was chipped out of petrified wood, a lizard skull, and a shrike feather.

A ten-gallon jerry can beside the stove contains drinking water. A coyote skull, a sheep vertebrae, a snakeskin line the window ledges. An old-fashioned milk bottle holds sprigs of delicate dry grasses.

Nondescript throw rugs partially cover the floor: I sleep in an old-fashioned tin bed I bought for twenty dollars in a secondhand store. The bed is made up with clean white linen sheets and old army blankets.

You and I enter this spare environment late one afternoon, carrying a six pack of Löwenbräu. We are feeling very sexy and happy and arrogant. Our intent is to while away a few hours talking about all the big and little things in life. Coincidentally, we plan to ball each other's brains out.

You have brought a small stash of the evil weed and some cigarette papers, because later on you'd like to get a little stoned. I never turn on myself, but I enjoy it when you do . . . although occasionally the intensity of your kinky sexual mood tips me out of kilter.

In drowsy half-light we relax on the doorstoop, drinking beer. As soon as evening shadows lengthen, crickets awaken and assert themselves. Small airplanes take off from the Taos airfield and fly overhead, heading south. We wave, but they do not tip their wings.

Coyotes prowl the arroyo a half-mile away, hunting in shoulder-high sagebrush. Their noisy barking chatter, always energetic, seems very excited and disorganized.

Closer by, nighthawks are hunting with their usual consummate grace.

I stroke my guitar, in the mood to sing a few songs. Some favorites, with which I greet the early stars, are "Yesterday," "Bridge Over Troubled Water," "The Mississippi Delta Blues," and "Delta Dawn." I'm no fantastic singer, but I can carry a tune, and tonight I think they sound all right.

I might also sing "Goodnight, Irene," and "Little Joe the Wrangler," and "On Top of Old Smokey," and "Little Town of Bethlehem."

Night develops clear and cloudless, without a moon. Snowy caps on the mountains are like white ivory. As for the stars?—well, as usual the only constellation I recognize is the Big Dipper. Nevertheless, all those astro-baubles are very lovely.

Of course, the Milky Way is a powerful spangled presence running across the sky, following the course of the Rio Grande Gorge, out of which it might have risen, a mythological spindrift misting off the huge boulders around which the white water churns.

Your simple lowcut white dress of flimsy jersey material is hiked up over your knees and bunched in your lap. Thin straps curl around your shoulders. Your feet are bare. My beer bottle is slippery and damp; I press it against your inside thigh. Inhaling sharply, you make no move to push the bottle away. Nor do you lower your eyes from the brilliant panoply of galaxies and constellations.

Time to go inside.

You light the kerosene lamp, turning the wick down low. We are hungry for each other in a lazy and very sensual way. My skin feels supersoft, my muscles are defined by a beautiful weariness. As if an orgasm gathered invisibly around us, eager to bathe our bodies in magic foam.

My hair prickles apprehensively. Your nipples harden without being touched. We luxuriate in wonderful anticipation, friendly and unthreatened. Mice scamper in the cupboard. Tiny feet dance through shadows against the far wall. My thinking is corny and poetic: *I'd like to huddle gratefully in the voluptuous cave of your body, and watch the storms go by.*

Something tiptoes outside. A bone scratches against the window. Cloth rasps slowly across the outside wall. The windows are mirrors reflecting our bodies. But I sense that death is out there, and I ain't afraid.

"Ha ha, death, you can't come in. We're busy. Better luck next time."

Teasingly, savoring the nuances, I pry the straps down off your shoulders. It is like this that we choose to celebrate life, give thanks to the mesa, or mourn the loss of a poet, a country, the destruction of a continent.

Moths flutter inanely against the window.

Sometimes a cruel and titillating sexuality takes over. I squirm uncomfortably, trapped in sadistic and pornographic fantasies. We acknowledge them in a kinky theater of childish make-believe, where nobody is ever hurt, and a gentle trust underlies pantomimed brutality. Our theater is exquisitely controlled. How we reached this balance, I don't know. But somehow we maneuver through the glittering knives without wounding each other. Orgasms are good, and often accompanied by peals of laughter. Your ample breasts threaten to break my fingers; your nipples tickle my kneecaps. I whisper weird tales into your ear and nibble your neck as you reach back between your legs to squeeze my balls. A transparent silky material undulates viciously against our bodies, responds to your arrogant salacious whims.

I often followed strange women in big cities, obsessed by the way cloth rippled between their buttocks and hair bounced off their shoulders. Nobody ever seemed neutral: I floundered in such rich agony. Afraid somebody would discover my horrible lusts, I desperately disguised my voyeuristic passions. Yet the slightest whiff of an old-fashioned high-school perfume knocked me out. Teen-age cheerleaders at high-school football games still torture me with their jazzy little shuffles against that background of stupid mayhem.

The hooded cloth scrapes against our walls. Icy bones slide across the windows, faintly squeaking. Coyotes laugh like frivolous maniacs. Reflected in a window, your face tilts back, slyly smiling as you quietly moisten your lips; the graceful curve of your throat extends down between swollen breasts through which the brightest stars of a cool constellation are shining.

Landscape and weather are masculine and feminine, profoundly sexual. The warm vanilla odor of sunny pines has much in common with the perfume of your intimate body. Halloween gusts that propel leaves clattering against windows in brittle noisy rage have always evoked the howls of hair-raising orgasms. I fear the delight your fingernails take in drawing fine bloody lines up the back of my muscular thighs.

Clouds boiling together in fervent copulation imitate the constricting pink muscles of your throat eagerly giving head. The traveling silvery wrinkles of wind-driven cat's-paws across the surface of lakes or little watering holes remind me of orgasms starting at the base of your spine and rippling urgently up your back and across your shoulders, exploding at the base of your neck with the impact of an erotic slug.

Once I was confused by the ferocious tenderness of grappling in your rich blood. I wanted to hit you. You said, "It's okay, if you like." But I was shocked, and couldn't go that far. Nevertheless, I love all these rambunctious fucks. I love it when we are playful and teasing, sly and sardonic; I love it when we giggle and whisper, babble nonsensically, and suddenly grow sober. I love all the sea changes that go down in an hour. I love it when we are virtuosos at innuendo, and I make you squirm just by breathing in your hair, or tonguing an earlobe, and you trigger my lusts by the nasty tone of your voice saying three crude words, just once. Mmmm . . . it sure is good to nuzzle, munch, lick, root about, follow directions, eat, gobble, suck on, slurp. I love mirrors, slithering across the kitchen floor, raising my hips to your face in the bathtub, parking in the dark, playing teen-agers at the movies.

Remember that time in the pines above the city when headlights swung off the highway, and we tumbled off the roof of the car stark-naked, landing in a bed of prickly-pear cactus, and we had mistakenly locked the car?

"Die? Me? *Never!*" once cried Tolstoi's sister-in-law, Tanya Behrs.

Something rustles outside, sniffing at the cracks in the wall. Footsteps? I hear dirt sifting between the skinny bones of bleached toes. Coyote cries echo mysteriously through invisible caverns.

When I am happiest, the tragedy of human existence flares up in me like a radiant and beautiful cancer. It kills nothing, though I weep; the knowledge gives great pain and heightens my awareness of the privileges I enjoy.

Did you see them, the shadows of passing horses? Reflected in the nearby window, your mouth is full, your eyes are wide, looking up at me, I am astraddle your chest, your breasts bulge tautly together up near your throat, and the Picuris reflection against my chest is momentarily blurred by the grave image of wild horses intent on a different destination.

A mouse squeaks. A breath of air sneaks through a crack, circles the smoky chimney of our lamp, and somehow causes the low flame to flicker. Thieves barely the size of molecules are plying their trade at random. Never have my shoulders been more tenderly kissed.

What *is* that outside our little house? Something weird scampered past, like a Christmas tree, and insanely giddy. It had wings, I think. They brushed against the roof, disoriented by the darkness, and by the disturbing vibrations of our passion.

Bones scraping against the window left behind a subtle rind of frost, as if from the smoke of an unholy brush wielded by a calavera trickster.

Your reflection is so lush it bruises the glass. You kneel on the bed, hands braced against your thighs, I kneel behind you, my hands fondling your breasts. I watch them bounce in my palms—*plop! plop!* You watch the process intently, eyes slightly narrowed and scornful and smug, queenly and prophetic, doomed by the powerful cravings of your body.

A lull. Air is cool and brittle. I douse the lamp, open the door. Stars cascade with melodious *pings!* off my shoulders like the weightless cool fireflakes from sparklers. Behind me, you press your belly into my buttocks, reach your hands around, and hold my penis while I take a leak, playfully trying to write *your* name in the sand. Then you kneel before me, sucking off the last yellow droplets. Rising, you poke a finger against my nose; whispering, "Don't go away, Johnny," you walk into the sage to pee. Why do you travel so far away? Your body shines like a radioactive doe.

The night is both lucid and perverse. I smell danger. Things are roaming around out there. But I am not frightened. For starters, I am not a tenth as vulnerable as the real denizens of this landscape.

You return, we embrace in the dark. Can you hear lizards sleeping? Without light to goad them, moths have quit their senseless fluttering. Somewhere a kangaroo rat lies helplessly beside a barrel cactus, bitten by a plague flea, dying horribly in cruel throes of mousey agony. Coyotes are farther away, now, barking north along the edge of the gorge, stopping occasionally to gaze down at the distant river where silver trout fan their fins behind boulders, cold-blooded and patient and voracious, waiting out the night.

You want to smoke a joint. All right, I'll roll it for you. You lie on your back on the bed; I straddle your hips. Your hands resting against my knees, you peer with drowsy anticipation as I tap the green mulch out of a small garlic salt bottle into the trough of a thin yellow cigarette paper.

No doper, I'm not real adept at it. I rolled my first joint at the age of thirty-nine. I am afraid to get high and lose control of my imagination. The few times we smoked together were fun. Sex was urgent and kinky, on the verge of being brutal. That unnerved me, even though I liked the offbeat intensity with which we nailed each other. Still, it was a different sexual realm, not really anchored—for me—in loving. It bothered me, and I honestly don't miss that particular thrill. But when only you are high, the balance is fine. Your quirky urgency turns me on. You are more innocent than I under that

influence. Love drools from your body like too many soap bubbles from a washing machine. My head is stuck through a hole in the canvas of a carnival contest area, and you are coming at me like a huge lemon-meringue pie traveling ninety miles an hour!

Tap, tap, twist, jiggle. Precious green flakes float onto your belly. Your palms are damp. I lick the cigarette paper, staring at your eyes regarding me while my tongue tip dampens stickum.

I twist the ends of the joint. Do you remember when they were called "reefers," and only jazz musicians and crazy criminals smoked them? And we knew that one puff opened wide the door to junkiedom's perdition? Geez, it's strange to look back on college days. All we ever did at Hamilton was get shit-faced drunk and kill each other in car accidents. Seven years later, my brother had a smack junkie roommate; everybody smoked dope openly, took LSD trips, and copped mescaline. I was still afraid to drop, shoot up, toot, smoke, or in any way ingest or inhale stuff that would blow my mind. Although I live in Taos, I have never read the Don Juan books, or attended a peyote meeting. I am very old-fashioned. I've never even sat still for hours on end mulling over a koan while a fierce jikijitsu waited for me to nod off so he could give me a whack with his oak kesaku.

Between your breasts I lay the doobie. Then brush together all the pot crumbs, pinch them up and drop them back in the jar. We hesitate, assessing each other. These days you look at me when we make love. At first your eyes were always closed: I asked you to open them. Now you like to watch our reflections. Or study my expression when I come.

Sitting, you light the cigarette. I fetch a tall glass of water, because you will get very thirsty. Then I lie back on the bed. Our little house is flooded with that odor. One whiff and I'm almost heady!

The coyotes have traveled far. I can still hear their faint barks, fading fast like morning stars. A mysterious force out there rearranges all the mesa bones. Tomorrow, the coyote bones in the arroyo will be on top of a hill. That horse jawbone near the tall anthill will have retreated to a bed of volcanic rocks near three ancient fence posts supporting a single strand of rusted barbwire.

While you are doing your doobie, three scenes involving important friends come to mind.

In the first scenario, Stephanie Sonora is sitting across from me at the Doña Luz Restaurant in Taos, nibbling on snails. She is all dressed up like a gorgeous gypsy, resembling a cross between the early Sophia Loren and bombastic Anna Magnani as she spins her delightful tale, her exaggerated eyes sparkling like those of a priceless female genie who has just popped clear of an ancient champagne bottle.

Her story takes place in 1958 on Madeira, where she happened, one evening, to watch a century plant bloom.

"We were in a Palladian villa, a type of pension, and the host invited us out to the garden—me and Aldo and three other couples. It was after dinner, I guess around ten, already dark, when we walked into the garden and assembled around this bush. What is it they say about century plants—that they only bloom once every hundred years? Well, there we were in this beautiful garden, so sculpted . . . as if it had a velvet lining . . . very English. And drenched in romantic moonlight, of course. And overlorded by a billion stars. Everybody was all dressed up, the women in beautiful silk dresses, the men strictly black-tie. I had on the most beautiful outfit in the whole world, a heavy cotton skirt with knifelike pleats and black embroidery—I had bought it in Lisbon. My black silk jersey blouse was tied at the shoulders . . . and of course I had on very *very* high heels."

Stephanie draws in a deep breath, and I can see the wheels turning busily behind her eyes as imagination and memory embellish and concoct with marvelous animated relish.

"Well, we all sat around in these spindly little antique chairs, eating very fragile and sweet cookies, and of course drinking a famous bottle of Madeira wine that had to have been at least a hundred years old. Our host was a very polite man. I think he was a botanist. And what an island on which to be a botanist! When people dream about an island, they *must* dream about a place like Madeira. Roses, passion flowers, apples and bananas all over the place. It's so lush and voluptuously green—like paradise. And there we were, sitting around this bush, our hands in our laps, waiting for it to bloom. And then right before our eyes it actually *happened*. It had such creamy, dense flowers, and it happened so slowly. We were absolutely mesmerized as those thick petals opened up. It was like a butterfly coming out of a cocoon as the buds bloomed. Extraordinary! At the end we were exhausted, because it took so long to open, but we tried to stay alert. I felt so . . . so *whole*. Who was it that said, 'When a flower opens, the heart revives' . . . ?"

I jump, from that image of Stephanie on Madeira, to Taos on a recent September evening at dusk. Doug Terry and I are playing tennis, trying to finish a match. We started playing tennis together a half-dozen years ago. At the start, I won easily because Doug had never previously held a racket. But he was determined. For two years, though, he could not win a match. Then he improved, and I seemed to grow older and more inept. Eventually, we became fairly equal. Then we kept a record of our contests, and competed for a garish gold-plated trophy Doug had located in the bowels of a local sporting-goods store. Each match became an exhausting do-or-die encounter as we played with the awkward insane passion of complete duffers elevating to art their amateur tomfoolery by the mere intensity of their feelings.

So it is dusk: the September light is quickly dying. We are racing to complete a match before dark. I won the first set, Doug won the second—now in the third we are tied six games apiece and it's seven-all in the tie breaker. Such a contest has not been seen since Borg outlasted McEnroe in the Wimbledon finals, 1980!

We are both real pooped. Wheezing stertorously, half crippled by asthmatic apoplexy and a fibrillating ticker, I am determined to die rather than lose. Doug's racket is bloody from torn blisters on his palm, an oft-separated shoulder is killing him, his trick ankle is swollen to twice its normal size, and his meniscusless knees aren't helping matters, yet he would rather leave his feet leaping for a ball (skidding painfully across the concrete on his nose and elbows) than give up a single point.

Neither of us can see the half-dead Wilson high-altitude offering, yet somehow we sustain one rally after another. To an outside observer, we must look like the Laurel-and-Hardy-meet-Jerry-Lewis Amateur Sweepstakes, but for us the game is high drama, life and death are on the line.

You see, we both used to be athletes whose bodies rarely let us down. We had many triumphs, and drank often from the cup of American sporting glory. But those days are long gone. I, for one, no longer feel, as an intimate part of my daily motivations, that almost crippling need to compete. Yet a wonderful, decidedly comic—almost absurd—theater of the old killer instincts describes Doug's and my contests together. We laugh at ourselves, and yet strain atrociously to conquer. Exalting in victory, we cringe and grovel despairingly in defeat. In a sense, it is a whacky last act of our athletic youths . . . and we love it.

So saying, I lunge for the shadow of a ball, and somehow connect, trying to lob it over the head of my friend, the wounded elephant who's gallumphing toward the net. With consummate lack of grace, he stretches onto tiptoes and takes a mighty whack at a spheroid he can only dimly perceive. The ball clatters noisily off the wooden frame of his racket, yet somehow bloops over the net into the opposite corner of my court . . . and at long last I have gone down to ignominious defeat.

I just sit where I have fallen, huffing noisily, soaked in sweat, and calling Doug Terry every foul epithet I can think of while he lies crumpled at the net, too tired to leap it, busily concocting a series of patronizing and obnoxious put-downs that will make my next half hour miserable. . . .

And both of us are as contented as we ever get these days.

My final scenario occurs at midnight. The phone rings, it is another good friend, Harvey Kalmeyer. For years he lived in Taos; recently he moved to Denver. We don't meet much anymore, but we have a love for each other, and try to stay in touch.

Harvey hails from Brooklyn, and always comes on something like a Yiddish gangster with a heart of gold. He inspired the maven pizza, an onion-and-green-chili concoction that for years was a favorite staple at the House of Taos Restaurant. These days Harvey is a burly big-city carpenter-contractor with a strong sense of responsibility to people and environment, a commitment to ethics and literature, a down-home sense of humor, a creative despair about the state of the world, and a mildly jaundiced but thoroughly upbeat lust for life.

Tonight, his phone call is in honor of Nelson Algren, who just died. "Hey," he says, "did you read Pete Hamill's eulogy on Algren? I got it right here. It was in the *Rocky Mountain News*."

I had not seen it. "Okay," he says, "then shut up for a minute, Nichols, 'cause I'm gonna read it to you."

And so he reads me the article over the telephone. Then we reminisce about Nelson Algren, who had died in Sag Harbor, Long Island, far from Chicago. For his last works he had been unable to find a publisher. His passing seemed to have gone unnoticed by an indifferent America to whom he gave such tough and beautiful classics as *The Man with the Golden Arm* and *Never Come Morning*.

"Shit! They shoulda took him back and buried him in Chicago," Harvey wails, and I wholeheartedly agree.

Further discussing Algren, we remember his book *Chicago: City on the Make*. In particular I recall a line right at the start: "I submit that literature is made upon any occasion that a challenge is put to the legal apparatus by a conscience in touch with humanity."

Nelson Algren was a good old boy and an important American writer. He was one of the people who lured me into literature and taught me what to strive for. And I am deeply touched that a friend like Harvey would call at midnight to commemorate his passing.

Now you turn to me, ready for love.

We nuzzle and tease, easy with each other, young and horny and happy. I never felt this confident or physically comfortable at eighteen or twenty-one. It takes time to accept a natural rhythm.

The night is as black as the bottom of the ocean at 12:00 A.M. Stars wink fiercely like the eyeballs of Samurai warriors. Our open door captures no music from the mesa. Imagine how the wind stops in treeless Outer Mongolia; and a desert horseman halts atop a sandy dune, afraid to budge for fear the crystal atmosphere will shatter.

One day when I was a small boy I up-ended a large rotten log, exposing two silky pink salamanders. Unaccustomed to brightness, they squirmed a little. Seldom have I witnessed anything so aggressively fragile, nor felt so gigantic as when I hovered above those tiny salamanders. Even though a child, I think I had insights into their extraordinarily heightened vulnerability. I realized, also, that I had invaded a cherished privacy. Carefully, I lowered the rotten log back onto those blind denizens of the mossy underworld.

That little boy appears right now, looming over our house on the mesa. Carefully taking the one-room dwelling between thumb and forefinger, he lifts it off the ground, exposing the miniature pink people linked together fucking. Fascinated, he breathes lightly so as not to disturb the lovers. They squirm in interesting curious ways, emitting faint passionate sounds.

Terribly small, completely defenseless.

Finally, they twitch violently and collapse. Will something else happen? After a moment, one of the precious beings drinks from a teeny water glass. After that, they lie still, cushioned against each other's bodies.

So much for the mystery at the heart of our universe. The gigantic little boy feels no further need to tarry. He replaces the house shell over the lovers, then quietly—in his ten-league boots—strides off for an ice-cream cone at the North Pole.

Sleep faster, sweetheart: the angels need our pillows.

The 5:00 A.M. landscape still quivers beneath a heel of implacable darkness. Wearily, I walk outside and stop for a moment, scratching my belly. Then I piss with a sigh; wonderful goose bumps scamper up my spine into the base of my brain. Tipping my head back, I stare aloft, happy to be mesmerized by the clarity of all those shooting stars.

I have a terrifying vision. . . .

It is 1882, the year of my grandmother's birth. We have slaughtered all the buffalo: only their bones remain. The bleached-white skeletons of animals killed for sport, slaughtered for tongues and heads, litter the rolling plains as far as the eye can see. Because fertilizer plants will buy the bones for phosphates, and sugar refineries can purchase them for carbon, buffalo bones have become big business. And the last survivors of once great Indian tribes now canvass the grassy barrens with bags over their shoulders, harvesting the remains. Shaggy, destitute and demoralized, sick and limping, the native people collect white bison bones for a buck, like janitors at the finish of a macabre carnival. They plod listlessly through that horrible American Dream, the logical outcome of our rapacious lust for milk and honey, a metaphor that grows more pertinent and frightening each hour.

That's it. My vision of the future set a hundred years ago. Those bands of defeated natives harvesting the spoils, dragging them off to railheads for shipment to eastern factories that will grind them up into salable commodities.

The 1882 sun is merciless: wind reverberates through gigantic rib cages with thin melancholy whines. Occasionally, a Cheyenne woman or a Kiowa brave gives a short tubercular cough . . . under the pitiless clarion-blue sky.

Sometimes I stand there in one of my special places, mystified by the natural world. And a cry rises in my throat: Why can't we keep our hands off? Why are we so compelled to "grow" and "change things," and rub them out? A pox on the invention of capitalism, the free-market economy, planned obsolescence, growth-for-the-sake-of-growth, expand or expire! If nobody had bulldozed dirt roads through the sagebrush, people would rarely visit Carson. Of course, I'd still hike over with my backpack and a sleeping bag. And I would know the landscape a thousand times more intimately.

Regularly, while setting up my camera, I know that I am a fool, a ripoff artist, a charlatan. Look at all the metals and chemicals torn from the earth to fashion my equipment: aluminum, steel, silver. How much pollution was created to forge the products with which I capture the mesa? How about the emissions released during fabrication of my automobile? Steel mills belched poisons, chemical factories discharged effluents into dying lakes and rivers, smokestacks spewed acid rain into countless reservoirs.

Sometimes the paradoxes leave me speechless. I can't make a move without murdering. Feverishly, I focus on a sunset and snap the shutter: *immortality!* But at the same instant I also kill the thing I venerate.

Rationalizations abound. If I transmit a sense of wonder to others, they will help save the earth. But in my darker moments I think: Bullshit! Admiring the planet, I destroy it. Monoxide from my tailpipe curdles the sage. "Here he comes," cry all the rabbits, kangaroo mice, and owls. "Here he comes," howl the coyotes and the wild horses.

"Here he comes," say the mountain, the crested wheat, and the snake-weed. "Here comes our lover, here comes our fancy-shmancy paramour, here he comes in his killing machine to regale our beauty, and, with his words and with his little camera, to slit our wild throats."

I turn off the motor, but the smell of hot oil disturbs me, so I walk away quickly. I am at one of a half-dozen hallowed places: on top of Tres Orejas, beside Del Valerio's stock pond, at the bottom of the Carson reservoir. Despite the lethal contradictions, I feel strong and hopeful; I soon relax absolutely. No need to ponder. I am just there, letting the landscape and weather happen however they will. A euphoria starts to build up in me, a sensation as precious as my childlike belief in Santa Claus a million years ago. Harsh contradictions drain out the soles of my shoes into the dusty earth. I accept the sky's magic, rejoice over odors. I hear no planes, no autos, I recall no lovers' quarrels, resurrect no guilt. Laziness floods my body with an almost sexual goo.

Early astronomers gazed at the stars, absolutely ignorant but profoundly intrigued. Face to face with the infinite universe, they refused to despair: and so their incredible observations fired up the brilliant foundations of modern imaginations.

I'm not ashamed to let Thoreau do the talking for me: "The west of which I speak is but another name for the Wild: and what I have been preparing to say is, that in Wildness is the preservation of the World."

So be it. I admire the texture of bones with my fingers; I thrust my face into the sage and inhale deeply; I trace with my eyes a ridge line carved over the millenniums; I play with the sky, making threads of it into cat's cradles between my fingers, I exhale it as a fine blue smoke, I mold wonderful carnival clouds . . . and throw beautiful birds—ravens, magpies, owls, shrikes, and zopilotes—across the curved fabular dome under which all the earthly elements are forever simmering.

It pleases me immensely to exalt in my capacity for wonder.

SEVENTEEN

A danger of a book like this is that it will attract more people to the Taos area, thus accelerating the despoliation of a fragile valley.

I have thought hard about this possibility. In the end, I concluded it would do no good to keep my mouth shut. People will move here no matter what. By the time I arrived in 1969, the rush was already on. All New Mexico lay on the block, as all of America has been on the block since the first Spaniards and the first Pilgrims came ashore bent on plunder. Taos history is no isolated story: what has happened and is happening here, went on and is going on across the nation.

Still, the change in twelve years has been real sobering. A majority of recent immigrants have only their self-interest at heart: it is the nature of our system to train people in this selfishness. Most territories are places to be exploited rather than cherished. Of course, some newcomers arrive with altruistic motives, like many Americans in Vietnam—and then they leave a shambles behind when they take a powder.

The shambles occurs when land and people are treated solely as commodities.

In the long run, I feel it will do more good than harm for me to plead the case of this valley. Longtime locals here are not fragile, but many of them are tired. The toughest of them cannot be defeated, but they are mortal, and will die off. When that happens I see the valley becoming monolingual and monocultural, homogenized into a McDonald's and Sonic Burger mindset.

Taos is a funky and passionate place, about to be massacred by the great American lust for Lack-of-Passion. In the few years since electricity entered the Pueblo, the stories of grandparents have been replaced by *The Dukes of Hazzard* and *Charlie's Angels*. Tract homes are creeping onto the mesas. A double chain-link fence, topped by barbwire concentration camp–style, was recently constructed around the grammar school football field, ostensibly to discourage vandals. I don't know yet if the budget provides armed guards: perhaps only Dobermans trained to dismember will patrol the perimeters.

Flexibility is leaving the system. Soon Colonel Sanders will annihilate memories of Padre Martínez; and Walt Disney will bury Joaquin Murieta and Reis Tijerina.

I am not a lonely old fool champing at a singularly unimportant bit. What is happening here reflects in microcosm the story of America.

Toward the end of his book *Disturbing the Universe*, the nuclear physicist Freeman Dyson has a chapter entitled "Clades and Clones." *Clade*, he writes, is "a Greek word meaning a branch of a tree, in this case the evolutionary tree on which the twigs are individual species. When some climatic or geographical revolution occurs, upsetting the established balance of nature, not just one new species but a whole clade will appear within a geologically short time."

He next explains that the major evolutionary changes on earth have been caused by "the formation of new clades, rather than by the modification of established species." This phenomenon occurs with cultural and social changes as well as within strictly biological evolutions. It accounts for the often frustrating, but incredibly rich and vital linguistic and cultural diversification on the globe.

A *clone*, Dyson then asserts, is the opposite of a clade. It is "a single population in which all individuals are genetically identical." In short, the makings of endless repetition.

"Clades are the stuff of which great leaps forward in evolution are made. Clones are evolutionary dead ends, slow to adapt, and slow to evolve. Clades can occur only in organisms that reproduce sexually. Clones in nature are typically asexual.

"All this," according to Dyson, "has its analog in the domain of linguistics. A linguistic clone is a monoglot culture, a population with a single language sheltered from alien words and alien thoughts." And, "in human culture, as in biology, a clone is a dead end, a clade is a promise of immortality."

Finally, he asks the question, "Are we to be a clade or a clone? This is perhaps the central problem in humanity's future."

It is certainly a central problem in the future of Taos. This was once a highly original valley, with dark and mysterious sides, with lullabies and murderous intentions, with a profound veneration for the disturbing vitality of nature and human beings.

Currently, the drive is to vapidify all these qualities, making Taos a clone of the rest of the United States, ending forever its originality and polyglot cultures, cutting those mesas and mountains down to size with Bellamah-type homes and Kawasaki dirt bikes.

For the record, I doubt Taos or the rest of America can be saved short of a radical social and environmental revolution. I dread a violent conflagration within our borders: I pray that the simple state of the planet's resources may force even the passionate capitalists of our time to give up on planned obsolescence, and on the worship of an expand-or-expire syndrome.

If, somehow, we retain enough of the clade in our energetic society, we may adapt instead of creating a useless holocaust to prolong our conspicuous consumption a few more years before all the oil runs out.

In the battle to change the destructive nature of our society, hope for the future is a potent weapon against the manipulative cynicism of the sauve-qui-peut, every-person-for-themselves mentality of our eco-nomic system, which depends on an alienated and ruthlessly competitive populace for its survival.

I insist on a hopeful outlook. I trust I will always have the courage to insist on this attitude, no matter how desperate the situation appears to be. This does not mean that I am a hopeless idealist, or an innocent romantic. It means simply that in order to work for the salvation of the planet, we *must* believe in its future. We must love life, love America, love the Taos Valley.

I think profit motives derive their strength from despair. If we accept the end of the world, what's to stop us from hastening the inevitable while making hay while the sun shines? I see capitalism founded on this principle: socialism makes a lot more human and ecological sense to me . . . although everyone is going to have to redefine the nature of materialism in the next fifty years, Communists included.

Pablo Neruda has said it for me:

I still have absolute faith in human destiny, a clearer and clearer conviction that we are approaching a great common tenderness. I write knowing that the danger of the bomb hangs over all our heads, a nuclear catastrophe that would leave no one, nothing on this earth. Well, that does not alter my hope. At this critical moment, in this flicker of anguish, we know that the true light will enter those eyes that are vigilant. We shall all understand one another. We shall advance together. And this hope cannot be crushed.

Momentary despair does not make me panic. Only an icy soul would not often despair over the cruel machinations that systematically massacre great sectors of humankind. Nevertheless, it is important not to wallow in the tragedies of Auschwitz and Vietnam. Those dark forces are constantly afoot, concocting plagues that riddle the human spirit— granted. Yet they are not all-powerful: Life . . . all the great tintinnabulations of the senses . . . plus the mighty adventures within the struggle each day to shape a new blossom . . . forbids it.

Therefore I am certain nobody is going to protect the dynamic and positive roots of Taos by hiding the fact that this area exists. That would leave it defenseless against the outer world. It must be very clear to all of us who feel a stake in the future of Taos and our country, and thus in the world, that, as Joseph Conrad once made indisputably clear in his novel *Victory,* the outer world always arrives.

Frankly, I don't think you can emphasize enough the beauty of what should be preserved for future generations. Too often we negate the simple things that once nourished our lives: repeatedly, our forgetful memories need jogging.

What I have to say about Taos pertains to everywhere. Taos is only a metaphor for that entire continent F. Scott Fitzgerald once imagined as the last piece of terrain wild and beautiful enough to be commensurate with our capacity for wonder. Hence, my defense of this small territory should speak to all of us, from the Arctic Circle to the lattermost mist-shrouded island south of Tierra del Fuego.

Often Spanish-speaking people approach me, asking, "How could you know so much about our culture—after living in Taos for only two and a half years—to write your novel, *The Milagro Beanfield War?*"

My response is that ninety percent of the novel is universal. Similar struggles, cultures, and people exist in such disparate places as New York City, rural Vermont, Virginia, France, Spain, and Guatemala.

This understanding was a part of my sensibility long before I arrived in New Mexico.

EPILOGUE

So we saunter toward the Holy Land, till one day the sun shall
shine more brightly than ever he has done, shall perchance shine
into our minds and hearts, and light up our whole lives with a great
awakening light, as warm and serene and golden as on a bankside in
autumn.

—Henry David Thoreau
"Walking"

Sometimes I wonder: how will I die?

Occasionally, I have playful fantasies about my demise. In the sixties, I saw myself dying in some Central American jungle, a rifle in my hand—shades of Che Guevara. Nowadays, the drama is less egotistical.

Inevitably, I develop incurable cancer. Of the prostate . . . or of my long-suffering intestines. Gathering friends and children around, I disperse the pertinent spiritual and physical legacies. Open and humorous, bawdy and lyrical, thoughtful and gentle, I fear not my impending doom—though it arrive next Monday . . . or at the age of eighty. With my death I teach the children to have no fear of dying. "His dignity is impeccable," they whisper. Utilizing an iron will, I live long enough to finish my current project, perhaps a great novel . . . or a last bittersweet memoir of the fading Taos hills.

When all is said and done, I struggle from bed, slip Louis Ribak's pistol into a pajama pocket, sneak out to the rattletrap VW bus, and take a final trip to Carson.

Somehow, I muster the strength to climb Tres Orejas. Ravens navigate disinterestedly through the still crepuscular air. As shadows lengthen a rattlesnake buzzes; I steer politely around it. Rain fell earlier, the strong scent of damp sagebrush flutters against me with truly physical intensity, like compassionate wings.

God, how my feeble heart soars!

I contain it, avoiding a prematurely fatal fibrillation . . . and push to the mountaintop, choosing the middle ear.

There stand I, shivering in the chilly autumn breezes I love. New snowcaps on the Sangre de Cristos are as beautiful as ever. Evening stars ride serenely above the quiet hills. An overlarge full moon rises behind Taos Mountain. Nighthawks are fluttering. The triple hoot of an owl cascades up from the piñon trees. Along the reservoir floor behind me, the unshod hooves of carefree galloping horses raise a cloud of dust.

I catch my breath as coyotes start barking. And touch the pistol to my temple . . . and utter a final benediction: "Hasta la victoria siempre." Then, with a grateful and sorrowful heart, I pull the trigger . . . and land forever relaxed among redolent boulders that fracture my cheekbones and shoulder blades with loving brutality.

Hopefully, nobody discovers me for days. First dibs on my flesh goes to the coyotes and rats and hawks and eagles, to the ravens and magpies who'll strip off my meat and muscles, leaving behind white and hollow bones.

I am haunted by dreams of utterly peaceful bones.

And so. . . .

It is dawn.

The noisy magpies are chattering. Duke is curled up under the red sleeping bag. In the other room Tina is snoring.

Outside, a strange sound: the twittering of birds—starlings—mingles with a mysterious thumping. After a moment I realize that a hundred birds have landed in the crab apple tree; their activity jiggles the branches, causing ripe fruits to fall.

So I wake up with a hardon, laughing, and the possibilities of this new day are limitless.

I roll over; you are beside me. I take your full breasts in hand, they burn with the fever of deep sleep and lazy dreams. Your entire body pulses, wonderfully peachy and on fire. I am so hard it feels brittle. You hug me between your thighs, and part your lips. We kiss, and I am tickled pink by the opulence you offer so ingenuously. I'd like to sing of your favors like Thomas Wolfe, Gaston Lachaise, Rodin. I wish we had an old-fashioned radiator, clanking and hissing out steam, while dry snowflakes ticktocked against the window . . . or wind-tumbled leaves scratched soporifically against our stove pipes.

Ahhh . . . the moment is perfect. I relax among the white contours of your drowsy flesh, woozy with incurable lusts. I nibble your neck and picture your breasts flattened out as wide as muffled saucers of marshmallow fluff against the rumpled sheet. Your buttocks fit exactly against my abdomen. Your smells are delicious—from your underarms, between your legs, within your blowsy hair. Juices! Muscles! Erotic secretions, tongues, and cigarette smoke—cancer and death on your sexy breath.

Through the open window come traces of horse dung, rotting apples, last night's skunk, cedar smoke, and the mysterious cottony odor of puffy white clouds.

Life as it should be, darlin'.

Purple prose and all.

The Last Beautiful Days of Autumn

Clouds over Taos Mountain

Lunch on November elm leaves

Grackles at kitchen feeder

Storm in my backyard

Duke

Loretta in the first snow

Half-frozen meadow grasses

My neighbor's cattle

Scrub-oak leaves

Wood nymph in Garcia Park

Just another aspen

November apple orchard

Raven in October snowstorm

Water-snake skeleton

The view on Power Line Trail

Brown Trout Alley

Mike Kimmel at Little Arsenic

Doug Terry, searching for sunglasses

Two-pound brown trout

Four-pound rainbow

Charley Reynolds

Mike Kimmel and a red admiral

Shel Hershorn at Little Arsenic

Taos Mountain from Suicide Slide

View south from the high bridge

The Rio Grande at Pilar

Sheep near the Martínez corral

Andrés Martínez atop Tres Orejas

Herding the sheep to water

Pacomio Mondragón and Andrés Martínez

Evelyn Mares Valerio and Isabel Vigil

Tanya Mares and two-headed calf

Pop on the Tres Orejas summit

Tania Nichols and Tanya Mares

Luke Nichols releases a magpie

Stephanie Sonora

Leo Garen and Billie Beach

Craig Vincent

Sylvia Landfair

Steve Reynolds and his mom, Lois

Doug Terry bags another dove

The author at Bernardin Lake

Bradley's horses

Road to the reservoir

Water tank in the Carson reservoir

Horse skeleton south of Los Cordovas

Tina, the baby bulldog

Taos Mountain from the Carson mesa

Sagebrush in limestone

Sheep moth (aka Hera moth)

Coyote bones

Rocks in a Carson arroyo

Old sheep trailer at Del Valerio's corrals

Tuft of mesa grass

Collared lizard

Arroyos at midday

Evening over Tres Orejas

December sunset over Tres Orejas

View west from Tres Orejas summit

Taos Mountain, Carson mesa, Del Valerio's stock pond

Almost wild horses

Frozen stock pond

December evening

January moonrise